Reproductive Rights of Women in India

Reproductive Rights of Women in India

DR. NEHA SINGH | DR. SEEMA GUPTA | DR. VERSHA VAHINI

Foreword by

HON'BLE JUSTICE UDAY U LALIT
49th Chief Justice of India

DR. PRASHANT BHALLA
President, Manav Rachna Educational Institutions

B L O O M S B U R Y
NEW DELHI • LONDON • OXFORD • NEW YORK • SYDNEY

BLOOMSBURY INDIA
Bloomsbury Publishing India Pvt. Ltd
Second Floor, LSC Building No. 4, DDA Complex,
Pocket C – 6 & 7, Vasant Kunj,
New Delhi 110070

BLOOMSBURY, BLOOMSBURY PRIME and the Diana logo are
trademarks of Bloomsbury Publishing Plc

First published in India 2023
This edition published 2023

ISBN: 978-93-56404-74-8
2 4 6 8 10 9 7 5 3 1

To find out more about our authors and books, visit
www.bloomsbury.com and sign up for our newsletters

Digitally Printed and bound in India by Replika Press Pvt. Ltd.

Contents

List of Cases

- *Air India v. Nergesh Meerza*, AIR 1981 SC 1829
- *Alberto R. Gonzales, Attorney General v. Carhart et al.* (2007) 550 U.S. 124
- *Amy AntoinetteMcgregor & Anr. v. Directorate of Family Welfare Govt. of NCT of Delhi* (2013) 205 DLT 96.
- *Anand Manharlal Brahmbhatt v. State of Gujarat*, 2015 lawsuit (GUJ) 2786
- *Anusha Ravindra v. Union of India*, W.P. (C) 934 / 2017 SC
- *Aschim Banga Khet Mazdoor Samiti v. State of West Bengal* 1996 (4) SCC 37
- *Asgarali Pradhania v. Emperor*. AIR 1933 Cal 893
- *Ashaben v. State of Gujarat*, AIR 2015 SC 3387
- *Ashok Kumar v. Anupama Sharma*, 2015 (3) RCR (CIVIL) 155
- *Attorney General v. X and Ors.* (1992) ILRM 401, (1992) 1 IR 1
- *Bhatou Boro v. State of Assam* (2018) 2 GAU LR 577
- *Bhupinder Kumar v. Angrej Singh*, Civil Appeal no. 5845, 2009, SLP (c) no. 17985, 2009
- *Binod Bihari Naik v. State of Orissa* (2018) CRI LJ 2676.
- *Carey v. Population Services International* (1977) 431 US 678
- *CEHAT & Ors v. Union of India* (2003) 8 SCC 412
- *Devika Biswas v. Union of India* (2016) 10 SCC 726
- *Dobbs v. Jackson Women's Health Organization*, 2022 U.S. LEXIS 3057
- *Dogra v. Malhotra*, CR No. 6337 and 6017 of 2011 (P & H).
- *Dr Jacob George v. State of Kerala* (1994) 3 SCC 430
- *Dr. Nikhil D Datar v. Union of India & Ors.*, SLP (civ) xxxx 2008 (SC).
- *Dr. Saraswathi v. State of Maharashtra*, 2013 (4) BOMCR (CRI) 461
- *E.P. Royappa v. Tamil Nadu* (1974) 4 SCC 3
- *Francis Coralie Mullin v. UT of Delhi* (1981) 1 SCC 60)
- *Gian Kaur v. State of Punjab*, 1996 SCC (2) 648 29
- *Gonzales v. Carhart*, 550 U.S. 124, 141 (2007).
- *Gopal Pattnaik v. State of Orissa*, Orissa High Court Writ Petition Criminal No. 68 of 2020

- *Govind v. State of Madhya Pradesh and Anr.* (1975)2 SCC148 30
- *Griswold v. Connecticut* (1965) 381 U.S. 479
- *Hallo-Bi @ Halima w/o Admin v. State of Madhya Pradesh* (2013) 1 MPHT 451.
- *Harris v. Mcrae* 448 U.S. 297, 302, 326 (1980)
- *High Court on its Own Motion v. State of Maharashtra* (2016) SCC Online Bom 8426
- *High court on its Own motion v. State of Maharashtra*, 2017 CRILJ 218
- *Hughes v. State* 868 p 2d 730 (1994).
- *In Re Polemis* (1921) 3 KB 560.
- *Jaitun v. Janpura Maternity Home* (2010) 172 DLT 9
- *Jane Roe v. Henry Wade* (1973) 410 U.S. 113
- *Javed v. State of Haryana*, 2003 (8) SCC 369 37.
- *Justice K.S. Puttaswamy (Retd) v. Union of India and Ors.*, (2017) 10 SCC 1
- *Kamla Devi v. State of Haryana*, WP (C) 2007/2015
- *Kavita v. State of Haryana*, 2015 (2) RCR (Criminal 606
- *Kharak Singh v. State of Uttar Pradesh and Ors.*, AIR 1963 SC 1295
- *Laxmi Mandal v. Deen Dayal Harinagar Hospital* (2010) 172 DLT 9.
- *Madhuben Arvindbhai Nimavat v. State of Gujarat*, 2016 SCC online GUJ 662.
- *Meera Santosh Pal v. Union of India*, 2017 SCC online SC 39
- *MP Sharma v. Satish Chandra*, AIR 1954 SC 300
- *Mr. Vijay Sharma and Ors. v. Union of India*, AIR 2008 BOM 29 49.
- *Mrs. A v. Union of India*, W.P. (Civil) No. 728/2017 (Order dated Aug. 31, 2017) (Supreme Court).
- *Ms. X v. India*, AIR 2016 SC 3525.
- *Ms. Z v. The State of Bihar and Ors.*, C.A. 10463 of 2017, 59-60, S.C.C.
- *Murari Mohan Koley v. State of West Bengal & Another*, 2005 (1) RCR (CR.L) 939 52.
- *Nand Kishore Sharma v. Union of India* AIR 2006 Raj. 166.
- *Navtej Johar v. Union of India* (2018) 10 SCC 1.
- *P and S v. Poland*. European Court of Human Rights (2012).
- *People's Union for Civil Liberties (PUCL) v. Union of India* (1996) Supp 10 SCR 321
- *Planned Parenthood of South Eastern Pennsylvania v. Casey* (1992) 505 U.S. 833
- *R v. State of Haryana*, W.P.(C), 6733 of 2016, H.C. P.& H., 74, 30 May 2017.

- *Raj Bokaria v. Medical Council of India*, (2010) SCC Online Del 4125.
- *Rama Soni v. State of MP & Ors.*, Madhya Pradesh High Court (Gwalior Bench) Writ Petition No. 25126 of 2018
- *Roe v. Wade* 410 US 113 (1973).
- *Sabu Mathew George v. Union of India*, (2017) 2 SCC 514
- *Sabu Mathew George v. Union of India*, (2018) 3 SCC 229.
- *Safoora Zargar v. State* 2020 SCC OnLine Del 664
- *Samar Ghosh v. Jaya Ghosh*, (2007) 4 SCC 511.
- *Sandesh Bansal v. Union of India*, (PIL) W.P. No. 9061/2008
- *Sarmishtha Chakraborty v. Union of India*, (2018) 13 SCC 339
- *Savita Sachin Patil v. Union of India*, (2017) 13 SCC 436
- *Shaikh Ayesha Khatoon v. Union of India* (2018) SCC Online Bom 11.
- *Sheetal Shankar Salvi v. Union of India*, (2018) 11 SCC 606
- *Sonali Kiran Gaikwad v. Union of India*, W.P. (C) 928/2017
- *State of Punjab v. Mohinder Singh Chawla* (1997) 2 SCC 83
- *Suchita Srivastava v. Chandigarh Administration*, AIR 2010 SC 235
- *Suparna Debnath v. State of West Bengal*, (2019) 1 CAL LT 349.
- *Surekha Gautam Khobragade v. State of NCT of Delhi*, Delhi High Court Writ Petition (Criminal) No. 69 of 2021
- *Suresh Kaushal v. Naz Foundation* (2014) 1 SCC 1
- *Tapasya Umesh Pisal v. Union of India* (2018) 12 SCC 57
- *Thakor Kinjalben Ragnathbhai v. State of Gujarat*, Gujarat High Court Special Criminal Application No. 2437 of 2020.
- *Voluntary health association of Punjab v. Union of India* (2013) 4 SCC 1
- *Webster v. Reproductive Health Services*, 492 U.S. 490 (1989)
- *X v. State of Madhya Pradesh & Ors.*, Madhya Pradesh High Court (Indore Bench) Writ Petition No. 4883 of 2020
- *Z v. State of Bihar & Ors.*, (2018) 11 SCC 5

Uday U. Lalit
Former Chief Justice of India

FOREWORD

One of the biggest challenges faced by women in India is the persistence of gender inequality. Women in India are often discriminated against in the homes, at the workplaces and in society at large. This discrimination can make it difficult for women to take decisions about their own bodies and lives. Access to quality reproductive health services is another major challenge. Many women in India do not have access to contraception, safe abortion services, or maternal health care. This is due to a number of factors, including poverty, lack of education, and social stigma, all arising from and further deepening the gender inequality.

Despite these challenges, there is a growing movement in India to promote and protect reproductive rights. The movement is working to ensure that all women in India have access to quality reproductive health services and that they are able to exercise their reproductive rights without fear of discrimination or violence.

This book is an important contribution to the movement to promote and protect reproductive rights in India. It provides a comprehensive overview of the challenges and opportunities facing women in India in terms of reproductive health and rights. The book also offers a number of recommendations for improving the situation.

I am confident that this book will be a valuable resource for policymakers, advocates, and anyone who is interested in promoting and protecting reproductive rights in India.

Heartiest Congratulations to the authors!

[UDAY UMESH LALIT]
11.08.2023

C-212, Sector-44, Noida - 201 301
Phone : 0120 - 4272444 e-mail : uday.lalit@gmail.com

MANAV RACHNA
|| vidyanatariksha ||

PRESIDENT
Manav Rachna Educational Institutions

CHANCELLOR
Manav Rachna International Institute of Research and Studies 'Deemed-to-be-University under section 3 of the UGC act.'
Manav Rachna University 'State Private University under section 2f of the UGC act.'

CHAIRMAN
Manav Rachna Dental College Recognized by Dental Council of India
Manav Rachna International Schools

CHAIRMAN
Kunskapsskolan Schools JV Manav Rachna and KED Sweden.

HONORARY PRESIDENT
BRICS Council of Exercise & Sports Science (BRICSCESS)

MEMBER
Scientific Advisory Board, Global Community Health (GCH)

DIRECTOR
Educational Rating and Assessment (ERA) Foundation

TREASURER
Education Promotion Society of India

MREI Campus:
Sector-43, Delhi Surajkund Road, Aravalli Hills, Faridabad, Haryana, INDIA
T +91-129-4198296, M+91 987 160 0009
chancellor@mriu.edu.in,
www.manavrachna.edu.in

Dr. Prashant Bhalla

FOREWORD

Discourse about reproductive rights is largely in the context of women because reproduction as a function affects women more than men. Reproductive rights are fundamental human rights that enable women to make informed choices about their own bodies and their own lives. These rights include the right to access safe and legal abortion, the right to contraception, and the right to maternal health care.

In India, reproductive rights are still far from being realized. According to a recent study, only 57% of women in India have access to modern contraception, and only 39% of women have access to safe abortion services. As a result, millions of women in India are at risk of unsafe abortion, maternal mortality, and other reproductive health problems.

This book provides an important empirical study of the challenges to reproductive rights in India. The authors draw on a wealth of data, including surveys, interviews, and focus groups, to paint a detailed picture of the situation on the ground. They show how the lack of access to reproductive health services, the stigma associated with reproductive health issues, and the social and economic constraints on women's autonomy all contribute to the denial of reproductive rights in India.

This book is a valuable contribution to the field of reproductive rights research. It provides a comprehensive and up-to-date overview of the challenges to reproductive rights in India, and it offers important insights into the ways in which these challenges can be overcome.

I hope that this book will be widely read and used to inform and inspire efforts to promote reproductive rights in India and around the world.

Congratulations to the authors.

Dr. Prashant Bhalla

Preface

Medical termination of pregnancy was legalised in India in as early as 1971. The MTP Act, 1971 provides women access to safe and legal abortion services and aims to prevent illegal abortions. It marked an important step in the recognition of women's right to reproductive and bodily autonomy. With two amendments to the act in 2002 and 2021, these rights have been expanded following a dynamic approach.

The Supreme Court of India has established that a woman's right to abortion is a fundamental right. The constitutional courts of the country have consistently recognized women's right to dignity, privacy, and bodily autonomy through their judgements. The courts have also observed that no one should force a woman to either carry or terminate a pregnancy against her will. Recently, the Supreme Court broadly interpreted the provisions of the MTP (Amendment) Act and permitted an unmarried woman to exercise her right to abortion.

On the contrary, the right to abortion has been seriously restricted in the USA recently. Abortion had been given constitutional protection by the SCOTUS in *Roe v. Wade* in 1973. The protection was rooted in privacy, which was reaffirmed in Casey 20 years after. Casey, however, based its protection in 'liberty' rather than privacy. Both these judgments were overturned in *Dobbs v. Jackson Women Health Organization* on June 24, 2022, where the US Supreme Court held that "procuring an abortion is not a fundamental constitutional right and that state may regulate abortion for legitimate reasons." Though the court accepted that abortion presents a profound moral question, it conceded that the constitution does not prohibit the citizens of each state from regulating or prohibiting abortion. After this judgment, women's right to abortion has been restricted to 15 weeks of pregnancy in the country. Indian laws and judgments have clearly come far away from the Dobbs judgement.

However, even though India's abortion laws are progressive, its effective translation into reality through improved access to safe abortion care is still underway. For the women undergoing abortions, morbidity and mortality continue to remain a serious issue. Further, women are unable to exercise larger autonomy in exercising this right due to ethical, religious, cultural, and social dilemmas. There are wide regional differences in literacy rate, availability of relevant and reliable information, and access to safe abortion services across the nation. The uneven rural–urban scenario makes it difficult for policymakers, administrators, and women's health advocates to create strategic interventions. These factors result in a thin research base as well due to the topic's sensitive nature.

It is, therefore, crucial to relook at various facets of abortion practices from the prism of women's human rights. While writing this book, women's experiences have been the central focus. The book contains a theoretical account of abortion practices and the challenges faced by women, which is supported by empirical data collected from women respondents from Delhi-NCR. The purpose of the study was to create an evidence-based body of credible knowledge about the current status of abortion rights and practices in India.

A questionnaire was developed based on an extensive literature review. The purpose of the questionnaire was to understand various aspects of rights and practices relating to abortions in India. The questions sought to obtain the views and opinions of women respondents as to their understanding about the deficiencies in abortion laws and policies, challenged faced by them in accessing abortion, and measures that may be taken to strengthen the rights. The questionnaire had 43 questions, each of which has answers to be measured on a 5-point Likert scale. The questionnaire was circulated to the respondents with prior consent considering its sensitive nature. A descriptive analysis of the survey responses was done by using SPSS 20.0. The bar graphs with the findings have been given in Chapter 10.

This empirical study was a part of the doctoral research titled 'Reproductive Rights and Abortion in India – An Empirical Study of Contemporary Issues' conducted at School of Law, Manav Rachna University, Faridabad.

With gratitude, we acknowledge the contribution of the respondents of the survey who poured their heart out in sharing their personal opinions. This book could not have been possible without them. We also acknowledge the consistent support extended by the School of Law, Ph.D. Office, and the library officials of Manav Rachna University. Our publisher has been exceptionally helpful. We humbly acknowledge their patience. We heartily thank our family members too. We, the co- authors worked together to give it the shape of a book. Each one went through the manuscript. Gave suggestions frankly. Discussed them and introduced them. There was meeting of minds. The whole idea was to make the work up-to-date, wholesome, readable and durable. Therefore, we mutually thank each other.

We are sure the book would be useful for students of law, researchers, and public-spirited people. Although sincere efforts have been made by the authors to avoid errors during the preparation of the book, they take responsibility for any mistakes.

Dr. Neha Singh
Dr. Seema Gupta
Dr. Versha Vahini

ONE

Prologue

The emphasis must be not on the right to abortion but on the right to privacy and reproductive control.

– Ruth Bader Ginsburg[1]

The idea of reproductive rights is based on the acceptance of the fundamental liberties of individuals and couples, including the freedom to determine how many children to have and how often, as well as the right to the best possible sexual and reproductive health. Though both the male and female participate in procreation, it is the female who has the biological responsibility of ensuring the complete development of the fetus. Pregnancy has a more lasting effect on the woman who is pregnant in comparison to her partner. In such a context, a woman's reproductive right to decide when to have children and choose what happens to her body assumes vital importance.

In respect of women's reproductive rights, several pertinent questions arise: Do women have control over their reproduction? Do women have the freedom to choose whether, when, and how many children to have? Do women have access to safe birth control methods? Do women have the right to safe abortion? Can sexuality be separated from reproduction?

This book intends to answer these and many such questions by analyzing theoretical frameworks, statutory provisions, precedents, and an empirical survey to understand the barriers faced by women in exercising their reproductive rights, especially their right to abortion. It has been observed that women remain unempowered when it comes to exercising control over their bodies and making fertility and motherhood choices. These results have been substantiated by examining the experiences of women through a survey using the quantitative research methodology. The responses comprise the experiences of women belonging to different

---

1 Joan Ruth Bader Ginsburg was an American lawyer and jurist who served as an associate justice of the Supreme Court of the United States from 1993 until her death in 2020.

age groups, marital statuses, educational backgrounds, professions, and familial structures. The conclusion shows that very little progress has taken place till now as far as reproductive rights are concerned and the autonomy enjoyed by women in this regard remains abysmally low. It is also observed that women's reproductive rights in general, and the right to abortion, are influenced by unequal power relations and undercurrents of coercion, social inequality, and discrimination that operate at the familial, societal, and state levels.

A recent 2023 United National Population Fund report titled "8 Billion Lives, Infinite Possibilities: the case for Rights and Choices" covers eight misconceptions about population growth and fertility matters. One common misbelief is that "these are demographic issues, not gender issues." The UNPF opines that "populations are about people and people are currently being born into a world of deeply entrenched gender inequality." It further says that human reproduction should be a choice but the latest data shows that it is often not. Around 44% of partnered women are unable to exercise bodily autonomy – meaning they are unable to make their own decisions over their healthcare, contraception, and sexual engagements. Nearly half of all pregnancies are unintended. Half a million births every year are accounted for by young girls aged 10 to 14 years. As few as one-fourth to one-third of women in low- and middle-income regions are having the number of children they planned, at their intended speed x. Yet, when faced with population-related challenges or concerns, rhetoric and policymakers often link population growth to fertility rates as a preferred solution. However, "How often do people proposing these solutions consider the fertility desires of women and girls?" the report asks. "Not often enough."[2]

This book aims to understand women's reproductive rights at the intersection of personal liberty, autonomy, privacy, equality, and social justice. Of all the lenses through which women's reproductive rights are viewed, privacy is the most common and influential one. Privacy broadly includes the right of an individual to safeguard and secure their personal life and affairs against intervention by others. The right to privacy stands for the right to make certain intensely personal, fundamental, and potentially life-changing decisions without interference from the government or society. Thus, privacy rights make way for women to make independent

[2] A report of United National Population Fund (2023) available at https://www.unfpa.org/news/population-bomb-bust-or-boon-new-unfpa-report-debunks-8-myths-about-world-8-billion

reproductive decisions, and the absence of privacy can restrain women from accessing information, advice, and treatment for their sexual and reproductive health.

However, as per reproductive justice activists like Loretta Ross and Dorothy Roberts[3], this singular focus on privacy fails to address the multidimensional nature of the problem. The concept of reproductive justice stems from the belief that marginalized groups, particularly vulnerable women, have historically been subject to structural inequalities that have influenced their reproductive choices. According to them, the right to privacy has its limitations in achieving reproductive autonomy for women, as demonstrated by the recent overturning of the *Roe v. Wade*[4] judgment by the US Supreme Court in *Dobbs v. Jackson Women's Health Organization.*[5] The former ruling laid the jurisprudential basis of women's reproductive rights on privacy by declaring that the right to privacy extends to the woman's right to control her pregnancy. Privacy, now, no longer provides the constitutional basis for reproductive autonomy for women in the USA.

Reproductive rights also, in part, derive their ground from the right to equality: "a right that enables women to be able to tread their chosen life paths on the same terms as men, without the fear of being forced into unplanned and unwanted childbearing." Contemporary feminist legal theory emphasizes gender equality, which in turn stresses reckoning with the differences between men and women existing in society. The theory, in general, objects to the acceptance of standards set by a male model. It argues that equality requires that the same interest is treated without discrimination and that different interests are treated in ways that respect those differences. Thus, equality is not a matter of guaranteeing women the same rights as men but ensuring the effective enjoyment of equal outcomes in health and well-being. In a nutshell, women's rights to health and healthcare rooted in equality encompass both compatible health needs as well as sex-specific health needs.

Legislative Framework

The provision of choice to undergo an abortion is embedded in the legal framework and social environment of a country. In India, the Medical

---

[3] Loretta J. Ross & Rickie Solinger, *Reproductive Justice: An Introduction* (University of California Press, 2017).

[4] 410 U.S. 113 (1973)

[5] 2022 U.S. LEXIS 3057

Termination of Pregnancy Act of 1971 (hereinafter referred to as the "MTP Act") is the first pertinent legislation in this regard. The MTP Act created an exception to the offence of abortion under the Indian Penal Code of 1860. Since voluntarily causing a miscarriage was a crime under the IPC and women were liable to be prosecuted by formalizing the procedure, the MTP Act created a basis that allowed a woman to access medical assistance/services without the fear of bodily harm. The Act took into consideration the mother's safety according to the medical technology available at the time. It set the gestational limit for abortion at 24 weeks (after the 2021 amendment) beyond which abortions would be performed only when there is a risk to the life of the pregnant woman.

While the Act has progressively broadened the scope of abortions, it lacks a rights-based framework. The MTP Act initially provided a qualified right to abortion and recognized termination of pregnancy as a normal recourse for pregnant women. However, due to the over-medicalized nature of abortions proposed by the Act, a pregnant person's ability to choose remains largely titular. The provision of seeking the opinion of the medical board is restrictive and intrusive. It tries to take away a pregnant individual's right to bodily and decisional autonomy and gives the power to medical practitioners.

Additionally, the government has failed to ensure that enough public healthcare facilities are equipped with the required infrastructure to support the implementation of this Act. Further, the regulatory framework remains insufficiently enforced. A vast majority of Indian women get aborted outside the legal framework due to the inherent restrictions associated with registered facilities and doctors' consent, which are built into the MTP Act. Their preference for unsafe abortions is further aided by the poor implementation of the Act by providers (health workers) and an even poorer understanding among women regarding their legal rights.

The original impetus behind the MTP Act was the growing fear of a population explosion. It was largely introduced as a way to control the population rather than to give people control over their own reproduction. The above-mentioned issues around the MTP Act were further compounded by the emergence and prevalence of sex-selective abortion. Strong son preferences in society led to sex-selective abortion and female feticide. As the MTP Act legalized abortion before 20 weeks of pregnancy, female feticide could not be banned per se, and hence the requirement of a new law was felt to prevent the misuse of the Act.

In response, the Pre-conception and Pre-natal Diagnostic Techniques (Prohibition of Sex Selection) Act of 1994 (hereinafter referred to as the "PCPNDT Act") was passed. To prevent the misuse of sex determination in prenatal diagnostic techniques – which could lead to female feticide – the PCPNDT Act (as amended in 2002) made it illegal to determine a child's gender either before or after conception.

Eventually, amendments were introduced to the five decades-old MTP Act through the MTP (Amendment) Act, 2021 in order to protect women from outdated abortion laws, which led them to opt for illegal and unsafe options. The MTP (Amendment) Act, 2021 was in line with the MTP Bills of 2014, 2017, and 2018, which had lapsed in the Parliament. However, the Amendment Act, 2021 was also doctor-centric with overly medicalized abortions. More significantly, it did not recognize abortion at will at any stage of pregnancy. Once again, the legislation fell short of being progressive and futuristic as it failed to secure reproductive rights. The MTP (Amendment) Act, 2021 has not done much to ease the barriers faced by women.

The legislative framework in India, especially the law regarding the termination of pregnancy, fails to embody the constitutional principles of equality and liberty and instead rests on regressive norms of social desirability. This framework requires an overhaul incorporating the evolving rights that govern individual bodily autonomy where a pregnant woman has a final say on her choice of reproduction.

Judicial Approach

The judicial approach, on the other hand, has actively contributed to the development of the reproductive rights of women. The court's affirmation of the right to privacy as a constitutional guarantee has compelled policymakers to revisit the notion about abortion as a method of population control. In interpreting health-related laws and policies, the Supreme Court has also condemned discrimination that limits women's authority and instead focused on women's rights to dignity, autonomy, and bodily integrity.

The courts in India have no doubt carried forward reproductive rights jurisprudence with the fundamental rights framework consisting of autonomy, bodily integrity, and privacy. Yet, pregnant women continue to face challenges in accessing reproductive health services. The Supreme Court and various High Courts have passed varied judgments relating to reproductive rights but have not settled on a standard procedure to define the parameters under which abortion may be permitted. In the MTP Act, of 1971, abortion was permitted up to 20 weeks of pregnancy. The term was recently increased to 24 weeks after the 2021 amendment. Abortion beyond this period may be carried out only with the permission of the court, which is based on the opinion of the medical board. Constitutional courts across the country have been conducting case-by-case reviews to determine whether to grant abortions to women. These cases typically involve pregnant women who are diagnosed with fetal impairment or pregnant adolescents who are a victim of rape. An ambiguous legal framework and an inconsistent approach can be noticed in various judgments.

In *Ghosh v. Ghosh*[6], the Supreme Court undermined women's reproductive autonomy when it held that a woman's decision to undergo abortion or sterilization without her husband's consent could constitute mental cruelty. However, the subsequent judicial decisions have moved towards greater constitutional protection of reproductive autonomy. By decriminalizing adultery and homosexuality in *Navatej Singh Johar v. UOI*[7], the Supreme Court gave further support to women's rights wherein it observed that "women have a right to sexual autonomy, which is an important facet of the right to personal liberty." The judgment in *Puttaswamy*[8] specifically recognizes the constitutional right of women to make reproductive choices as a part of personal liberty under Article 21. In *Independent Thought v. Union of India*[9], the Supreme Court held that a girl child's rights, independent of her marital status, deserve recognition and acceptance. *Navtej Singh Johar and Joseph Shine*[10] have relied on the concept of substantive equality, which is crucial in order to extend equal protection to historically disadvantaged groups.

Though the apex court has advanced reproductive rights jurisprudence, the judiciary generally has only allowed abortion in difficult cases, perhaps exclusively in ones that were strictly based on grounds mentioned in the MTP Act. The judiciary, as can be gauged from the various judgments, has remained glued to the rule book, and has given no concession to genuine cases. The majority of court decisions allowing abortions

---

[6] *Samar Ghosh v. Jaya Ghosh* (2007) 2004 S.C. 151

[7] AIR 2018 SC 4321

[8] (2017) 10 SCC 1

[9] (2017) 10 SCC 800

[10] *Joseph Shine v. Union of India* (2018) SCC OnLine SC 1676.

have focused on issues of life and liberty, while individual choice and reproductive autonomy have received less attention. This seems to denote that a colonial moral framework that seeks to preserve heteropatriarchal power structures through the control of sexuality and reproduction is still at play. It is the responsibility of the legislature as well as the judiciary to identify such restrictions and recognize reproductive rights within the framework of fundamental and human rights.

TWO

Understanding Reproductive Rights

Reproductive freedom is critical to a whole range of issues. If we cannot take charge of this most personal aspect of our lives, we can't take care of anything. It should not be seen as a privilege or as a benefit, but a fundamental human right."

– Faye Wattleton[1]

Concept of Reproduction

Reproduction is a biological process in which an organism produces an offspring that is biologically identical to the mother. It ensures a species' continuity over generations and is the primary characteristic of life on Earth. There are two modes of reproduction: sexual and asexual.

'Reproducing' means 'producing again' as defined in Section 3 (65) of the General Clauses Act, 1897. According to *Dorland's Illustrated Medical Dictionary*, reproduction is defined as the process by which organized bodies produce offspring or the act of creating a similar object or situation, duplication, and replication.[2] Termination of pregnancy, as defined in Section 312 of the IPC, 1860, is the "premature delivery or expulsion of a human fetus" before it is capable of supporting life (that is, at any period of gestation short of the full term).

The Black's Law Dictionary defines 'reproduction' as the creation of children, and 'pregnancy' as the condition caused by a fertilized ovum that begins with conception and ends with the delivery of the child.[3] Sexual reproduction is a type of reproduction that involves the production of an offspring by the fusion of male and female gametes. In comparison

---

[1] Faye Wattleton is an American reproductive rights activist; she who was the first African American and the youngest elected president of the Planned Parenthood Federation of America, and the first woman since Margaret Sanger to hold the position

[2] Dorland, W. A. N. Dorland's illustrated medical dictionary (28th ed.). Philadelphia: W.B. Saunders Co. 1 (1994).

[3] Centennial (ed.), *The Black's Law Dictionary*, 8th ed. 1179, 1207 (1991)

to asexual reproduction, this process is typically slow and complex. The organisms generated in this manner are genetically diverse. As a result, they can adapt to changing climatic conditions. Humans and a large number of multicellular organisms reproduce sexually.

Women have always been at the center in this regard – in the era of monarchy, she bore the heir to the throne and ascertained the dynasty's legacy; in the world wars, she was referred to as a "childbearing machine;" and in modern times, she undertakes in-vitro fertilization and surrogacy.[4] Frequently, womanhood is reduced to motherhood.

Reproduction appears to have been a contentious issue throughout history. The woman has traditionally been highly regarded as a mother and reprimanded in some cultures for being infertile or incapable of bearing a son. Frequently, womanhood has been reduced to motherhood, and the cultural permissibility of granting women the right to reproduce or not has long been a point of contention. It encompasses traditions, religion, and science and has ramifications for international obligations. Over time, the State's objective to control the population became a ground for limiting fertility and impinging on an individual's reproductive choices. In the 1990s, policies focusing on population control began to shift toward reproductive freedom and bodily integrity.

Notion of Reproductive Rights

Reproductive rights are human rights that directly relate to sexual and reproductive health. These rights are protected by different instruments such as international conventions and declarations, constitutions, domestic legislations, and subordinate legislations. They are not only important for achieving health and development goals, but also important in and of themselves as human rights that are meant to protect each person's dignity.[5]

The World Health Organization (WHO) sums up reproductive rights as follows:

> *Reproductive rights rest on the recognition of the basic right of all couples and individuals to decide freely and responsibly the number, spacing, and timing of their children and to have information to do so, and right to*

---

[4] M. Unnithan-Kumar, "Reproduction, Health, Rights: Connections and Disconnections." *Human Rights in Global Perspective: Anthropological Studies of Rights, Claims and Entitlements*, edited by R. Wilson and J. Mitchell, 183-209. London: Rout (2003).

[5] J.N. Erdman, R.J. Cook, in International Encyclopedia of Public Health, 2008.

> *attain the highest standard of sexual and reproductive health. They also include the right of all to make decisions concerning reproduction free of discrimination, coercion, and violence.*[6]

The following categories of rights are included in reproductive rights:[7]

- The right to self-determination in reproductive functions
- The right to make reproductive choices freely and without fear of coercion, discrimination, and violence
- The right to legal and safe abortion
- The right to access contraceptive methods as well as the right to be free of coerced sterilization and contraception
- Protection against gender-based practices such as female genital mutilation and male genital mutilation

Reproductive rights, including the choice of if and when to have children, are important for women's health and economic well-being. Research shows that being able to shape one's own reproductive life is linked to more stable and happy relationships, more work opportunities, higher wages, and better career advancement for women.[8] Further, being able to choose when and how many children to have can have a huge impact on a young woman's pursuit of higher education.[9] A woman's ability to plan her family could mean the difference between living in poverty and being financially stable in the long run. [10]

The abovementioned broad categories of the legal and ethical framework of reproductive rights are far less evident and can even be deficient when it comes to genetic screening, embryo selection, or (in the future) genome editing. Assisted reproduction and common genetic selections raise numerous moral dilemmas, including the commodification of the body, the use of anonymous gamete donors, and sperm and egg selection. While the right to bear children is accepted within certain

---

[6] Gender and Reproductive rights, available at: http://who.int/reproductive-health/gender/index.html.

[7] SVAM Amnesty International, "Stop Violence Against Women: Reproductive Rights" (USA, 2007) available at: http://www.amnestyusa.org

[8] A.R. Miller, "The Effects of Motherhood Timing on Career Path", 24(3), *Journal of Population Economics*, 1071–1100 (2011).

[9] H. Hock, "The Pill and The College Attainment of American Women And Men, Working Paper", *Mathematical Policy Research*, Washington, DC (2008).

[10] J Bronte-Tinkew, ME Scott and A Horowitz, "Male Pregnancy Intendedness and Children's Mental Proficiency And Attachment Security During Toddlerhood", 71(4), *Journal of Marriage and Family*, 1001–1025 (2009).

biological constraints, it does not follow – and cannot be argued – that someone has a right to deliver a child with certain preselected genetic characteristics. This amounts to a form of consumerist reproduction or even self-reproduction. Apart from this extreme version, ordinary reproductive rights relating to abortion or surrogacy are circumscribed by a country's legislative framework, which tends to lessen the control of women over their procreation.[11]

Approaches to Understanding Reproductive Rights

Reproductive rights can be understood via different approaches.

As Bodily Integrity

A woman's body is a fiercely contested territory across the world. It may be constructed differently in different contexts, but it remains a site of power play. While the body is intensely 'personal' in the sense that it is contained within individuals, its manifestation is shaped by the same variables that shape social relationships: gender, age, class, and ethnicity. The dichotomy between a woman's body and mind is a socially constructed one. This partitioning of the mind and body into mutually exclusive categories results in the loss of 'personhood,' the loss of control and autonomy over their bodies, and the violation of bodily integrity.

Women's inherent right to exercise control and autonomy over their bodies is included in bodily integrity. This includes (i) the right to a life free of fear of violence and the right to live in safe environments; (ii) the right to be not treated with physical, sexual, or emotional violence by intimate partners and others, including those acting on behalf of the State; (iii) geographic mobility and the ability to choose where to go, whom to go with, and how and when to travel; and (iv) the right to make informed sexual and reproductive health choices, including whether to marry, whom to marry, and when (age) to marry and the desire that sexual and reproductive health services are sensitive to their rights and needs. Viewed from the lens of the right to bodily integrity, the right to abortion affords women protection against being compelled to sacrifice their womb for the State's ostensible interest in potential life.[12]

---

[11] M. Unnithan-Kumar, "Thinking through Surrogacy Legislation in India: Reflections on Relational Consent and the Rights of Infertile Women", 1(3), *Journal of Legal Anthropology*, 287–313 (2013).

[12] R. A Destro "Abortion and the Constitution: The Need for a Life-Protective Amendment", 63(5), *California Law Review*, 1250–1351 (1975).

Women are constantly threatened with violence: they face discrimination and exploitation; they are deprived of the right to spatial mobility and the ability to make well-informed choices concerning their bodies and their sexuality. Control and regulation of these spaces by society compromise their bodily integrity, rendering them powerless. Thus, respect for one's bodily integrity is a necessary condition for female empowerment in any scenario.[13]

Sexual health and the right to sexuality must be healthy and self-affirming, and free of violence and coercion. Women need to be afforded the opportunity to pursue a sexual life that is satisfying, safe, and pleasurable. Education and awareness would not only address the dangers of bodily integrity violations but also enable them to care for and take great pride in their bodies as well as construct an identity and social behavior on their terms. This would also encompass their emotional, psychological, religious, and physiological spaces and wants.[14]

In the Indian context, the female body is a space inscribed with culturally labelled and socially authorized ideals of the desirable woman. The socialization of the girl child[15] happens through a multifaceted process whose primary objective is to instill appropriate codes of conduct, including self-effacement and self-denial. They are trained to view their lives primarily through the lens of service to others. The rules for presenting the submerged bodily self in daily life are well-defined, and children are socialized into compliance from an early age. Thus, women's identification with their bodies becomes the primary reason for their oppression in patriarchal cultures. A woman is primarily identified by her bodily functions and viewed as a vehicle for male sexual satisfaction and reproduction as well as a medium for its natural individual corollary: childbearing, rearing, and nurturing. This biological function defines her entire life, her roles, her position, and her status in society. Nearly half of the girls between the ages of 10 and 14 are married in many rural areas. Women are compelled to demonstrate their fertility by getting pregnant as soon as possible following marriage. Adolescent marriage is

---

13 Kanchan Mathur, "Body as Space, Body as Site: Bodily Integrity and Women's Empowerment in India", 43(17), *Economic and Political Weekly*, 54–63 (2008)

14 S. Madhok, *Rethinking Agency: Developmentalism, Gender and Rights* (Routledge, New Delhi: 2013)

15 Gender socialization is the process of teaching members of society how to behave according to gender expectations or gender roles.

interchangeable with adolescent childbearing where approximately 10–15% of all births occur to teenagers.

Virginity and modesty are virtues that are ingrained in girls' socialization patterns. The perception of bravery or 'macho' behavior associated with men is interpreted and accepted as the right to commit violence in contrast to the acceptance of violence on the part of women, who are expected to be not only chaste but also obedient and 'good.' The traditional image of a 'good woman' remains one who upholds the family's honor and the domain's "culture of silence," and is obedient and sacrificing.[16]

From childhood, the girl child is conditioned to conform to certain norms of behavior, such as how to speak, how to dress, for whom to dress, and how to sit and behave in the existence of males. Her mobility is restricted where leaving the house frequently requires prior permission. The modesty of a woman reflects the community's masculinity. She becomes a "symbol of violence" because she embodies her community's shame and subjection. Paradoxically, the common denominator across all communities and social classes continues to be female modesty.

A woman's identity is intimately connected to her role as a mother, wife, or daughter. The expectation from her is a denial of her femininity and submergence of her existence in the male. As a matter of fact, her survival in the mainstream is called into question after her husband's death, even if she is financially self-sufficient.

Thus, women lack the right to express their urges, and discussions – particularly about their bodies and sexuality – are taboo. Society dictates that women have no right to challenge or make independent choices regarding their labor, bodies, and sexuality. They are conditioned to believe that everything that occurs within the four corners of the house is 'personal' and thus should not be made 'public' as disclosing family matters will bring 'shame' and 'dishonor' to the family. Women also discipline themselves, both consciously and unconsciously, to be the heralds of tradition, harmony, and familial and social honor. Thus, the female body becomes the edifice upon which gender inequality is constructed and legitimized. As a result, her primary concern/responsibility becomes negating the self for the sake of the family/community. She is socialized throughout her life to accept her 'lower' status. Even if she faces severe

[16] B Subha Sri, "Women's Bodies and the Medical Profession", 45 (17), *Economic and Political Weekly* (2010).

discrimination or physical violence, she accepts her fate. Thus, the woman's body is constantly shaped and moulded to conform to societal expectations, leading to a severe lack of rights and a constant violation of her bodily integrity.

As Reproductive Autonomy

Reproductive autonomy is defined as the right of women (regardless of their marital status) to choose whether to have children, and if they do, the right to determine the number of children, when, and with whom as well as the freedom to choose the means and methods by which they exercise their reproductive management choices.[17] Access to sex education, birth control, maternal and reproductive healthcare, and pregnancy termination services, and economic independence are some of the key determinants of whether a legal system secures reproductive autonomy for women.[18]

The right to reproductive autonomy has indeed been regarded as a constitutionally protected fundamental right by Indian courts. From the 1990s when the Supreme Court refused to comment on women's right to abort an unwanted pregnancy in *Jacob George v. the State of Kerala*[19] to the Delhi High Court's decision in the 2010 *Laxmi Mandal v. Deen Dayal Harinagar Hospital*[20] case where the court stated that the Constitution protects women's right to access public health facilities and the enforcement of their reproductive rights, the judicial attitude toward the right to abortion has shifted significantly. In *Suchita Srivastava and Another v. Chandigarh Administration*,[21] the Supreme Court went so far as to declare that reproductive autonomy is an aspect of personal liberty protected by Article 21. It stated:

> *It is important to recognize that reproductive choices can be exercised to procreate as well as to abstain from procreating. The crucial consideration is that a woman's right to privacy, dignity, and bodily integrity should be respected. This means that there should be no restriction whatsoever on the exercise of reproductive choices such as a woman's right to*

---

[17] *Montgomey v. Lanarkshire Health Board* (2018) 105 UKSC 11.

[18] Cook, J. Rebecca, M. Bernard Dickens, and F. Mahmoud Fathalla, *Reproductive Health and Human Rights: Integrating Medicine, Ethics, and Law* (Clarendon Press, 2003).

[19] 1994 (2) SCALE 563.

[20] 172 (2010) DLT 9.

[21] (2009) 9 SCC 1.

> *refuse participation in sexual activity or the insistence on [the] use of contraceptive methods. Furthermore, women are also free to choose birth control methods such as undergoing sterilization procedures. Taken to their logical conclusion, reproductive rights include a woman's entitlement to carry a pregnancy to its full term, to give birth, and to subsequently raise children.*[22]

However, the right to reproductive autonomy in India needs to be understood in light of the limitations placed on women's agency by the social fabric as well as the economic circumstances of the women.[23] The gendered nature of poverty is affecting women disproportionately in terms of education, employment, and property ownership, which further contribute to the denial of autonomy in the decision-making process. As a result, women have neither economic independence nor a voice in the decision-making process with respect to the affecting her body.

Meghan Campbell, who is a renowned lecturer in Law at the University of Birmingham and Deputy-Director of the Oxford Human Rights Hub, pointed out that 'being a woman' both causes and perpetuates poverty.[24] When blended with a patriarchal social structure and a strong social preference for male children, many women report living in coercive environments that force them to seek abortions, particularly if they are pregnant with a female fetus. In 2004, the Abortion Assessment Project performed comprehensive social research on the prevalence of formal and informal abortion in India, utilizing community-based household surveys, qualitative studies, and working papers. The data collected confirmed the widespread use of sex determination and abortion of female fetuses.[25]

---

[22] (2009) 9 SCC 1.

[23] A similar argument was put forward by Fredman with reference to women's agency in choosing to wear religious attire. She believes that given the evident role of culture in both sex selection and the manifestation of religious values, the comparison is applicable. Sandra Fredman, Comparative Human Rights Law (n 62) 452.

[24] Meghan Campbell, "CEDAW and Women's Intersecting Identities: A Pioneering New Approach to Intersectional Discrimination", 11(2), *Revista Direito GV*, 479–504 (2015), available at SSRN: https://ssrn.com/abstrAct=2726534

[25] Duggal, Shalini, Tulsi Das Chugh, and Ashish Kumar Duggal, "HIV and Malnutrition: Effects on Immune System", *Clinical and Developmental Immunology* (2012).

Reproductive autonomy was defined and discussed in the case of *K.S. Puttaswamy v. Union of India*[26] as the capacity to exercise free will and 'control over the body' by consenting to or refusing medical procedures. In the context of reproductive rights, autonomy also refers to a woman's right to make her own reproductive and sexual health decisions without fear of coercion or violence. Informed consent and confidentiality are critical components of ensuring women's freedom of choice.

The right to health, as defined in *Paschim Banga Khet Majdoor Samiti v. State of West Bengal*[27], was sought to be expanded to include reproductive rights in *Laxmi Mandal.*[28] This case focused on the refusal of maternal healthcare services and did not overtly recognize abortion as a component of reproductive rights. In any case, mere legal recognition is insufficient to ensure that reproductive rights are enforced.

In *Javed v. the State of Haryana* 2003,[29] "the petitioners challenged the constitutionality of a Haryana State law prohibiting anyone with more than two living children from retaining certain public offices. The Supreme Court determined that the law was not arbitrary and that its purpose was population control, which was covered by the constitutional exception for "public order, morality, and health." Notably, the court overlooked significant barriers to contraceptive services and information, particularly for marginalized women and girls. The court also rejected numerous demonstrations on how Indian women lack the autonomy to make decisions regarding having children within the family.

In 2009, reproductive autonomy was recognized as a fundamental right by the Supreme Court in the case of *Suchita Srivastava*, where a young woman with moderate intellectual disabilities got raped and became pregnant while residing in a government-run welfare institution. This was the first time that the Supreme Court of India recognized reproductive rights within the framework of reproductive choices. The apex court held that a woman's right to make reproductive choices is also an aspect of personal liberty under Article 21 of the Constitution of India which provides that, "No person shall be deprived of his life or personal liberty except according to procedure established by law."

---

[26] (2017) 10 SCC 1.

[27] 1996 SCC (4) 37.

[28] 172 (2010) DLT 9.

[29] AIR 2003 SC 3057.

In 2016, in the case of *Devika Biswas v. Union of India*,[30] the apex court found that "coercive and substandard sterilization procedures used mostly by public healthcare professionals violated women's reproductive rights." Beyond the reproductive health framework, the court also recognized women's autonomy and gender equality as essential components of women's reproductive rights. While concluding that coercive sterilization practices violate a woman's fundamental and human right to dignity and health, the court emphasized the critical role of a 'meaningful choice' for a woman.

In 2017, the *Puttaswamy* judgment[31] marked a watershed moment in the court's understanding of fundamental rights.[32] It rejected a purely spatial and relational understanding of privacy and made an appreciable shift toward a more individualistic understanding of privacy. This ruling has the potential to improve the entire framework due to its emphasis on autonomy and bodily integrity. However, its practical application is still uncertain.

Abortions continue to be regulated by the MTP Act, which transfers abortion decision-making authority from women to their doctors. This is a violation of a woman's right to reproductive autonomy, and thus of her right to life and privacy. By mandating that women obtain permission from a medical service provider before having an abortion, the MTP Act makes it more difficult for women to exercise their reproductive autonomy at any stage of pregnancy.

On top of this, there has always been an implicit contradiction between the MTP Act and the PCPNT Act. The MTP Act allows women to seek the termination of their pregnancies, whereas the PCPNDT Act prohibits sex determination. Although the latter prohibits only sex determination and makes no provision for abortion, it is widely accepted that India's sex ratio is the result of abortions performed following sex determination based on a preference for a male child. This correlation sometimes negatively influences the provision of rights granted under the former Act.

Reproductive choices are the perhaps most private and intimate decisions women make in their lives that also have undeniable public

---

[30] (2016) 10 SCC 726.

[31] *Justice K.S. Puttaswamy v. Union of India* (2017) 10 SCC 1.

[32] Alok Prasanna Kumar, "The Puttaswamy Judgment: Exploring Privacy Within and Without", 52, *Econ. & Pol. Wkly.* 34 (2017).

dimensions.[33] Thus, decisions regarding reproduction (particularly whether and how to use one's reproductive capacity and whether or not to 'bear and beget' children) are not made in a vacuum; they are influenced by a variety of factors, including political, ideological, socioeconomic, and health and healthcare concerns.

Nowadays, due to technological advancements, there are more choices available when it comes to various facets of reproduction. In essence, having a child is no longer a matter of chance; it is typically the result of a deliberate choice. This aspect of medical advancement has substantially impacted the individual's reproductive decision-making. With technological advances in contraception, pregnancy termination, and in-vitro pregnancy initiation, progressive amendment in laws for women's protection and quality control are required. Here, it is to be noted that state intervention in reproductive decision-making is essential, but it can also have a deleterious impact on individuals and society as a whole.

As a Reproductive Choice

Women's reproductive choice is a fundamental right protected under Article 21 of the Indian Constitution. It is also governed by factors such as official family planning and abortion policies and their implementation; the steep decline in family size desires and falling fertility rates as well as their impact on the demand for contraception and abortion; and social and gender-related pressures and expectations about accepted reproductive behavior.[34]

In the 2023 report titled "8 billion Lives, Infinite Possibilities: the case of Rights and Choices," on the eighth belief that "rights and choices are great in theory, but unaffordable in reality", the UNPF opines that "Failing to support reproductive rights always comes with costs – and those costs are borne, disproportionately by women and the most marginalized. We must work toward providing a full range of reproductive healthcare services – from contraception to safe delivery to infertility care – in all settings. These interventions can help people and societies thrive and prosper."[35]

---

33 Erin Nelson, *Law, Policy and Reproductive Autonomy* 1 (Harte Publishing, Oxford, 2013).

34 A Malhotra, L Nyblade, S Parasuraman et al., "Realizing Reproductive Choice and Rights: Abortion and Contraception in India", *ICRW* (Washington, DC, 2003).

35 A Report of United National Population Fund (2023) available at https://www.unfpa.org/news/population-bomb-bust-or-boon-new-unfpa-report-debunks-8-myths-about-world-8-billion.

The report further raises concern over the quantitative approach used to view the population: "Too many people? Too few? What is the right number?" The UNPF says that we are asking the wrong questions. What we should be asking is: are people, especially women, able to freely make their own reproductive choices? The answer, unfortunately often, is no.

The right to abortion is multifaceted, encompassing a variety of different rights. It is most famously described as a right to privacy,[36] which refers to the freedom to make certain incredibly personal, fundamental, and potentially life-changing decisions without government interference. It also comes under the right to equality, with the stance that women must have equal decision-making power as men without fear of being forced into unplanned and undesired childbearing.

Unequal decision-making power in the family may limit women's autonomy in reproductive health matters. This could result in increased fertility rates, unwanted pregnancies, forced abortions, a lack of prompt healthcare seeking, or insufficient birth spacing.[37] Sex-selective abortions occur in certain contexts due to the strong preference for sons. Complications from abortion may result in disability or death, particularly if the abortion is performed in unsafe conditions.

Women's lower social status contributes to their limited ability to negotiate with sexual partners about condom use, marriage age and timing, and pregnancy spacing. Child marriage exposes girls to intimate partner violence, social isolation, and decreased educational attainment[38]. Additionally, maternal mortality and the incidence of obstetric fistula are higher for adolescent girls. Transactional or 'survival' sex erodes low-income girls' bargaining power for contraception or condom use. All such situations may result in unintended pregnancy, HIV infection, or another

---

[36] (2017) 10 SCC 1.

[37] World Health Organization, *Mental Health Aspects of Women's Reproductive Health: A Global Review of the Literature* (WHO, Geneva, 2009). Available at http://www.who.int/reproductivehealth/publications/general/97892415663567/en/index.html.

[38] World Health Organization, *Making A Difference in Countries: Strategic Approach to Improving Maternal and New Born Survival and Health* (WHO, Geneva, 2006). Available at http://www.who.int/making_pregnancy_safer/documents/wa3102006ma/en/index.html.

STI.[39] Undesired pregnancies have been linked to low birth weight and premature births.

Capacity[40] determination is inextricably linked to the right to autonomy and self-determination, which is a recognized fundamental legal right. Nevertheless, millions of women worldwide lose their legal capacity as a result of stigma and discrimination. Women also lose autonomy through a judicial declaration of incompetency or simply because a doctor determines that the woman "lacks the capacity" to make a decision.

As a Matter of Privacy

Reproductive rights, as a component of the right to privacy, are an essential cornerstone of personal and family life. The subject of information, awareness, privacy, and confidentiality regarding abortion as well as access to healthcare services that are free of legal and cultural barriers are critical in establishing women's reproductive rights.

In a nutshell, privacy refers to an individual's right to protect and secure their private life or affairs against intrusion by others. Without privacy, women may be unable to access information, advice, and treatment regarding sexual and reproductive health issues.[41] As a result, it is critical to safeguard women's privacy. The right to privacy is also codified and protected by international human rights instruments.

In the landmark case of *Roe v. Wade,*[42] the United States Supreme Court held that the right to abortion was a component of women's constitutional right to privacy and the State could interfere with such a right only to advance its compelling interest. The State was held to have a strong interest in protecting women's health. Thus, the Court apprehended that a woman's right to privacy is sufficiently broad to include her choice on whether or not to terminate her pregnancy. *Eisenstadt v. Baird*[43] had held that "a statute prohibiting the dissemination of contraceptives to unmarried persons violated the equal protection clause because the

[39] M Temin and R Levine, "Start with a Girl: A New Agenda for Global Health", *Centre for Global Development* (Washington DC, 2009).

[40] Capacity is defined as a functional determination that settles whether an individual is capable of making a medical decision within a given situation.

[41] A Report on Your Health, Your Choice, Your Rights: International and Regional Obligations on Sexual and Reproductive Health and Rights (2018).

[42] 410 U.S. 113 (1973).

[43] 405 U.S. 38 (1972).

Court determined that no rationale or legitimate distinction between married and unmarried contraceptive users can be made." Thus, this case established that the right to privacy in the area of procreation did not apply exclusively to married couples.

In Indian cases, the *Roe* judgement has been cited as a seminal decision on abortion rights. In *Ashaben v. the State of Gujarat*[44], the Gujarat High Court noted that, *in Roe*, the United States Supreme Court held that "the pregnancy period into three trimesters. During the first trimester, the decision to terminate the pregnancy was solely at the discretion of the woman. After the first trimester, the state could "regulate procedure." During the second trimester, the state could regulate (but not outlaw) abortions in the interests of the mother's health. After the second trimester, the fetus became viable, and the state could regulate or outlaw abortions in the interest of the potential life except when necessary to preserve the life or health of the mother." In *K.S. Puttaswamy v. Union of India*[45], the Supreme Court unanimously asserted privacy to be a constitutionally protected right as an intrinsic element of the right to life and personal liberty under Article 21. At its core, the right was deemed to include the 'preservation of personal intimacies,' including, but not limited to, 'procreation' and the 'right to be alone.' The apex court's decision's relevance and applicability to reproductive rights are self-evident. The exercise of a person's reproductive rights, including the right to abortion, can now be said to be firmly rooted in the right to privacy through the beliefs of liberty, autonomy, and dignity.

However, as declared in the *Puttaswamy* case, the right to privacy undermines the constitutional foundations of the current legal framework governing abortion and reproductive rights extensively. Although the MTP Act, 1971 decriminalizes abortion in certain circumstances, no legal right to abortion on demand exists. The Supreme Court of India had already held authoritatively in *Govind v. State of M.P.*[46] that privacy is primarily concerned with the individual and is connected to and entwined with the concept of liberty. The court ruled that the sanctity of the domestic sphere, including the home, family, marriage, motherhood, procreation, and childrearing, must be protected under the right to privacy. Thus, the

---

[44] 2015 SCC OnLine Guj 6198.

[45] (2017) 10 SCC 1

[46] 1975 SCR (3) 946

recognition of a constitutional right to privacy may provide a privacy-based justification for a self-contained right to abortion.

The *Puttaswamy* judgment has served as the foundation for ground-breaking decisions on reproductive rights around the world and feminist legal theorists have made significant critiques of privacy,[47] most notably in attaining reproductive autonomy. Also, American feminist academicians have repetitively expressed concern about the dependence on privacy for reproductive rights, arguing that privacy can be interpreted as a negative right, as indicated by the US Supreme Court's jurisprudence.[48] It is believed that viewing privacy solely as a negative right would preclude the State from enacting affirmative measures to ensure that all women and girls have access to reproductive health services in practice.[49] Certain legal experts have criticized the historical framing of privacy in terms of spaces and relationships rather than individuals. Thus, privacy rights do not guarantee women's reproductive rights. It is respected within safeguarded institutions/relationships such as family or marriage, where their priorities may differ from those in positions of authority in those spaces. However, other feminist perspectives believe that the right to privacy establishes a zone of autonomy within which women can make autonomous reproductive choices and realize their personhood.[50]

As Reproductive Health Rights

The right to health and the right to timely and sufficient medical care are inextricably linked to the right to life, but the right to reproduction is not explicitly recognized as a fundamental right in the Indian Constitution.

In India, women's health is intimately connected to their lower social status. They are expected to eat last, save the best food for the family's men, and ignore their illnesses in order to manage the entire household. This frequently results in malnutrition, which is one of the primary reasons for women's high rates of morbidity and mortality.[51] Food distribution

---

[47] Ratna Kapur, "Erotic Justice: Law and the New Politics of Postcolonialism", 29 (2005).

[48] A.L. Allen, "Tribe's Judicious Feminism (*Review of Abortion: The Clash of Absolutes*, by L.H. Tribe)", 44(1), *Stanford Law Review*, 179–203 (1991).

[49] *Harris v. McRae*, 448 U.S. 297 (1980).

[50] Michele Estrin Gilman, "Welfare, Privacy, and Feminism", 39, *U. BALT. L.F.* 1, 16 (2008).

[51] Aparajita Mohanty, Shashikala Gurpur, Chaitra R. Beerannavar "Rethinking Inclusive Development: A Human Rights Critique of South Asia", 157, *Social and Behavioral Sciences*, 128–136 (2014).

within households continues to reflect societal gender biases. As the household's patriarchal culture and social norms govern intra-household resource allocation, women's wellness, including health and nutrition, becomes secondary not only to the household's survival but also to the male members' well-being.

Reproductive health issues affecting girls/women during the pre-puberty stage or associated with menstruation are frequently interconnected with other health problems. Stress and depression affect women's reproductive cycles.[52] Moreover, it is not uncommon for chronic conditions to be labelled as psychosomatic, particularly in women.

The United Nations Committee on Economic, Social and Cultural Rights (CESCR), in its General Comment No. 14,[53] has discussed the right to health. It asserts that the right to health is an all-encompassing right that includes not only appropriate and timely healthcare but also the underlying determinants of health, including access to safe drinking water and adequate sanitation; an adequate supply of safe food, nutrition, and housing; safe working and living conditions; and access to health-related education and information, including about sexual and reproductive health.

In India, the right to healthcare has been considered a fundamental right. Several Supreme Court rulings have perceived the right to health and the right to timely and adequate medical treatment as being integral to the right to life. The Supreme Court held in *Parmanand Katara v. Union of India*[54] that Article 21 requires the State to protect life and thus doctors at government hospitals are obligated to extend medical assistance to preserve life. This case arose out of a public interest petition involving the question of emergency medical treatment to injured victims of motor accidents. The court further observed that neither law, procedure, nor State action can nullify or impede medical professionals' obligations. In *Paschim Banga Khet Samity v. State of West Bengal*,[55] it was held that "the State is required to provide adequate medical facilities, and the denial of

---

52 S. Shaikh et al., "Lean Body Mass In Preschool Aged Urban Children In India: Gender Difference", 57(3), *European Journal of Clinical Nutrition*, 389–393 (2003).

53 UN Committee on Economic, Social and Cultural Rights (CESCR), General Comment No. 14: The Right to the Highest Attainable Standard of Health (Art. 12 of the Covenant). Doc. E/C.12/2000/4 (2000).

54 1989 SCC (4) 286.

55 1996 SCC (4) 37.

timely medical intervention by a government hospital to a person in need of such treatment violates Article 21."

Various provisions of the Directive Principles of State Policy deal with health-related issues. According to Article 47, one of the primary responsibilities of the State is to improve the nutritional status and standard of living of its citizens as well as public health. Article 39I mentions that the State's policy should be directed toward ensuring that the health and strength of men and women workers, as well as children, are not compromised and that citizens are not compelled by economic necessity to enter occupations that are unsuitable for their age or strength. Article 39(f) requires the State to take measures to ensure that children have the opportunities and facilities necessary for healthy development.

The Constitution of India (1950) – Articles 47, 39(e), and 39(f)

- **Art. 47** – Duty of the State to raise the level of nutrition and the standard of living and to improve public health. The State shall regard the raising of the level of nutrition and the standard of living of its people and the improvement of public health as among its primary duties and, in particular, the State shall endeavour to bring about prohibition of the consumption, except for medicinal purposes, of intoxicating drinks and of drugs which are injurious to health.
- **Art. 39(e)** – "That the health and strength of workers, men and women, and the tender age of children are not abused and that citizens are not forced by economic necessity to enter avocations unsuited to their age or strength."
- **Art. 39(f)** – That children are given opportunities and facilities to develop in a healthy manner and in conditions of freedom and dignity and that childhood and youth are protected against exploitation and against moral and material abandonment.

Article 42 provides that the State shall ensure just and humane working conditions and maternity leave. According to Article 45, the State shall make every effort to provide early childhood care and education to all children until they reach the age of six. While these provisions are not enforceable in any court, the State is obligated to apply them when enacting laws and policies as they are critical to the country's governance.

The term 'women's reproductive health' falls squarely within the definition of the term 'health.' This human rights-based approach demonstrates an inextricable link between reproduction and health, which serves to protect reproductive rights while also achieving reproductive health. Reproductive health is discussed as a component of everyone's right to the best possible physical and mental health.

The Constitution of India (1950) – Articles 42 and 45

- **Art. 42** – Provision for just and humane conditions of work and maternity relief. The State shall make provision for securing just and humane conditions of work and for maternity relief.
- **Art. 45** – Provision for free and compulsory education for children. The State shall endeavour to provide, within a period of ten years from the commencement of this Constitution, for free and compulsory education for all children until they complete the age of fourteen years.

Reproductive health is defined as "a state of complete physical, mental, and social well-being, and not merely the absence of disease or infirmity, in all matters related to the reproductive system and its functions and process." Reproductive health encompasses all aspects of human sexuality and reproductive processes, functions, and systems, and implies that people can have "a responsible, satisfying, and safe sexual life" as well as the ability to reproduce and the freedom to choose whether, when, and how frequently to do so. Men and women possess the right to know about and have access to safe, effective, affordable, and legal ways to regulate their fertility. They also have the right to healthcare services that promote safe pregnancy and childbirth and give couples the best chance of having a healthy baby. Reproductive health is a lifelong process that begins long before women and men reach sexual maturity and extends well beyond women's childbearing years.

Realization of reproductive rights is tied to and depends on the protection and fulfillment of other human rights, such as the right to life, the right to health, the right to be treated equally, and the right to be free from gender-based violence. In India, peoples' and couples' reproductive rights are protected by a complex set of laws and policies that promote health, employment, education, food, nutrition, and protection from gender-based violence.

Abortion too may be viewed as a healthcare right. It is a right to access a safe medical procedure without harm, even if that procedure is for the termination of potential life. Reproductive rights, along with the right to contraception, have been conceptualized in this way for a long period. This conventional understanding of reproductive rights as healthcare rights has been brushed aside by both courts and reproductive rights advocates in pursuit of rhetoric focused on personal autonomy, equality, and dignity.

Within the family and community, the stigma associated with the body and reproductive health issues prevents women from accessing information about their bodies. Further, women tend to disregard chronic conditions such as mental stress, reproductive difficulties, weakness, and aches and pains amid low self-esteem. Against this backdrop, the concept of 'caring' for one's body is alien to most women. While they continue to demonstrate alarmingly low levels of awareness about health (including maternity services, contraception, immunization, and nutrition during pregnancy), the health delivery system also persists to be insensitive to the needs of poor women and lacks outreach, particularly in remote and distant areas. Thus, a sizable proportion of women continue to lack access to healthcare facilities.

The absence of appropriate social structures that enable women to access and exercise their reproductive rights practically renders legal recognition of women's reproductive rights insufficient. Rights violations caused by restrictions that disproportionately affect marginalized women call for a thorough review of autonomy. Intersectionality accounts for the compounded discrimination caused by multiple oppressive structures.

Thus, in order to make truly informed decisions, people need to be free from bias, become empowered, and have access to a wide range of options.

THREE

Reproductive Rights of Women in India

Sexual and reproductive health is very much a basic right, especially for women. If women do not have rights over their body and sexuality, and if they do not get proper health services throughout their lives, they will not be able to live and function in a dignified way.

– Shanta Laxmi Sretha
Beyond Being Committee, Nepal[1]

State of Reproductive Rights in India

Nowhere in Indian legal texts is the term "reproductive rights" used. However, India retains the concept of women's reproductive rights. Though the Constitution, the statutory framework, and the judiciary have recognized some forms of reproductive rights, as detailed later, there has been a failure on numerous fronts to make these rights a reality for a sizable segment of women. The gaps in the laws and their implementation are a source of concern.

It is worth noting that the government acknowledged in its October 2005 report to the United Nations Committee on the Elimination of Discrimination Against Women (CEDAW) that "women rarely have any say in decisions about having children or the number and spacing of children. These decisions are frequently made by the family and male members, and women are further encumbered by the obligation to produce male children."[2]

---

1 She is an advocate of gender equality, women's human rights and sustainable development. She is one of the SRHR champions and initiated She Decides movement in Nepal in March 2019 in cooperation with the ARROW. She had worked in the government and in non-government organizations in Nepal, Eritrea, Tanzania, and Zambia.

2 Committee on the Elimination of Discrimination Against Women (CEDAW Committee), Consideration of reports submitted by States parties under article 18 of the Convention on the Elimination of All Forms of Discrimination against

About once every four minutes, a pregnant woman in India loses her life due to lack of medical attention.[3] Despite the fact that abortion was made legal in 1971, access is so limited that an estimated 6.7 million women end up having to undergo unsafe abortions performed by unauthorized practitioners annually. During 1970, in view of the strong focus on population control, women were being forced to undergo sterilization procedures in horrifyingly unclean government buildings. Many state governments, instead of ensuring access to a full range of contraceptive services, had adopted coercive population policies that barred families with more than two children from receiving welfare and government jobs, contesting for political roles, and gaining comprehensive access to education and healthcare.[4]

In the current scenario in India, however, various policies and laws are in place to safeguard the reproductive rights of individuals and couples in the areas of health, employment, education, food and nutrition, and safety from gender-based violence.[5] These rights endow couples or people with autonomy in health decision-making, which may be exercised without undue interference from others. Although the rights to health and reproductive rights are not explicitly recognized as fundamental rights in the Indian Constitution, the Supreme Court has repeatedly ruled that access to timely and adequate health care is a vital human right. In a landmark decision in *Suchita Srivastava v. Chandigarh Administration*,[6] the Supreme Court declared that reproductive autonomy is a component of personal liberty protected under Article 21. It is up to women to decide whether to procreate or abstain from procreating using their reproductive choices. The primary concern is to preserve a woman's right to bodily integrity as well as her right to privacy and dignity. This indicates that a person should be free to choose their own method of reproduction and birth control, including sterilization procedures. Deduced logically,

---

Women (CEDAW), Combined second and third periodic report of State parties, India, para. 333, U.N. Doc. CEDAW/C/IND/2-3

[3] World Health Organisation, *Maternal Mortality in 2000: Estimates Developed by WHO, UNICEF, UNFPA* 24 (2004), available at http://www.who.int/reproductive-health/ publications/maternal_mortality_2000/mme.pdf.

[4] Shruti Pandey et al. (eds.), "Coercion Versus Empowerment", *Human Rights Law Network*, vii, xxii (2006).

[5] SAMA, "Resource Group for Women And Health, Beyond Numbers: Implications of the Two-Child Norm", 7 (2005).

[6] (2009) 9 SCC 1.

reproductive rights include a woman's right to bear and bring up children (holding a pregnancy to its full term, giving birth, and rearing the child). This case upheld the right to personal liberty and advanced the right to special treatment based on individual and female preferences.

Furthermore, in 2015, in *T. Sivakumar v. the Inspector of Police*,[7] the High Court of Madras delivered a landmark judgment recognizing child marriage as a violation of human rights as well as girls' fundamental rights under Articles 14 and 15 of the Indian Constitution. Subsequently, the verdict in *M. Mohamed Abbas v. the Chief Secretary*[8] established that the Prohibition of Child Marriage Act (PMCA), which sets 18 as the minimum legal age for girls to marry, supersedes personal laws without violating Article 25 of the Constitution (freedom of religion). Additionally, the Court stated in its decision that all girl children should have the same right to education and empowerment as the men in society, as guaranteed by Articles 14, 15, 16, and 21 of the Constitution.

Numerous cases in India involve issues relating to the denial of maternal healthcare. Depriving women of maternal healthcare services directly violates their inalienable survival rights, which are a component of the right to life. The Supreme Court's positive and productive decisions directed toward preserving fundamental rights help close the gaps and overcome the barriers to reproductive rights in India.

Gateways to Reproductive Rights in India

Termination of Pregnancy

Termination of pregnancy refers to the procedure of ending pregnancy medically. In the early stages of pregnancy (7–9 weeks), it can be terminated with the help of medicines; during the later weeks, surgery may be needed. Legally, only the consent of the pregnant woman (who is an adult) is required for terminating the pregnancy; no other person's consent needs to be obtained. Surgical termination should be performed by experienced medical professionals due to the high risk involved in the procedure, even if it is minor in itself. It is also important to visit a gynecologist to ascertain and be aware of the risks and complications that may arise in a particular case. In the non-surgical approach, doctors usually recommend a pill named Mifeprex (mifepristone). This pill is either administered by injection or taken orally.

---

[7] AIR 2012 Mad 62.

[8] 2015 (4) CTC 132.

Before 1971, abortions were primarily regulated by Sections 312–314 of the IPC, 1860 and were illegal unless the life of the mother was under exigent circumstances[9]. The MTP Act of 1971 was passed to prohibit abortions performed by untrained individuals or in unsanitary conditions, as well as to reduce maternal morbidity and mortality.

The Supreme Court clarified in *Jacob George v. the State of Kerala*[10] that the IPC's miscarriage provisions are subordinate to the MTP Act. The Rajasthan High Court also dismissed the petition challenging the constitutional validity of the MTP Act on the grounds that it violates an unborn child's fundamental right to life in *Nand Kishore Sharma v. Union of India.*[11] The High Court held that "the MTP Act was consistent with Article 21 of the Constitution of India because its primary objective was to save pregnant women's lives, prevent harm to their physical or mental health, and avoid possible birth defects." The Supreme Court in *Suchita Srivastava v. Chandigarh Administration*[12] observed that as per Article 21, a woman has the right to choose whether or not to have children. This case attempted to recognize the choice to abort as a part of a woman's right to freedom. In another case involving *High Court on its Motion v. the State of Maharashtra,*[13] the Bombay High Court too reaffirmed the stance stated in *Suchita Srivastava*[14] and made the following observations:

> *A woman's decision to terminate a pregnancy is not a frivolous one. Abortion is often the only way out of a very difficult situation for a woman... These are decisions taken by responsible women who have few other options. They are women who would ideally have preferred to prevent unwanted pregnancy but were unable to do so. If a woman does not want to continue with the pregnancy, then forcing her to do so represents a violation of the woman's bodily integrity and aggravates her mental trauma, which would be deleterious to her mental health.*

The right to abortion got further strengthened with the passage of the Medical Termination of Pregnancy (Amendment) Act, 2021, which

---

[9] In the criminal procedure context, exigent circumstance refers to an emergency situation requiring swift action to prevent imminent danger to life or serious damage to property, or to forestall the imminent escape of a suspect, or destruction of evidence.

[10] 1994 SCC (3) 430.

[11] (1977) ILLJ 430 Del.

[12] AIR 2010 SC 235.

[13] Suo Motu public interest litigation No. 1 of 2016.

[14] AIR 2010 SC 235.

extended the period during which abortions may be performed legally. The amended statute now permits abortion up to 20 weeks on the advice of one doctor and between 20 and 24 weeks on the advice of two doctors for certain categories of women. To terminate a pregnancy after 24 weeks due to significant fetal anomalies, the approval of the state-level medical board is essential.

Sterilization and Other Contraceptives

Sterilization is a permanent method of birth control and is another gateway to the realization of reproductive autonomy of parents and women in particular. It is the most preferred method of family planning in India as it is the most beneficial birth control method for both men and women when done safely and ethically. The fact that the public is not very aware of alternative temporary contraceptive methods also adds to its prevalence. Further, there are numerous complaints about the unavailability of alternative contraceptives.

While sterilization is a safer and more convenient choice for men, the stigma associated with vasectomy – that it renders men impotent – hinders its adoption. So, female sterilization continues to be the most popular method. In India, state governments promote sterilization as a population control measure and actively provide sterilization services through the fixed day static model[15] as well as camps, mostly free of cost. Under these state-run programs, sterilization is carried out on a large scale and people are given nominal incentives for undergoing sterilization. Health workers specifically target women from 'backward communities' to meet the sterilization targets assigned to them.

However, sterilization must not be viewed as a method of population control. The current family planning program's objective is to empower individuals to make informed decisions and provide them with effective and safe methods of contraception.[16]

In *Ramakant Rai v. UOI*,[17] the apex court was approached through a PIL on government practices regarding female sterilization, which lacked counseling or informed consent as well as pre-and post-operative

---

[15] The fixed day static (FDS) approach in sterilization services is defined as providing sterilization services in a health facility by trained providers posted in the same facility, on fixed days, throughout the year on a regular and routine manner.

[16] Issues of Sterilization, available at https://reproductiverights.hrln.org/issues/sterilization/.

[17] (2009) 16 SCC 567.

care and included unhygienic and unanesthetized operating conditions, sterilization of minors, coercion, and cruelty. The PIL requested the court to direct the governments to strictly follow the GOI guidelines on female sterilization enacted in October 1999 in letter and spirit. The petitioners asserted that current sterilization conditions violated not only the guidelines but patient's reproductive rights, women's rights, and health rights as articulated in international instruments ratified by India, including the Alma-Alta Declaration, CEDAW, ICPD Programme of Action, and Beijing Platform for Action. They further contended that the current conditions violated the constitutional right to health, which is part of the right to life enshrined in Articles 14, 15, 21, and 47.

In March 2005, the court issued an interim order to ensure that the guidelines were followed finding a lack of uniformity in procedures and norms. It ordered all states in India to "establish an approved panel of doctors to carry out sterilization procedures, prepare and circulate a checklist with information on each patient, circulate uniform copies of the proforma of consent, set up a Quality Assurance Committee, maintain overall statistics, hold an inquiry into every case of breach of the Union of India guidelines and take punitive action against them, and bring into effect an insurance policy." The Union of India was directed to, within four weeks, outline "uniform standards to be followed by the state governments, including the norms for compensation and the format of the statistics, checklist, consent proforma, and insurance." All the state governments and the central government submitted their respective compliance report and the matter was finally closed in December 2007.

Some incidents have come to the fore where surgeries did not follow the *Ramakant Rai* guidelines for procedure and quality. This resulted in adverse side effects, failure of sterilization, and even death. In numerous instances, sterilization was conducted without the consent of the women and by keeping them in complete ignorance of alternative methods of birth control, thus taking away their ability to make a decision and live a healthy, dignified life.

Later in 2006, the GOI published a manual on "Standards on Female and Male Sterilization" as well as updated the Quality Assurance Manual based on the prevailing technical and programmatic modifications as well as the directions of the Supreme Court. In 2014, the Ministry of Health and Family Planning, GOI issued a revised manual for standards and quality assurance in sterilization services[18] in order to improve and assure the quality of sterilization services in public and accredited private/NGO facilities in the country. The government emphasized that family planning interventions hold one of the keys toward fulfilling India's commitment to MDGs for lowering maternal and child morbidity and mortality. The government claims that there has been a substantial decline in the failure, complication, and death rates of sterilization as centers are now ensuring adherence to quality guidelines and SOPs.

Despite this, in January 2012, around 53 women in Bihar were sterilized in an incredibly negligent manner. The sterilization camp was organized by an NGO that had been accredited by the District Health Society, seemingly without following any formal or transparent process. The women had received no counseling regarding the risks and complications associated with the sterilization procedure. The surgeries were performed in a school instead of a hospital, in an unsanitary and unethical manner, by a single surgeon under torchlight on top of a desk without access to running water or sanitary gloves. Almost all the women reported severe physical pain following the operation and filed police reports. State authorities conducted a subsequent investigation and determined that the camp was tremendously successful, except for the use of expired medication. The court found that the incident violated two very important rights under Article 21 (Protection of Life and Personal Liberty) – the right to health and the right to reproductive autonomy. It held that the right to exercise reproductive rights includes the right to make an informed decision about sterilization free of coercion. In its deliberations, the court cited the CEDAW's 2004 decision in *A.S. v. Hungary*,[19] which held that fully informed consent to sterilization is required.[20]

Surrogacy as a Means to Enhance Reproductive Choices

Surrogacy represents an interesting field for studying reproductive rights, but it is generally analyzed through feminist discourses and experiences. Surrogacy has provided an option to intended mothers to overcome the problems of fertility and widened the scope of reproductive

---

[18] Manual of National Health Mission, GOI available at /https://nhm.gov.in/images/pdf/programmes/family-planing/guidelines/Standards_and_Quality_Assurance.pdf.

[19] Communication No. 4/2004, CEDAW/C/36/D/4/2004.

[20] *Devika Biswas v. Union of India & Others*, AIR 2016 SC 4405.

choices. It allows women to conceive a child and escape possible societal discrimination associated with childlessness. It also allows unmarried couples or single men to have a child, thereby making parenthood more accessible and equitable. In India, surrogacy is a legal arrangement in which a woman agrees to become pregnant after being implanted with a man's sperm and another woman's oocyte, or she gives her oocyte to the man who wants to have a child. The Surrogacy (Regulation) Act 2021 defines surrogacy under section 2(zd) as "a practice whereby one woman bears and gives birth to a child for an intending couple with the intention of handing over such child to the intending couple after the birth." The surrogacy arrangement can be of different types – traditional or gestational surrogacy, compensated or altruistic surrogacy, domestic or international surrogacy, and agency-based or independent surrogacy.[21] In traditional surrogacy, the egg of the surrogate mother is fertilized during the process. In gestational surrogacy, the surrogate woman (mother) only serves as a host or carrier for the zygote until it develops into a baby, at which point she gives the child back to its real parents. The Surrogacy (Regulation) Act, 2021 permits gestational surrogacy for altruistic purposes, with a host of conditions. The Act defines under section 2(b) altruistic surrogacy and 2(g) commercial surrogacy.

Surrogacy (Regulation) Act, 2021 – Sections 2(b) and 2(g)

- **Section 2(b)** – Altruistic surrogacy means the surrogacy in which no charges, expenses, fees, remuneration, or monetary incentive of whatever nature, except the medical expenses and such other prescribed expenses incurred on surrogate mother and the insurance coverage for the surrogate mother, are given to the surrogate mother or her dependents or her representative.
- **Section 2(g)** – Commercial surrogacy means commercialization of surrogacy services or procedures or its component services or component procedures, including selling or buying of human embryo or trading in the sale or purchase of human embryo or gametes or selling or buying or trading the services of surrogate motherhood by way of giving payment, reward, benefit, fees, remuneration or monetary incentive in cash or kind, to the surrogate mother or her dependents or her representative, except the medical expenses and

[21] About Surrogacy: The Different Types of Surrogacies, available at https://surrogate.com/about-surrogacy/types-of-surrogacy/types-of-surrogacy/.

such other prescribed expenses incurred on the surrogate mother and the insurance coverage for the surrogate mother.

The Act permits only gestational surrogacy, which has been described in Explanation to Section 4 as "a practice whereby a surrogate mother carries a child for the intending couple through implantation of the embryo in her womb and the child is not genetically related to the surrogate mother." Further, according to sections 4(b) & (d), gestational surrogacy can be availed only for altruistic purposes and not for purposes of commercialization or production of children for sale, prostitution, or any other form of exploitation.

Notably, surrogacy can be availed by intended couples or intending women. Men alone are not allowed to avail of surrogacy. Section I(r) defines intending couple as a couple who have a medical indication necessitating gestational surrogacy and who intend to become parents through surrogacy. The intending couple must be legally married, where the age of the female is between 23–50 years and that of the male is 26–55 years. They should not have had any surviving child biologically or through adoption or through surrogacy earlier. However, a couple with a child who is mentally or physically challenged or suffers from a life-threatening disorder or fatal illness with no permanent cure approved by the appropriate authority with due medical certificate can also avail surrogacy. Intending woman in section 2(s) means an Indian woman who is a widow or divorcee between the age of 35–45 years and who intends to avail surrogacy.

Advances in the medical field of assisted reproductive technology have resulted in the development of effective techniques, including donor insemination and embryo transfers,[22] which has increased the popularity of surrogacy as a reproductive process among couples, especially in India.[23] However, the significant economic strain associated with surrogacy affects its accessibility to people with meagre means struggling with infertility. The total cost of the procedure varies between INR 10 and

---

[22] The transfer of one or more embryos, selected from a larger cohort of available embryos. See World Health Organization, International Committee for Monitoring Assisted Reproductive Technology (ICMART) and the World Health Organization (WHO) revised glossary of ART terminology (2009), available at https://www.who.int/reproductivehealth/publications/infertility/art_terminology2.pdf?ua=1.

[23] A Report on Centre for Social Research, *Report on Surrogate Motherhood – Ethical or Commercial*, available at: http://www.womenleadership.in/Csr/SurrogacyReport.pdf.

16 lakhs, depending on the clinic,[24] location, and level of technological advancement.

Before the passing of the Surrogacy (Regulation) Act, 2021, the absence of a legally binding regulatory mechanism allowed for the widespread exploitation of low-income women, such as forced implantation in postmenopausal women, provision of disgraceful living conditions and conveyance of limited information about the potential health risks of participating in the surrogacy process. Preeclampsia, gestational diabetes, postpartum complications like hemorrhaging and depression, and the risk of mortality for surrogate mothers were not addressed.

The Parliament passed the Surrogacy (Regulation) Act, 2021 to legalize and regulate surrogacy in response to years-long activism. On January 25, 2021, the Act became law after the union government published it in the official gazette. The legislation regulates surrogacy, protecting the rights and dignity of surrogate mothers while allowing couples and certain categories of women who have been unable to conceive despite trying a variety of fertility treatments to achieve their goal of becoming parents.

The Surrogacy (Regulation) Act, 2021 is the first law in India that regulates surrogacy practices. However, societal discomfort around surrogacy remains, especially in cases where an egg or sperm donor is required. Conversely, the progressive law, which aims to make surrogacy available to people who cannot have children, fails to be progressive by its very nature because it excludes a certain category of persons and uses vague language that leaves it open to much debate and misinterpretation. It is argued by many that the Act is restrictive in nature and needs to be more inclusive by allowing traditional surrogacy and permitting non-binary people to avail surrogacy.

The government also passed the Assisted Reproductive Technology (Regulation) Act in 2021 to aid reproductive technology clinics and laboratories.

Assisted Reproductive Technologies and Reproductive Rights

Innovative and sophisticated diagnostic instruments and medicines & drugs for fertility treatment have the potential to improve the reproductive health and reproductive choices of couples and women. There has been a global rise in the utilization of assisted reproductive technologies (hereinafter referred to as ART) mainly due to increased emphasis on

---

[24] Natalia Alvarez & Romina Packan, "Surrogacy Laws in India – Cost, Process & Requirements", *Babygest* (2019), available at: https://babygest.com/en/india/.

reproductive rights and justice as well as an increase in prominence of and accessibility to medical technologies. ART methods continue to be an option for those who want to become parents without giving birth in addition to assisting couples and individuals who are unable to conceive despite fertility treatments. The traditional conceptions of motherhood and paternity are changing with time. Their broadened definitions have resulted in a substantial improvement in the distinction between biological and sociological parentage. A larger number of people around the world, primarily those in the upper middle class, are now able to make purposeful use of these technologies as a result of the above-mentioned shift in societal consciousness, contemporary, fast-paced lifestyles, and increased disposable incomes.[25]

In-vitro Fertilization

In-vitro fertilization (hereinafter referred to as IVF) is a widely used ART technique involving medical intervention during the natural process of fertilization. The fertilized egg is placed into the uterus of the commissioning mother. It is used in cases of male or female infertility, such as those induced by blocked fallopian tubes, ovulation disorders, genetic disorders, tubal diseases, endometriosis, immunological issues, cervical problems, or uterine disorders. In India, the price of IVF ranges from INR 2 to 4 lakhs (about USD 2,500 to USD 4,500). In most cases, health insurance does not cover the expense of IVF or any other fertility treatment; so, the decision to undergo such treatment requires significant out-of-pocket expenditures. Due to the fact that gametes are exposed in vitro and embryos initially develop outside the human body, IVF remains a risky procedure despite its widespread use today. Additionally, multiple gestations, ectopic pregnancies, spontaneous[26] abortions, and premature births are some of the risks associated with ART procedures, including IVF.

An IVF cycle consists of several steps. The appointing mother is required to take medicines to mature the eggs in her body as the first step. This is called ovulation induction, and the patient's body is constantly

---

[25] F. James Smith et al., "Socioeconomic Disparities in the Utilization and Success of Fertility Treatments: Analysis of Data from a Prospective Cohort in the United States", 96(1), *Fertil. Steril.* (2011).

[26] F. Zergers & Hochschild et al., "International Committee for Monitoring Assisted Reproductive Technology (ICMART) and the World Health Organization (WHO) revised glossary of ART terminology, 2009", 92(5), *Fertility and Sterility* (2009).

monitored for hormone levels and egg production. Drugs used to stimulate hormone production include follicle-stimulating hormone (FSH) and luteinizing hormone (LH).[27] To avoid ovarian hyperstimulation syndrome, the hormones must be administered with extreme caution as their effects may vary on each woman. An exaggerated systemic response to ovarian stimulation is characterized by a wide spectrum of clinical and laboratory manifestations. It is classified as mild, moderate, or severe according to the degree of abdominal distention, ovarian enlargement, and respiratory, hemodynamic, and metabolic complications. During this point, the process of egg retrieval begins, in which the eggs are surgically removed from the body. This method involves inserting a needle into the vagina and then using a suction device to remove the eggs. Next, sperms – of either the commissioning father's or a donor's – are added to the eggs under the insemination stage. After three to five days, the embryos formed from the fertilized eggs are harvested and implanted.[28] Pregnancy develops after an embryo successfully implants in the uterine wall. Human chorionic gonadotropin levels are measured to verify the pregnancy.

Gene Therapy

Gene manipulation can refer to gene selection and gene editing. Preimplantation genetic diagnosis (PGD) is a technique to test cell(s) from embryos created outside the body by IVF for a genetic disorder. Under the procedure, an embryo's chromosomes and genes are analyzed in a petri dish to screen the ones carrying genetic disorders like sickle cell anemia and Down syndrome. Tests are carried out for the specific disorder that the embryos are known to be at significant risk of inheriting. Unaffected embryos are selected for transfer to the uterus in the hope that a normal birth will ensue.[29] Since the embryo is reimplanted via IVF, all of the medical risks involved with IVF are applicable.[30]

---

[27] Gottumukkala Achyuta & Rama Raju et al., "Luteinizing Hormone and Follicle-Stimulating Hormone Synergy: A Review of Role in Controlled Ovarian Hyper-Stimulation", 6(4), Hum. Reprod. Sci. (2013).

[28] What is IVF?, planned parenthood, available at https://www.plannedparenthood.org/learn/pregnancy/fertility-treatments/what-ivf

[29] National Health Service ('NHS'), Clinical Commissioning Policy: Pre-implantation Genetics Diagnosis (April 2013), available at https://www.england.nhs.uk/wpcontent/uploads/2013/04/e01-p-a.pdf

[30] Pre-implantation genetic diagnosis (PGD), Human Fertilisation & Embryology Authority, available at https://www.hfea.gov.uk/treatments/embryo-testing-and-treatments-for-disease/pre-implantation-geneticdiagnosis-pgd/

Gene editing is subdivided into somatic gene therapy and germline editing. Somatic gene therapy is the editing of cells that are not reproductive, such as gametes, germ cells, or gametocytes. This implies that the intervention is not passed on to the patient's descendants. It is more frequently used than germline therapy and is effective in treating cystic fibrosis,[31] adenosine diseases,[32] certain types of cancer, and hemophilia. While cystic fibrosis is an inherited condition that causes sticky mucus to build up in the lungs and digestive system, which causes lung infections and problems with digesting food, ADA-SCID is caused by mistakes (mutations) in the ADA gene, which results in absent or very low levels of the ADA enzyme. Enzymes are protein substances that help speed up chemical reactions in the body. Lack of the ADA enzyme causes a build-up of a toxic substance called deoxyadenosine. This prevents cells from dividing effectively.

CRISPR-Cas9 is a highly complicated, novel gene-editing technique. It entails the synthesis of RNA with a sequence complementary to the target DNA sequence in a genome. Additionally, it interacts with the Cas9 enzyme. Cas9 is an endonuclease enzyme that has immunological functions in the body. The enzyme cuts the DNA at the specified location, which is recognized by the modified RNA. After this is done, the DNA repair machinery is employed to make changes to the genetic material of the cell. Besides that, a new sequence can replace an old one in a piece of DNA.[33] The CRISPR/Cas9 system occurs naturally in bacteria and attains its DNA-cutting abilities from its role as part of the bacterial immune system. Snippets of DNA from invading viruses are cut and stored in the bacterial genome as part of the CRISPR (clustered regularly interspaced short palindromic repeats) array. The Cas9 protein (short for CRISPR-associated protein 9) uses those snippets to recognize future invaders and cuts their genetic material, killing them. The CRISPR/Cas9 array allows the bacteria to recognize future attacks and, because it becomes part of the bacterial genome, to pass that immunity on to its offspring. Jennifer

---

[31] Cystic fibrosis (CF) is a genetic condition that affects a protein in the body. People who have cystic fibrosis have a faulty protein that affects the body's cells, tissues, and the glands that make mucus and sweat.

[32] Adenosine deaminase (ADA) deficiency is an inherited disorder that damages the immune system and causes severe combined immunodeficiency (SCID). People with SCID lack virtually all immune protection from bacteria, viruses, and fungi.

[33] Brown TA. Genomes. 2nd edition. Oxford: Wiley-Liss; 2002. Chapter 14, Mutation, Repair and Recombination.

Doudna, one of the leading researchers of the technique, has developed strategies to combat the unethical and unbridled use of CRISPR-Cas9.[34] Some of the experts[35] have proposed a global moratorium, while others have suggested additional consequences for misuse, such as loss of funding and abrogation of publication privileges. Although there is no binding legislative framework in India to govern or regulate gene therapy, the ICMR published the *National Guidelines for Gene Therapy Product Development and Clinical Trials* in November 2019.

Legal Framework

ART have generated considerable enthusiasm worldwide over the last four decades. As more and more sophisticated techniques continue to develop under ART, important questions persist about the impact of ART on reproductive rights. New developments such as preimplantation screening, germline editing, gene selection, embryo splitting, sperm injection, extracorporeal gestation and posthumously birthing, and other technology-mediated procreation methods raise complex legal, ethical, and policy concerns. In India, ART are regulated through the Assisted Reproductive Technology (Regulation) Act, 2021. The Act provides a framework to supervise ART clinics and banks so as to ensure safe and ethical practices and prevent the technologies' misuse. It defines the term ART under section 2(a) as "… with its grammatical variation and cognate expressions, means all techniques that attempt to obtain a pregnancy by handing the sperm or the oocyte outside the human body and transferring the gamete or the embryo into the reproductive system of a woman." Broadly, in vitro fertilization-embryo transfer (IVF-ET), gamete intrafallopian transfer (GIFT), zygote intrafallopian transfer (ZIFT), and frozen embryo transfer are the types of assisted reproductive technologies. These techniques also apply to egg donation and gestational carriers. When other treatments (such as intrauterine insemination) fail or when there is extreme male factor infertility, severe endometriosis, or tubal obstruction, ART may be recommended. The Act envisages that

[34] Hannah Shelby, "Renowned scientists address ethics, 'twin scientific revolutions' of AI and CRISPR", *The Stanford Daily*, November 21, 2019, available at https://www.stanforddaily.com/2019/11/21/renownedscientists-address-ethics-twin-scientific-revolutions-of-ai-and-crispr/.

[35] Niall Firth, "CRISPR experts are calling for a global moratorium on heritable gene editing", *MIT Technology Review*, March 13, 2019, available at https://www.technologyreview.com/s/613120/crisprexperts-are-calling-for-a-global-moratorium-on-heritable-gene-editing/.

ART services, including in-vitro fertilization and gene therapy, are used to ensure reproductive health and treat infertility while addressing social and medical concerns.

The ART and Surrogacy Board is being constituted at the national and state levels under sections 3 and 6 of the 2021 Act. The composition of the national board and state boards are prescribed in sections 4 and 7, respectively. Some of the functions of the national board include advising the central government and reviewing and monitoring the implementation of the Act. The national board is also tasked with laying down the code of conduct and standards for ART clinics, banks, employees and the national registry.

The national registry is a database of all clinics and banks of the country, which includes details about the nature, types, and outcomes of services offered by them. This data shall be used by the national board for conducting research in ART and other fields, identifying new research areas, and making policies and guidelines. Additionally, the ART and Surrogacy Authority is being set up in each state and union territory (as per section 12) for regulating registration and compliance by clinics and banks within their bounds. The Act provides the procedure for the registration of clinics and banks in Chapter III (sections 15–20) and the duties thereof in Chapter IV (sections 21–31). The offences and penalties are described in Chapter V (sections 32–41).

FOUR

Nature and Scope of the Right to Abortion

The state shall constitute medical boards in each district in order to examine cases of women seeking medical termination of pregnancy. The state has also been directed to focus on providing facilities to women in rural areas with regard to their hygiene and health.

– *XYZ v. Union of India*[1]

In 1971, the Parliament of India enacted the Medical Termination of Pregnancy Act (MTP Act), making India one of the liberal countries to legalize abortion. Consequently, unwanted pregnancies could be legally terminated by women under certain circumstances. The Act enabled women to assert basic control over their bodies and health, without the fear of physical harm.

However, this has not resulted in the availability of affordable and safe abortion services for women. While all public sector amenities of a certain category are presumed to provide abortion services for free, the reality is quite different – with pregnancy termination facilities largely run by the private sector, thereby making it difficult for women with limited financial resources to access them.

Women prioritize privacy over their physical health when it comes to such a sensitive and socially unapproved issue as abortion. In the majority of states in India, public health centers do not consistently offer abortion pills as part of their medical services.[2] Several registered medical practitioners promote surgical over medical abortion so that other procedures can be done alongside. Pressure on a woman to undergo permanent sterilization along with abortion is an example. Due to a lack of awareness of the MTP Act, there are delayed actions from women to seek medical care. In cases where minor girls, survivors of sexual assault, and women with limited access to medical services are involved, these

---

[1] WPC No. 10835 of 2018, High Court of Bombay.

[2] Handbook on Medical Methods of Abortion, Ministry of Health & Family Welfare Government of India, 2016.

factors make the mechanism ineffective. Unsafe abortion is one of the leading causes of maternal death in India.

This chapter covers the concept and practice of abortion in India. To give a deeper insight, the chapter also describes the notion of abortion through different facets, including human and socio-cultural rights.

Meaning of Abortion

The term abortion means "the act of terminating a pregnancy, either by removing an embryo or a fetus before maturity."[3] Abortions are conducted using surgical instruments, modern medicines, or other traditional methods. Miscarriage is the term used to refer to an abortion that occurs accidentally. An abortion that is planned or intended is referred to as induced abortion. Induced abortion is sometimes referred to as 'delayed pregnancy termination' where the fetus is removed despite its ability to survive. The terms 'medical termination of pregnancy' and 'abortion' have distinct connotations. The former refers to the procedure prescribed by law, while the latter is associated with women's autonomy. Abortion has been legalized in developed countries within certain circumstances and is carried out using modern medical methods that address the individual's future health, and physical, biological, and psychological needs.[4]

Abortions can be classified broadly into three categories: spontaneous, therapeutic, and criminal.

(a) A **spontaneous or natural abortion** occurs as a result of an abnormal condition in the fetus or mother, or as a result of some other medical cause.

(b) A **therapeutic abortion** is carried out with due diligence by a medical expert who is convinced that continuing the pregnancy would put the mother's life in jeopardy or cause serious health problems for her. This kind of abortion is also performed when there is a cause to believe that the fetus is physically or mentally disabled.

(c) A **criminal abortion** occurs in case of deliberate interference during the prenatal period in circumstances where there is no legal justification.

---

[3] Bongani Tshuma et al., "Abortion: A Concept Analysis", 7(5), *Journal of Nursing and Health Science*, 20–23 (2018).

[4] M. Forster, "Long-Term Physical and Psychological Health Consequences of Induced Abortion", *Journal of Obstetrical & Gynaecological Survey*, 67 (2012).

The term 'miscarriage' is used synonymously with 'abortion' under Sections 312 to 316 of the Indian Penal Code, 1860. Section 312 IPC, which prohibits the unlawful termination of pregnancy, uses the term 'miscarriage' to refer to pregnancy that is terminated prematurely by artificial means.

Around the globe, there is an ongoing debate on abortion's social, cultural, ethical, legal, and economic implications. The moral and religious perspectives on abortion are diverse. Abortion is legal in some countries under certain conditions, such as rape, fetal abnormalities, or threat to the mother's health.[5]

Each year, approximately 56 million abortions are performed worldwide,[6] with slightly less than half performed in unsafe conditions. Maternal morbidity and mortality associated with unsafe abortion complications have been identified as significant public health problems.[7] It is to be noted that medical reporting of abortion is unreliable in various countries where abortion is illegal or stigmatized.

There are numerous and varied reasons for abortion. People frequently assert that they cannot afford to raise a child, that the father is not supportive, that having a child would interfere with their education, that it would hurt their relationship with their partner or that they are too young to have a child. Certain abortions are performed in response to social challenges. These can include a preference for a child of a specific gender, opposition to single or early motherhood, marginalization of disabled people, inadequate economic assistance from families or lack of access to birth control methods.

Understanding the Right to Abortion

The right to abortion is a subject that has been extensively debated at both the national and international levels. The dilemma is whether a mother

---

[5] A.J. Adler et al., "Incidence of Severe Acute Maternal Morbidity Associated with Abortion: A Systematic Review", 17(2), *Tropical Medicine & International Health*, 177–190 (2012).

[6] J Bearak, A Popinchalk, B Ganatra, A-B Moller et al., "Unintended Pregnancy and Abortion by Income, Region, and the Legal Status of Abortion: Estimates from a Comprehensive Model for 1990–2019", 8(9), *Lancet Global Health*, e1152-e1161 (2020).

[7] World Health Organization Report, "Health Worker Roles in Providing Safe Abortion Care and Post-Abortion Contraception" (WHO: Geneva, 2015).

has the right to terminate her pregnancy or whether the fetus has a right to life.

Under the Constitution of India

Any discrimination based on sex is expressly forbidden by the Constitution of India under Article 15. Differential treatment of women based on pregnancy has been recognized by the courts as a violation of the right to equality.[8] The implications of restricted abortion on the right to equality have been indirectly addressed by the Supreme Court.[9] In *X v. Principal Secretary, Health and Family Welfare Department, Govt of NCT Of Delhi*,[10] the Supreme Court held that the artificial distinction between married and unmarried women prior to the MTP (Amendment) Act, 2021 was not constitutionally sustainable. "The benefits of law extend equally to single and married women. If women with unwanted pregnancies are forced to carry them out to term, the State would be stripping them of their right to determine the immediate and long-term paths their lives would take."

Article 21 of the Indian Constitution recognizes the right to life and personal liberty. The right to abortion has been recognized as a subset of the right to personal liberty. However, the question of whether an unborn child should be regarded as a human being and provided the status of a person continues. Many facets of the right to abortion are governed by religious, ethical, moral, and legal values.

In *Nand Kishore Sharma v. Union of India*,[11] the petitioner challenged the constitutionality of the MTP Act for violating the rights of the unborn child under Article 21 of the Constitution. The question of law and morality in abortion was dealt with. The Court upheld the validity of the MTP Act, stating that "the object of the Act being to save the life of the pregnant woman or relieve her of any injury to her physical and mental health, and no other thing. The Act is rather in consonance with Article 21 of the Constitution of India than in conflict with it."

In *Suchita Srivastava v. Chandigarh Administration*,[12] the Supreme Court recognized the right to reproductive autonomy under Article 21. It was held that the right to reproductive autonomy includes the right

---

[8] *Navtej Johar v. Union of India* (2018) 10 SCC 1.

[9] *NALSA v. Union of India* (2014) 5 SCC 438.

[10] SLP (Civil) No. 12612 of 2022, Decided on 21-7-2022.

[11] AIR 2006 Raj. 166.

[12] (2009) 9 SCC 1.

to "make reproductive choices, to procreate as well as to abstain from procreating."

The landmark decision of *Justice K.S. Puttaswamy (Retd.) and Anr. v. Union of India and Ors.*[13] stated that Article 21 of the Constitution protects the right to life with dignity and the right to privacy, which includes the right to procreate or abstain from procreating. The Supreme Court acknowledged that "privacy of the body entitles an individual to the integrity of the physical aspects of personhood. The intersection between one's mental integrity and privacy entitles the individual to freedom of thought, the freedom to believe in what is right, and the freedom of self-determination. The family, marriage, procreation, and sexual orientation are all integral to the dignity of the individual. Above all, the privacy of the individual recognizes an inviolable right to determine how freedom shall be exercised."

In *Independent Thought v. Union of India,*[14] the Supreme Court acknowledged the reproductive autonomy and right to bodily integrity of minor girls and held that "the discussion on the bodily integrity of a girl child and the reproductive choices available to her is important only to highlight that she cannot be treated as a commodity having no say over her body."

On April 29, 2019, the constitutionality of sections 3(2), 3(4), and 5 of the MTP Act was challenged in *Swati Agarwal v. Union of India.*[15] The petitioners argued that these provisions are in violation of Articles 14 and 21 of the Constitution. The petition sought to widen women's access to safe abortions and grant them greater reproductive choices. It also asserted that the State has a positive obligation to guarantee the right to health under Article 21. The Supreme Court is yet to decide on this matter.

Life of a Fetus and Abortion

According to the WHO, a fetus of 500 grams after a minimum of 22 weeks of gestation is considered viable. However, individuals are only legally protected under the right to life from birth to death, and not during pregnancy. Further, the term 'fetus' is not mentioned in international

[13] (2017) 10 SCC 1.

[14] (2017) 10 SCC 800.

[15] W.P. (C) 825/2019 Supreme Court.

human rights treaties. Thus, human rights are not considered applicable before birth.[16]

On the contrary, the UN Convention on the Rights of the Child argues that, "the child, due to his physical and mental immaturity, requires special safeguards and care, including appropriate legal protection both before and after birth."[17] Similarly, the rights of the unborn child were voiced by the members of the Right to Life Movement in the United States of America. They emphasized that no individual or government should deny a fetus his or her constitutional and moral rights.[18]

Pro-life groups argue that science has proven that human life begins with fertilization beyond a reasonable doubt. From the moment it is conceived, the fetus is a new human being with a genetic code that is distinct from that of its parents. The new human being requires development and growth, and women only give birth to that new human being. Thus, abortion always puts an innocent person's life to an end. In the end, future generations rely on the actions of the present generation for survival.[19]

The pro-choice lobby argues that the moral and legal rights of all affected parties should be considered, and not just the fetus.' Further, it raises questions such as: Is it ethical to allow the fetus to live but to let the mother die? Is it moral to insist on the birth of a deformed child? Who has the authority to make decisions?

The dilemmas raised by the abortion debate are complex. Those who oppose abortion assert that a fetus is a human being with a right to life and an abortion can be compared to murder, whereas those who advocate for abortion legalization assert that a woman has autonomy over her own body.[20]

According to international human rights law, a person is vested with human rights only at birth. In *High Court on Its Own Motion v. State of*

---

[16] World Health Organization (1979).

[17] UN General Assembly, *Convention on the Rights of the Child*, 1577 United Nations, Treaty Series, 3 (1989).

[18] R.N. Karrer, "The National Right to Life Committee: Its Founding, its history, and the Emergence of the Pro-Life Movement Prior to Roe v. Wade", 97(3), *The Catholic Historical Review*, 527–557 (2011).

[19] J. P. Sterba, "Abortion, Distant Peoples, and Future Generations", 77(7), *The Journal of Philosophy*, 424–440 (1980).

[20] L. Say et al., "Global Causes of Maternal Death: A Who Systematic Analysis", 2(6) *Lancet Global Health*, e323-e333 (2014).

Maharashtra, the Court also resonated with the idea and held that "an unborn fetus cannot be put on a higher pedestal than the rights of a woman."[21]

Human Rights and Abortion

Human rights do not belong to man alone, they belong to humanity at large. Men and women both have been guaranteed the right to life, liberty, equality, food, shelter, work, recreation, education, and equal social and political participation. However, gender discrimination, specifically regarding reproductive rights, has emerged as the most serious threat to women's enjoyment of human rights. It is widely accepted that women do not enjoy the same socio-economic, civil, and political rights as men, and male dominance over women's sexuality, fertility, and reproductive health continues to be a reality.[22]

In developed countries, abortion reforms were primarily motivated by the desire to emancipate women's status. The need for reforms was recognized due to poverty, overpopulation, women's mortality rate, and sex selection. The reforms aimed to grant reproductive autonomy and the right to self-determination to women. Abortion laws are governed by state welfare laws, which are obligatory with the overarching goal of attaining welfare. In practice, they remain confined to a State's socio-economic and political interests.

In a pro-life country, a woman who chooses abortion to end a problematic pregnancy may face greater social stigma than she would in a pro-choice country. Women may have to pay more, travel a greater distance, or wait for a longer period to get aborted in the former. For instance, an Indian woman will face rarer barriers to abortion than an Irish woman, but her barriers will be greater than those of a British woman. Only 39.3% of the global population lives in countries that permit abortion for any reason.[23]

The UN Treaty Monitoring Bodies (UNTMBs) regularly call for governments to decriminalize abortion. UNTMBs have highlighted the State's obligation to remove barriers to safe and legal abortion access.

---

21 2017 Cri LJ 218 (Bom HC).

22 Cook, Rebecca, "The International Protection of Women's Reproductive Rights", 24(2), *New York University Journal of International Law and Politics*, 645–727 (1992).

23 S Singh et al., "The Incidence of Abortion and Unintended Pregnancy in India, 2015", *Lancet Global Health* (2017).

They have reported on the direct link between criminalization and restrictive abortion laws and violations of human rights norms. The identified barriers include mandatory waiting periods, biased counseling requirements, and third-party authorization requirements.

Under Article 6 of the International Covenant on Civil and Political Rights (ICCPR), abortion got recognized as a violation of the right to life. The Human Rights Committee (HRC) confirmed that "although States parties may adopt measures designed to regulate voluntary terminations of pregnancy, such measures must not result in violation of the right to life of a pregnant woman or girl." The HRC said that States should not punish women or medical providers for abortions. The Committee also observed that imposing a criminal charge on women who get abortions further forces them to get illegal abortions done.[24]

According to the Committee on the Elimination of Discrimination Against Women (CEDAW), the criminalization of abortion prevents women and girls from taking medical help for their mental and physical health. Due to a lack of access to contraceptive services and information, women fail to fully enjoy their sexual and reproductive health. Resultantly, women remain deprived of fair legal protections. The CEDAW also observed that making abortion illegal is a form of violence and discrimination against women.

The Committee on Child Rights (CRC) also called on countries to decriminalize abortion. The committee aims to ensure adolescent girls' access to safe abortions and post-abortion care. As per CRC directives, girls should also be allowed to make their abortion-related decisions fearlessly.[25]

The Special Rapporteur on Health of the United Nations General Assembly (UNGA) stated that "criminal laws penalizing and restricting induced abortion are the paradigmatic examples of impermissible barriers to the realization of women's right to health and must be eliminated."[26] The Rapporteur mentioned that "marginalization and vulnerability of women intensify violations of their rights by the unfriendly service providers."[27] The Rapporteur also highlighted the significance of countries fulfilling

[24] Human Rights Committee, General Comment No. 36 (n. 23), para 8.

[25] Committee on Child Rights, General Comment No. 20 (n. 27), para 60, 2016.

[26] United Nations General Assembly (UNGA), Interim Report of the Special Rapporteur on the Right of Everyone to the Enjoyment of the Highest Attainable Standard of Physical and Mental Health, para 21, UN Doc A/66/254 (2011).

[27] *Mellet v. Ireland*, CCPR/C/116/D/2324/2013.

their responsibility to ensure access to reproductive health information and the availability of safe and legal abortion services.[28] It was also recommended that all women should get quality obstetric delivery services, and sexual and reproductive health services should take gender into consideration.[29] UN human rights bodies have asked India to live up to its international obligations to protect sexual and reproductive health rights (SRHR), including the right to safe abortion.

Abortion Practices in India

The MTP Act, 1971 was the first law to legalize induced abortion in the country. It gave a conditional right of abortion to women up to 20 weeks of pregnancy.[30]

Women in India face a number of social and domestic constraints that limit their ability to make reproductive decisions. These consist of social pressure of early marriage and childbearing, limited access to contraception knowledge, and a lack of decision-making power in the home. Further, their limited physical mobility to access services, violence in the family, and coercive sexual relationships add to their vulnerability.[31]

According to the Ministry of Health and Family Welfare, approximately 4.6 lakh abortions were performed in the country from 1996 to 1997.[32] As per data, 5.8 lakh spontaneous abortions happened in 2017–2018 and 5.9 lakhs in 2019–2020.[33] Estimates for the contribution of unsafe abortions to maternal death range between 8% and 20%.[34] Approximately 6.7 million abortions are performed outside of government-recognized

---

28 HRC, General Comment No. 36 (n. 23); WHO, 'Safe Abortion: Technical and Policy Guidance for Health Systems' (2nd ed., 2012) 94.

29 HRC, Report of the Working Group on Universal Periodic Review: India, para 138, 153; UN Doc A/HRC/21/10 (2012).

30 J. R Steinberg & L. R Rubin, "Psychological Aspects of Contraception, Unintended Pregnancy, and Abortion", 1(1), *Policy Insights from The Behavioral and Brain Sciences*, 239–247 (2014).

31 National Family Health Survey (NFHS-2), 1998-1999.

32 MOHFW, 1997.

33 MOHFW, 2020.

34 K Dahiya, S Madan, R Hooda et al., "Evaluation of The Efficacy of Mifepristone/ Misoprostol and Methotrexate/ Misoprostol for Medical Abortion", 6, *Indian J Med Sci*, 301 (2017).

institutions each year, often by untrained individuals in unfavorable conditions.[35]

Although the legality of the MTP Act never got contested, still the majority of women obtained abortions outside of this legal framework. Multiple factors contributed to the prevalence of this illegal practice, such as inherent restrictions on registered service providers and failure of service providers to provide optimum facilities. Despite the policy's stated commitment to informed choice principles, service providers frequently did not adhere to them. The legal requirement of prior consent from the physician for the abortion also proved to be a barrier. Women's poor understanding of their legal rights was another major contributor to illegal abortions. Thus, the policy debate about abortion in India focuses on women's ignorance of their legal rights and inadequate implementation of the Act.[36]

Overall, the decision to terminate a pregnancy is frequently shadowed by cultural, religious, socio-economic, and societal pressures in India. Despite medical advancements, women have been forced to continue pregnancies on moral grounds on numerous occasions. According to limited research, some states have been hesitant to abandon the target-based approach, and some service providers have been hesitant to adopt informed choice principles.[37]

Abortion has been viewed as more of a social issue than a personal one. Normal pregnancy, for example, is necessary, and a woman should refrain from seeking an abortion. However, if a divorced or unmarried woman becomes pregnant, abortion is not only acceptable but is expected to protect the reputation of the family. The right to choose whether or not to have an abortion is inextricably linked to the family's honor.

Consequently, the MTP Act remained an abortion law for years only in documents and frequently denied an abortion to women as a right.[38]

---

[35] Susheela Singh, et al., "Abortion & Unintended Pregnancy in Six Indian States Findings and Implications for Policies and Programs", *Guttmacher Institute* (New York, 2018).

[36] M.A. Hall, R.B. Stephenson, & S. Juvekar, "Social and Logistical Barriers to the Use of Reversible Contraception Among Women in a Rural Indian Village", 26(2), *Journal of Health, Population, and Nutrition*, 241–250 (2008).

[37] M. Stillman et al., "Abortion in India: A Literature Review", *Guttmacher Institute* (New York, 2014).

[38] R.K. Jones and J. Jerman, "Abortion incidence and service availability in the United States 2011", 46(1), *Perspectives on Sexual and Reproductive Health*, 3–14 (2014).

As a result, the unconditional right to abortion for women remained elusive.[39] However, over the last three decades, as the government of India sought to shift away from its long-standing emphasis on fertility reduction to a more responsive system to individual needs, there has been marked progress in the application of the Act. For example, in *Anusha Ravindra v. UOI*,[40] the apex court granted a rape survivor the right to terminate her pregnancy in the twenty-fourth week.

In India, the right to abortion and reproductive autonomy got better recognition through the MTP (Amendment) Act, 2021. With changing times, the right to bodily sovereignty will keep expanding. It means that women are closer to enjoying the absolute right to choose what they want for their bodies – without the fear of interference from someone else.[41]

Socio-cultural Aspects of Abortion

Women have consistently used abortion (safe or unsafe) as a last resort to avoid unwanted pregnancies. Despite the universal practice of abortion, there are significant differences among countries in terms of legalization of and access to the procedure as there are varied moral and ethical views about abortion in societies.[42]

Currently, the right to abortion is a conditional right. It can be exercised if there is a significant risk of the child being born with a physical or mental disability, or if contraception has failed.[43] If the mother chooses to keep the baby, she is solely responsible for all associated costs. The mother will require ultrasounds, maternity clothing, and prenatal care, among other things. The father is morally obligated to assist.[44] Assuring the baby's health and personal well-being adds up to a

---

39 S. Bhattacharya, M.A. Bashar, A. Singh, "So Near, Yet So Far: Access to Safe Abortion Services Remains Elusive for Poor Women in India", *BMJ Case Rep.* (2017).

40 W.P. (C) 934/2017 SC.

41 Nivedita Menon, "Sexuality, Caste, Governmentality: Contests Over 'Gender' in India", 91(1), *Feminist Review*, 94–112 (2009).

42 A.M. Niță & C Ilie Goga, "A Research on Abortion: Ethics, Legislation and Socio-Medical Outcomes. Case Study: Romania", 61(1), *Romanian Journal of Morphology and Embryology*, 283–294 (2020).

43 M. Berer, "Abortion Law and Policy Around the World: In Search of Decriminalization", 19(1), *Health and Human Rights*, 13–27 (2017).

44 Franklin, Jenae, "A Mother's Paradox: Choosing a Birthing Method in the 21st Century", *Pitzer Senior Theses Paper*, 57 (2014).

significant financial and emotional investment. Forcing her to have the baby is equally inhumane as forcibly terminating her pregnancy.[45] The law does not take into account all the consequences of what it imposes on an individual. The enactment of restrictive abortion laws makes abortion a riskier option. Moreover, by denying the right to abortion, women are deprived of their bodily autonomy. The only way to end illegal abortions and exploitation by private clinics is to make abortion legal, accepting it as a legitimate choice for women.[46] Thus, the logical conclusion is that abortions should be permitted as a personal decision and not be viewed as a point of contention.

---

[45] P. Muttreja, & S. Singh, "Family planning in India: The way forward", 148 (Suppl.), *The Indian Journal of Medical Research*, S1–S9 (2018).

[46] Sugandha Nagpal, "Sex-Selective Abortion in India: Exploring Institutional Dynamics And Responses", 3, *McGill Sociological Review*, 18–35 (2013).

FIVE

Abortion Laws in India

"Reproductive autonomy requires that every pregnant woman has the intrinsic right to choose to undergo or not to undergo an abortion without any consent or authorization from a third party."

– *X v. Principal Secretary*, Health and Family Welfare Department, Govt. of NCT of Delhi[1]

Reproductive rights are a contentious issue regardless of the population's socioeconomic status, religion, or culture. However, laws have begun to address women's rights, recognizing the years of oppression women have endured. Reproductive autonomy is the foundation for gender equality, and above all, it is a fundamental right. It is about choice, power, and dignity. Therefore, women and girls must not only have access to comprehensive reproductive health services and information but also have reproductive autonomy with positive health outcomes.

This chapter deals with the legal framework for abortion that governs women's reproductive rights in India.

The Constitution of India, 1950

The reproductive rights of women are protected under the Constitution of India. Article 14 provides that the State must protect the fundamental right to equality. The fundamental right to non-discrimination promised under Article 15 and Article 15(3) specifically gives power to the State to enact special provisions for women and children as per need.

The Constitution of India, 1950 – Article 14

- **Art. 14:** The State shall not deny to any person equality before the law or the equal protection of the laws within the territory of India.

The Constitution of India, 1950 – Article 15

- **Art. 15:** Prohibition of discrimination on grounds of religion, race, caste, sex or place of birth – (1) The State shall not discriminate

[1] SLP (C) No 12612 of 2022, decided on 29th September, 2022.

against any citizen on grounds only of religion, race, caste, sex, place of birth or any of them. (2) No citizen shall, on grounds only of religion, race, caste, sex, place of birth or any of them, be subject to any disability, liability, restriction or condition with regard to (a) access to shops, public restaurants, hotels and places of public entertainment; and (b) the use of wells, tanks, bathing ghats, roads and places of public resort maintained wholly or partly out of State funds or dedicated to the use of the general public. (3) Nothing in this article shall prevent the State from making any special provision for women and children. (4) Nothing in this article or in clause (2) of Article 29 shall prevent the State from making any special provision for the advancement of any socially and educationally backward classes of citizens or for the Scheduled Castes and the Scheduled Tribes.

The right to life and personal liberty under Article 21 has been expanded through judicial interpretations to secure women's reproductive rights. Article 21 now includes the right to dignity, which is inclusive of reproductive rights (the right to become pregnant, to bear children, to decide the number of children, to have an abortion, to use or not use contraceptives, to be or not be sterilized, to be or not be a parent, etc.). The right of a woman to make reproductive choices is also deduced from the right to privacy and bodily integrity. Privacy, at its core, does include the preservation of personal intimacies, including sexual orientation.[2] In *Suchita*, the Supreme Court determined that privacy was a necessary component of the right to live in dignity. As a result, three fundamental values were identified to underpin this right: autonomy, bodily integrity, and dignity. In *Puttaswamy*, the Supreme Court relied on both personal liberty and non-discrimination principles to establish the right to privacy as a fundamental right emerging primarily from Article 21.[3]

The Constitution of India, 1950 – Article 21

- **Art. 21:** No person shall be deprived of his life or personal liberty except according to a procedure established by law.

Article 39 of the Indian Constitution mandates the State to secure adequate means of livelihood for men and women equally while framing policies and regulations.

---

[2] *Suchita Srivastava v. Chandigarh Administration* (2009), 14 SCR 989.

[3] *K.S. Puttaswamy v. Union of India* (2017), 10 SCC 1.

The Constitution of India, 1950 – Article 39

- **Art. 39:** The State shall, in particular, direct its policy towards securing (a) that the citizens, men and women equally, have the right to an adequate means to livelihood; (b) that the ownership and control of the material resources of the community are so distributed as best to subserve the common good; (c) that the operation of the economic system does not result in the concentration of wealth and means of production to the common detriment; (d) that there is equal pay for equal work for both men and women; (e) that the health and strength of workers, men and women, and the tender age of children are not abused and that citizens are not forced by economic necessity to enter avocations unsuited to their age or strength; (f) that children are given opportunities and facilities to develop in a healthy manner and in conditions of freedom and dignity and that childhood and youth are protected against exploitation and against moral and material abandonment.

Majority of the human rights are promised under fundamental rights. Human dignity is an integral part of the constitutional culture of India. Under Article 32 and Article 226, the Supreme Court and High Courts, respectively, have the power to provide remedies for violations of fundamental rights under Part III of the Constitution. Under Article 32(2), the Supreme Court has the power to issue directions or orders or writs.

The Constitution of India, 1950 – Article 32

- **Art. 32:** Remedies for enforcement of rights conferred by this Part – (1) The right to move to the Supreme Court by appropriate proceedings for the enforcement of the rights conferred by this Part is guaranteed. (2) The Supreme Court shall have the power to issue directions or orders or writs, including writs in the nature of habeas corpus, mandamus, prohibition, quo warranto and certiorari, whichever may be appropriate, for the enforcement of any of the rights conferred by this Part. (3) Without prejudice to the powers conferred on the Supreme Court by clause (1) and (2), the Parliament may by law empower any other court to exercise within the local limits of its jurisdiction all or any of the powers exercisable by the Supreme Court under clause (2). (4) The right guaranteed by this article shall not be suspended except as otherwise provided for by this Constitution.

The Constitution of India, 1950 – Article 226

- **Art. 226:** Power of High Courts to issue certain writs – (1) Notwithstanding anything in Article 32, every High Court shall have powers, throughout the territories in relation to which it exercises jurisdiction, to issue to any person or authority, including in appropriate cases, any Government, within those territories directions, orders or writs, including writs in the nature of habeas corpus, mandamus, prohibitions, quo warranto and certiorari, or any of them, for the enforcement of any of the rights conferred by Part III and for any other purpose. (2) The power conferred by clause (1) to issue directions, orders or writs to any Government, authority or person may also be exercised by any High Court exercising jurisdiction in relation to the territories within which the cause of action, wholly or in part, arises for the exercise of such power, notwithstanding that the seat of such Government or authority or the residence of such person is not within those territories. (3) Where any party against whom an interim order, whether by way of injunction or stay or in any other manner, is made on, or in any proceedings relating to, a petition under clause (1), without (a) furnishing to such party copies of such petition and all documents in support of the plea for such interim order and (b) giving such party an opportunity of being heard, makes an application to the High Court for the vacation of such order and furnishes a copy of such application to the party in whose favour such order has been made or the counsel of such party, the High Court shall dispose of the application within a period of two weeks from the date on which it is received or from the date on which the copy of such application is so furnished, whichever is later, or where the High Court is closed on the last day of that period, before the expiry of the next day afterwards on which the High Court is open; and if the application is not so disposed of, the interim order shall, on the expiry of that period, or, as the case may be, the expiry of the aid next day, stand vacated. (4) The power conferred on a High Court by this article shall not be in derogation of the power conferred on the Supreme court by clause (2) of Article 32.

Article 51(c) of the Constitution provides that the government is required by law to follow international law and treaty obligations. India is a signatory to a number of international agreements that recognize reproductive rights. These include the Convention on the Elimination of

All Forms of Discrimination Against Women (CEDAW),[4] the International Covenant on Civil and Political Rights (ICCPR),[5] the International Covenant on Economic, Social, and Cultural Rights (ICESCR),[6] and the United Nations Convention on the Rights of the Child (UNCRC). When determining the scope and nature of basic rights, the courts heavily consider international human rights standards.

Indian Penal Code, 1860

Considering the religious, moral, social, and ethical background of the Indian community, abortion had been a crime under the Indian Penal Code, 1860. Abortion law is primarily governed by Sections 312–316 of the IPC. The provisions criminalize abortion. The woman herself, or anyone else including a medical practitioner, could be prosecuted for participating in an abortion under the penal provisions.

Section 312 makes voluntarily causing miscarriage an offence in two circumstances when a woman is 'with child' (which means as soon as gestation begins) and when she is 'quick with child' (motion of the fetus is felt by the mother). Even if the pregnant woman causes herself to miscarry, the same is punishable. Section 312 permits abortion only on medical grounds to protect the life of the mother.

Indian Penal Code, 1860 - Section 312

- **Section 312: Causing miscarriage** - Whoever voluntarily causes a woman with child to miscarry, shall, if such miscarriage be not caused in good faith for the purpose of saving the life of the woman, be punished with imprisonment of either description for a term which may extend to three years, or with fine, or with both; and, if the woman be quick with child, shall be punished with imprisonment of either description for a term which may extend to seven years, and shall also be liable to fine.

---

[4] An international treaty adopted in 1979 by the UN General Assembly. It came in force on 3 September 1981 and has been ratified by 189 States.

[5] A multilateral treaty adopted by UN General Assembly Resolution 2200A (XXI) on 16 December 1966 and in force from 23 March 1976 in accordance with Article 49 of the covenant.

[6] A multilateral treaty adopted by the UN General Assembly on 16 December 1966 through General Assembly Resolution 2200A (XXI), and came in force on 3 January 1976.

As per Section 313, whoever commits a miscarriage without the consent of the woman is punished with imprisonment for up to ten years with a fine. Similar punishment is imposed upon the defaulter under Section 314 if death is caused by the act done with intent to cause miscarriage. Section 315 criminalizes an act done with the intent to prevent the child from being born alive or to cause it to die after birth. Section 316 imposes punishment on a person whose act caused death. The person would be guilty of culpable homicide as by such an act, he/she caused the death of a quick unborn child. The term 'abortion' has not been used in the IPC. Terms such as 'miscarriage' and 'unborn child' are also undefined in the code.

In the 1960s, due to the increasing number of induced abortions, the government ordered the establishment of the Shantilal Shah Committee to deliberate on the legalization of abortion in the country. As overpopulation was a grave issue, the State ignored the religious forces too.[7] The Committee carried out a comprehensive review of the sociocultural, legal, and medical aspects of abortion. In 1966, it recommended legalizing abortion to protect women's health and lives, on both compassionate and medical grounds.[8] It was also viewed as a population control measure. The term 'medical termination of pregnancy' (MTP) was used to counter opposition from socio-religious groups who were averse to abortion.

Consequently, in order to reduce maternal mortality owing to unsafe abortions, the Medical Termination of Pregnancy (MTP) Act was brought into force in 1971. This law was introduced as an exception to Sections 312 and 313 of the IPC, 1860.

Medical Termination of Pregnancy Act, 1971

The MTP Act, 1971 elaborated the provisions for how and when a medical abortion can be carried out. Even so, abortion became legal in limited circumstances only.

Section 3 of the MTP Act, 1971 originally provided that pregnancy could be terminated in the first trimester (within 12 weeks) if a doctor was of the opinion that it was safe for the woman to undergo an abortion. Beyond 12 weeks and up to 20 weeks, the opinion of two doctors was

---

[7] S.K. Banerjee et al., "Accreditation of Private Sector Health Facilities for Provision of Comprehensive Abortion Care Services: A New Initiative of the State Government of Bihar, India", *Ipas Development Foundation* (New Delhi, 2013).

[8] Shantilal Shah Committee Report, "Report of The Committee on Legalization of Abortion" (1966).

required to perform the abortion. Beyond that, pregnancy could not be terminated as it was very risky and might cause harm or even death to the pregnant mother. It could only be performed in extreme situations when it was necessary to abort the fetus to save the life of the mother. While deciding whether or not to perform the abortion, the doctors ascertained the risk of harm to the health of the pregnant mother. The law was physician-centric as the doctor's permission to perform the abortion was mandatory to be recorded in writing. Section 3(4) provided that if the pregnant woman was below 18 years or was incapable of giving valid consent (person of unsound mind), the consent of the guardian was required. If the woman was above 18 years, she could consent to the abortion herself. The consent of the husband was not required to undergo an abortion.

MTP Act, 1971 – Section 3: When Pregnancies may be terminated by registered medical practitioners

- When Pregnancies may be terminated by registered medical practitioners – (1) Notwithstanding anything contained in the Indian Penal Code (45 of 1860), a registered medical practitioner shall not be guilty of any offence under that Code or under any other law for the time being in force, if any pregnancy is terminated by him in accordance with the provisions of this Act. (2) Subject to the provisions of sub-section (4), a pregnancy may be terminated by a registered medical practitioner, (a) where the length of the pregnancy does not exceed twelve weeks if such medical practitioner is, or (b) where the length of the pregnancy exceeds twelve weeks but does not exceed twenty weeks, if not less than two registered medical practitioners are, of opinion, formed in good faith, that (i) the continuance of the pregnancy would involve a risk to the life of the pregnant woman or of grave injury to the physical or mental health; or (ii) there is a substantial risk that if the child were born, it would suffer from such physical or mental abnormalities as to be seriously handicapped. Explanation 1 – Where any, pregnancy is alleged by the pregnant woman to have been caused by rape, the anguish caused by such pregnancy shall be presumed to constitute a grave injury to the mental health of the pregnant woman. Explanation 2 – Where any pregnancy occurs as a result of failure of any device or method used by any married woman or her husband for the purpose of limiting the number of children, the anguish caused by such unwanted pregnancy may be presumed to constitute a grave injury to the mental health of the pregnant woman. (3) In determining whether the continuance of pregnancy would involve such risk of injury to the health as is mentioned in sub-section (2), account may be taken of the pregnant woman's actual or reasonable foreseeable environment. (4) (a) No pregnancy of a woman, who has not attained the age of eighteen years, or, who, having attained the age of eighteen years, is a lunatic, shall be terminated except with the consent in writing of her guardian. (b) Save as otherwise provided in C1(a), no pregnancy shall be terminated except with the consent of the pregnant woman.

Section 4 specified that pregnancy could only be terminated at government-approved hospitals under the MTP Act.

MTP Act, 1971 – Section 4

- **Section 4:** No termination of pregnancy shall be made in accordance with this Act at any place other than (a) a hospital established or maintained by Government, or (b) a place for the time being approved for the purpose of this Act by Government.

Section 5 gave an exception to sections 3(2) and 4. Section 5 established two key conditions pertaining to abortion. The conditions were that if the concerned doctor acted in good faith and determined that it was absolutely essential to carry out the termination of pregnancy, it would not be compulsory by law to obtain the medical opinions of two registered medical practitioners. Secondly, if it was discovered that the termination was conducted by a non-registered healthcare professional, it would constitute a criminal offence.

MTP Act, 1971 – Section 5

- **Section 5:** Sections 3 and 4 when not to apply – (1) The provisions of section 4 and so much of the provisions of sub-section (2) of section 3 as relate to the length of the pregnancy and the opinion of not less than two registered medical practitioners, shall not apply to the termination of a pregnancy by the registered medical practitioner in case where he is of opinion, formed in good faith, that the termination of such pregnancy is immediately necessary to save the life of the pregnant woman; (2) Notwithstanding anything contained in the Indian Penal Code (45 of 1860), the termination of a pregnancy by a person who is not a registered medical practitioner shall be an offence punishable under that Code, and that Code shall, to this extent, stand modified.

Under section 7, the doctors or the hospital authority were not permitted to disclose to the public any information about the woman who underwent termination of her pregnancy. This information had to be kept confidential.

MTP Act, 1971 - Section 7

- **Section 7:** Power to make regulations – (1) The State Government may, by regulations (a) require any such opinion as is referred to in sub-section (2) of section 3 to be certified by a registered medical practitioner or practitioners concerned, in such form and at such time as may be specified in such regulations, and the preservation or disposal of such certificates; (b) require any registered medical practitioner, who terminates a pregnancy, to give intimation of such termination and such other information relating to the termination as may be specified in such regulations; (c) prohibit the disclosure, except to such persons and for such purposes as may be specified in such regulations, of intimations given or information furnished in pursuance of such regulations.

The Medical Termination of Pregnancy Act, 1971 failed in one of its basic objectives of providing safety to pregnant women and empowering them by providing a qualified right to terminate the pregnancy of their free will. The MTP Act was amended twice since then, in 1975 and 2002.

The highlights of the amendment were that abortion services were decentralized, and criminal penalties for unapproved abortions were added. A committee that operated at the district level was to be responsible for deciding whether to allow private establishments to provide abortion services. The time and location of performing the services had to strictly comply with the provisions of the Act; violation would lead to harsher penalties. To deal with psychological illnesses that did not amount to mental disabilities, the term 'lunatic' was substituted with 'mentally ill person.' However, there was still a need to upgrade the conditions of the private hospitals that provided abortion services. In order to regularize operations at private hospitals, The MTP Rules, 2003 were promulgated.

The Medical Termination of Pregnancy Rules, 2003

In the exercise of powers conferred by section 6 of the MTP Act, 1971, the central government notified MTP Rules on June 13, 2003. The rules provided the composition and tenure of the district-level committee. Out of the four members, one member was to be a gynecologist/ surgeon/ anesthetist and the other three members were to be from a local medical profession, non-governmental organization, and Panchayati raj institution of the district, respectively. The rules also provided that the committee must have a woman member. All the members had two calendar years of tenure.

The 2003 Rules provided that whoever was registered in a state medical register immediately before the commencement of the Act and had a minimum of three years of experience in the practice of gynecology and obstetrics was eligible to serve as the medical practitioner on the committee. Another important addition was the requirement of a government-approved place for the procedure to be done. The government approved a place when it was assured that the MTP would be conducted in safe and hygienic conditions with the prescribed equipment.

The Medical Termination of Pregnancy Regulations, 2003

In the exercise of powers conferred by section 7 of the MTP Act, 1971, the central government formulated the MTP Regulations in 2003. These regulations increased women's access to healthcare, especially in the private sector. The regulations provided for streamlining the process so as to bring about transparency and accountability. Regulation 3 of the MTP Regulations 2003 specified that the registered medical practitioners are required to certify their opinion for the termination of pregnancy in Form I. The same is to be certified by the medical practitioner who terminates any pregnancy within three hours of doing the procedure. To maintain confidentiality, the consent given by a pregnant woman together with the certified opinion recorded in Form I shall be placed in an envelope and sealed by the registered medical practitioner under Rule 4. The sealed envelope is required to be sent to the chief medical officer of the state through the head of the hospital. Rule 7 provides that no entry shall be made in any case sheet, operation theatre register, or follow-up card or register other than the admission register maintained at any hospital.

Pre-conception and Pre-natal Diagnostic Techniques (Prohibition of Sex Selection) Act, 1994

Preference for a male child led to a rise in sex-selective abortions. Sex selection is the act of identifying the sex of the fetus and eliminating the fetus if it is of the unwanted sex. Families opted for abortions of female fetuses after determining the sex of the child through sonography. Female feticide could not be prohibited as abortion prior to the twentieth week of pregnancy was legal under the MTP Act, 1971, whose provisions were frequently abused for this purpose.

To prohibit sex selection, the government passed the Pre-conception and Pre-natal Diagnostic Techniques (Regulation and Prevention of Misuse) Act, 1994. The Act was passed to regulate the use of pre-natal diagnostic techniques. The use of these techniques is permitted only to detect genetic abnormalities, metabolic disorders, chromosomal abnormalities, certain congenital malformations, and sex-linked disorders.

The mandate of the PCPNDT Act is that no laboratory, center, or clinic would conduct any test, including ultrasonography, for the purpose of determining the sex of the fetus. The provisions lay that no person, including the one who was conducting the procedure as per the law, will communicate the sex of the fetus to the pregnant woman or her relatives by words, signs, or any other method.

Any person who puts an advertisement for pre-natal and pre-conception sex determination facilities in the form of a notice or document, through the media, or by means of hoarding, etc., can be imprisoned for up to three years and fined Rs. 10,000. An offence under section 3A of the PCPNDT Act included conducting or helping in the conduct of pre-natal diagnostic (PND) techniques in unregistered centers and conducting PND tests for any purpose other than the ones mentioned in the Act. Sale, distribution, supply, renting, etc., of any ultrasound machine or any other equipment capable of detecting the sex of the fetus is also an offence.

Under section 23 of the PCPNDT Act, the penalty for any violation of the act by a service provider is up to five years imprisonment with a fine of up to Rs. 50,000. The appropriate authority is obliged to report the registered medical practitioner's name to the State Medical Council for necessary action. The action includes suspension of registration, conviction, and removal of the service provider's name from the council's register for the prescribed period.

PCPNDT Act, 1994 – Section 23

- **Section 23:** (1) Any medical geneticist, gynecologist, registered medical practitioner or any person who owns a Genetic Counselling Centre, a Genetic Laboratory or a Genetic Clinic or is employed in such a Centre, Laboratory or Clinic and renders his professional or technical services to or at such a Centre, Laboratory or Clinic, whether on an honorary basis or otherwise, and who contravenes any of the provisions of this Act or rules made thereunder shall be punishable with imprisonment for a term which may extend to three years and with fine which may extend to ten thousand rupees and on any subsequent conviction, with imprisonment which may extend to five years and with fine which may extend to fifty thousand rupees. (2) The name of the registered medical practitioner shall be reported by the Appropriate Authority to the State Medical Council concerned for taking necessary action, including suspension of the registration, if the charges are framed by the court and till the case is disposed of and on conviction for removal of his name from the register of the Council for a period of five years for the first offence and permanently for the subsequent offence. (3) Any person who seeks the aid of any Genetic Counselling Centre, Genetic Laboratory, Genetic Clinic or ultrasound clinic or imaging clinic or of a medical geneticist, gynaecologist, sonologist or imaging specialist or registered medical practitioner or any other person for sex selection or for conducting pre-natal diagnostic techniques on any pregnant woman for the purposes other than those specified in sub-section (2) of section 4, he shall be punishable with imprisonment for a term which may extend to three years and with fine which may extend to fifty thousand rupees for the first offence and for any subsequent offence with imprisonment which may extend to five years and with fine which may extend to one lakh rupees. (4) For the removal of doubts, it is hereby provided, that the provisions of sub-section (3) shall not apply to the woman who was compelled to undergo such diagnostic techniques or such selection.

In 2003, the PCPNDT Act was amended and renamed as Pre-conception and Pre-natal Diagnostic Techniques (Prohibition of Sex Selection) Act, 1994.

In *CEHAT & Ors. v. Union of India*,[9] the Supreme Court directed the central and state governments to launch awareness campaigns in rural and urban areas. The NGO, Centre for Enquiry into Health and Allied Themes (CEHAT), had filed a writ petition contending that medical science was being abused to abort female fetuses prior to birth. The NGO

[9] (2003) 8 SCC 412.

argued that influential medical practitioners indulged in female feticide but managed to escape the punishments.

Medical Termination of Pregnancy (Amendment) Act, 2021

The MTP Act, 1971 stipulated a gestational limit of 20 weeks for termination of pregnancy, beyond which abortion of a fetus was statutorily impermissible. Abortion is not merely a medico-technical issue but initiates a much broader ideological struggle. The struggle revolves around the meanings of family, State, motherhood, and women's reproductive health and autonomy. To address these issues along with the increase in maternal mortality and morbidity caused by unsafe abortions and associated complications, the MTP (Amendment) Act, 2021 was notified by the government on March 25, 2021.

The amended provisions have brought positive changes in women's right to abortion. The amendment aims to broaden the scope of safe abortion services available to women. It aims to ensure dignity, autonomy, secrecy, and justice for women who need to end their pregnancies. New sections and clauses were inserted under existing sections of the MTP Act, 1971. Some of the important amendments are discussed as under:

Amendment in Section 3 of the MTP Act, 1971

Section 3 of the MTP Act, 1971 has been amended to increase the gestation period from 20 to 24 weeks for particular categories of women such as rape survivors or other vulnerable women. The 'categories of women' have been listed under 3B of MTP Rules, and not in the MTP (Amendment) Act, 2021.

Only one registered medical practitioner's opinion is required for termination of pregnancy up to 20 weeks. In cases of gestation between 20 and 24 weeks, the advice of two registered medical practitioners is required. However, the "24-week gestation" mark for terminating pregnancy does not apply in cases of significant fetal abnormalities diagnosed by a medical board. As per rule 3A, the medical board is to either accept or reject the proposal for medical termination of pregnancy within three days of receiving the request. The abortion procedure has to be done within five days of the board receiving the request for the same.

MTP (Amendment) Act, 2021 – Section 3(2)

- **Section 3(2):** Subject to the provisions of subsection (4), a pregnancy may be terminated by a registered medical practitioner, (a) where the length of the pregnancy does not exceed twenty weeks, if such medical practitioner is, or (b) where the length of the pregnancy exceeds twenty weeks but does not exceed twenty-four weeks in case of such category of woman as may be prescribed by rules made under this Act, if not less than two registered medical practitioners are, of the opinion, formed in good faith, that (i) the continuance of the pregnancy would involve a risk to the life of the pregnant woman or of grave injury to her physical or mental health or (ii) there is a substantial risk that if the child were born, it would suffer from any serious physical or mental abnormality. Explanation 1 – For the purposes of clause (a), where any pregnancy occurs as a result of failure of any device or method used by any woman or her partner for the purpose of limiting the number of children or preventing pregnancy, the anguish caused by such pregnancy may be presumed to constitute a grave injury to the mental health of the pregnant woman. Explanation 2 – For the purposes of clauses (a) and (b), where any pregnancy is alleged by the pregnant woman to have been caused by rape, the anguish caused by the pregnancy shall be presumed to constitute a grave injury to the mental health of the pregnant woman.

MTP (Amendment) Rules, 2021 – Rule 3B

- **Rule 3B:** Women eligible for termination of pregnancy up to twenty four weeks – The following categories of women shall be considered eligible for termination of pregnancy under clause (b) of subsection (2) of Section 3 of the Act for a period of up to twenty-four weeks, namely (a) survivors of sexual assault or rape or incest; (b) minors; (c) change of marital status during the ongoing pregnancy (widowhood and divorce); (d) women with physical disabilities [major disability as per criteria laid down under the Rights of Persons with Disabilities Act, 2016 (49 of 2016)]; (e) mentally ill women, including mental retardation; (f) the fetal malformation that has substantial risk of being incompatible with life or if the child is born it may suffer from such physical or mental abnormalities to be seriously handicapped; and (g) women with pregnancy in humanitarian settings or disaster or emergency situations as may be declared by the Government.

Under Section 3(2C) of the amendment, each state and union territory shall be required to establish a medical board. Under section 3(2D), the medical board shall be composed of a gynecologist, pediatrician, radiologist, and other such members as the state government or union territory may notify in the official gazette.

MTP (Amendment) Act, 2021 – Section 3 (2C)

- **Section 3 (2C):** Every State Government or Union territory, as the case may be, shall, by notification in the Official Gazette, constitute a Board to be called a Medical Board for the purposes of this Act to exercise such powers and functions as may be prescribed by rules made under this Act.

It is applaudable that the MTP Act, 2021 has amended the Explanation to Section 3 (2) to include unmarried women by replacing the term 'married woman' with 'any woman' and the term 'husband' with 'partner.' With this change, the presumptive exception created by this section now applies to all women and their partners, regardless of whether or not they are married.

Insertion of Section 5A

According to Section 5A, the registered medical practitioner is not permitted to reveal the name or other identifying information of a woman whose pregnancy has been terminated. The information can only be shared with a person authorized by any law in force. In case the medical practitioner fails to comply with the provisions under section 5A, he/she shall be liable to a punishment of imprisonment of up to one year with a fine.

MTP (Amendment) Act, 2021 – Section 5A

- **Section 5A:** (1) No registered medical practitioner shall reveal the name and other particulars of a woman whose pregnancy has been terminated under this Act except to a person authorised by any law for the time being in force. (2) Whoever contravenes the provisions of sub-section (1) shall be punishable with imprisonment which may extend to one year, or with fine, or with both.

While society and the State are primarily responsible for protecting the exercise of the right to abortion through institutional, legal, and medical support, they also have the authority to regulate it through the imposition of restrictions. Abortion continues to be a restrictive right, and not an absolute one. Nonetheless, India's abortion laws, led by the MTP (Amendment) Act, 2021, are a welcome step in the right direction and an indicator that the country is addressing women's issues more fiercely than ever.

SIX

Changing Contours of Abortion Laws in India – From 1971 to 2021

The woman alone has the right over her body. A woman can become pregnant by choice irrespective of her marital status... Importantly, it is the woman alone who has the right over her body and is the ultimate decisionmaker on the question of whether she wants to undergo an abortion.

– *X v. Principal Secretary*, Health and Family Welfare Department, Govt. of NCT of Delhi[1]

Abortion is a global phenomenon. Its practice has evolved through changes in demographic patterns, family structure, and religious influences. Factors like urbanization, unemployment, sex and marriage practices, educational levels, and women's status have all influenced the social and legal perspective on induced abortions. The reasons for abortion and the methods used have also differed depending on socio-economic factors.

Before the notification of the MTP Act, 1971, approximately one-seventh of pregnant women resorted to unsafe termination processes at the hands of quacks and paramedical staff. Around 5 million terminations were conducted annually in India, among which 3 million were illegal.[2] Such unsafe terminations resulted in increased morbidity and mortality among pregnant women and their children. The MTP Act aimed to give women a qualified right to abortion and make termination of a pregnancy a legal option.[3]

To establish a legal framework for medical abortion, the Government of India established the Shantilal Shah Committee to propose the draft

---

1 SLP (C) No. 12612 of 2022, decided on 29th September 2022.

2 N.R. Madhava Menon, "Population P olicy, Law Enforcement and the Liberalization of Abortion: A Socio Legal Inquiry into the Implementation of the Abortion Law in India", 16, *Journal of Indian Law Institute*, 632–33 (1974).

3 *Suchita Srivastava v. Chandigarh Administration* (2009) 9 SCC 1.

law. The Shah Committee's report observed that "whatever moral and ethical feelings society as a whole may have on the subject of induced abortion; it is a fact that several mothers are willing to risk their lives by having an illegal abortion instead of carrying that particular child to term." The committee submitted a comprehensive report outlining numerous circumstances that justify a legal abortion, which was deemed necessary not only to save the pregnant woman's life but also to avoid serious harm to her long-term health.

In this chapter, the current MTP Act along with all its amendments has been analyzed at length. The amended provisions have brought positive changes in women's right to abortion. The paradigm shift in the exercise of abortion rights can be better judged by comparing the scenario before and after its enactment.

Scenario Before the MTP (Amendment) Act, 2021

The MTP Act, 1971 guaranteed women the right to choose to have an abortion based on her own informed consent, physical and mental health, and the best interests of her unborn child. According to section 3 of the MTP Act, if a pregnancy does not exceed 12 weeks, it can be terminated based on the opinion of one registered medical practitioner (RMP). The pre-condition is that continuing the pregnancy would put the woman's life at risk or cause serious harm to her physical or mental health, or the baby would be born with severe physical or mental defects. If the length of the pregnancy falls between 12 and 20 weeks, the opinion of two registered doctors is required to terminate it.

MTP Act, 1971 - Section 3: When pregnancies may be terminated by registered medical practitioners

(1) Notwithstanding anything contained in the Indian Penal Code (45 of 1860), a registered medical practitioner shall not be guilty of any offence under that Code or under any other law for the time being in force, if any pregnancy is terminated by him in accordance with the provisions of this Act.

(2) Subject to the provisions of sub-section (4), a pregnancy may be terminated by a registered medical practitioner (a) where the length of the pregnancy does not exceed twelve weeks, if such medical practitioner is, or (b) where the length of the pregnancy exceeds twelve weeks but does not exceed twenty weeks, if not less than two registered medical practitioners are, of opinion, formed in good faith,

that (i) the continuance of the pregnancy would involve a risk to the life of the pregnant woman or of grave injury to her physical or mental health; or (ii) there is a substantial risk that if the child were born, it would suffer from such physical or mental abnormalities as to be seriously handicapped.

- Explanation 1 – Where any pregnancy is alleged by the pregnant woman to have been caused by rape, the anguish caused by such pregnancy shall be presumed to constitute a grave injury to the mental health of the pregnant woman.
- Explanation 2 – Where any pregnancy occurs as a result of the failure of any device or method used by any married woman or her husband for the purpose of limiting the number of children, the anguish caused by such unwanted pregnancy may be presumed to constitute a grave injury to the mental health of the pregnant woman. It is crucial to highlight that the grounds for termination listed in Section 3, except the second explanation, apply to all women irrespective of their marital status.

Section 5(1) states an exception to section 3(2) noting that if the termination seems immediately necessary to save the woman's life, regardless of the length of the pregnancy, the opinion of a single medical practitioner will suffice.

The MTP Act, 1971, before the 2021 amendment, provided that abortions could only be done up to 20 weeks of pregnancy. Post that, abortions could only be done if the woman's life was in danger. In such cases, permission has to be taken from the court. For permission, a writ petition has to be filed in the High Court or the Supreme Court of India, under Article 226 or Article 32 of the Indian Constitution, respectively. Consequently, the court orders the creation of a medical board, which is responsible for gathering information and submitting a report to it. Based on this report, the court decides whether or not to grant permission for medical termination. Some instances where the apex court relied upon the opinion of the medical board and decided for or against abortion are discussed below.

In *Meera Santosh Pal v. Union of India*,[4] a woman in her twenty-fourth week of pregnancy approached the Supreme Court to aid her to terminate the pregnancy. The Supreme Court established a medical board. The board determined that continuing the pregnancy would cause grave harm to the woman's physical and mental health and the fetus would be

[4] (2017) 3 SCC 462.

unable to survive due to abnormalities. The Court permitted the woman to undergo medical termination of pregnancy.

In *Sarmishtha Chakraborty v. Union of India*,[5] the medical board, established by the Supreme Court, approved the abortion because the woman would suffer severe mental injury if the pregnancy continued and the child, if born alive, would require immediate corrective surgery for a life-threatening cardiovascular condition. In *Sheetal Shankar Salvi v. Union of India*,[6] the Supreme Court declined permission to undergo medical termination based on the medical board's report. The Supreme Court stated that the medical board was unable to determine the period for which the baby was likely to survive without endangering the mother's life.

The primary objective of the MTP Act, 1971, seemed to be population control and family planning instead of rendering abortion rights to women. Further, the opinion of an RMP was decisive. It was on the basis of the opinion formed by the medical practitioners, either under Section 3 or under Section 5, that a woman could terminate a pregnancy. The subjectivity of an RMP's opinion affected the final decision taken regarding abortion. Consequently, it impeded access to safe and legal abortions and the actualization of women's fundamental right to reproductive autonomy.

Scenario After the MTP (Amendment) Act, 2021

The Medical Termination of Pregnancy (Amendment) Act, 2021 has been enacted to expand access of women to safe and legal abortion services on therapeutic, eugenic, humanitarian, or social grounds. The amendment included the insertion of certain new clauses in the existing MTP Act, 1971.[7] Its goal is to strengthen access to comprehensive abortion care without compromising the service and quality of safe abortion.

Comparison Between the MTP Act, 1971 and MTP (Amendment) Act, 2021

Time since Conception	*Requirements for Termination of Pregnancy*	
—	MTP Act, 1971	MTP (Amendment) Act, 2021
Up to 12 weeks	The advice of one doctor	The advice of one doctor

[5] (2018) 13 SCC 339.

[6] (2018) 11 SCC 606.

[7] Refer to Chapter 05 of the book.

12 to 20 weeks	The advice of two doctors	The advice of one doctor
20 to 24 weeks	Not allowed	Two doctors for some categories of pregnant women
More than 24 weeks	Not allowed	Medical board in case of substantial fetal abnormality
Any time during the pregnancy	One doctor, if immediately necessary to save a pregnant woman's life	

Analysis of the MTP (Amendment) Act, 2021

The highlight of the amendment is the increase in the permissible upper limit for terminating a pregnancy from 20 to 24 weeks of pregnancy. The reason for this extension might be the probability of fetal complications at a later gestation period. Women with fetal irregularities discovered after the twentieth week of pregnancy can now discontinue their pregnancy with legal and medical backing.

Under Section 3(2)(b), the phrase 'in case of such categories of women' indicates that the right to abortion between 20–24 weeks is available only for rape victims, incest victims, and women with severe physical and psychological conditions such as depression, physical disability, or insanity. Women who do not fall into one of the above-mentioned categories will need special permission from a medical board to have an abortion.

The amendment retains the requirement for doctors' approval for abortions and specifies certain conditions under which the approval may be granted. However, instead of two doctors, only one doctor is required to approve abortions for up to 20 weeks of pregnancy. There is a relaxation of the pre-condition of consultation with two doctors mandated under the MTP Act, 1971. This change eases the mental, physical, and financial burden on women.

According to the All-India Rural Health Statistics (2018–2019), there were 1,351 gynecologists and obstetricians in rural community health clinics across India, with 4,002 vacancies. This clearly indicates a 75% shortage of qualified doctors.[8] Women's access to safe abortion services may continue to be restricted due to the unavailability of qualified

[8] Government of India, Report on "Rural Health Statistic 2018–2019", Ministry of Health and Family Welfare Statistics Division.

medical professionals. The amendment has kept the pool of service providers unchanged. There is a need to expand the provider base. AYUSH practitioners and staff nurses may be trained additionally to conduct abortions up to 12 weeks of pregnancy.

Under section 3(2b), the termination of pregnancy, beyond 24 weeks of gestational age, can only be permitted by the medical board. The medical board permits such termination only in case the pregnant woman is diagnosed with substantial fetal abnormalities. If a woman desires to terminate a normal pregnancy post 24 weeks, she must file a writ petition in the appropriate court.

For uneducated and vulnerable women, approaching the medical board might prove to be a barrier. Moreover, in case of significant fetal abnormalities, the amendment does not mention the time period within which the board must submit its report. Terminating a pregnancy is a time-sensitive procedure. Any delays in the medical board's decision-making process may result in additional abnormalities for the pregnant woman along with mental trauma. However, Rule 3A(b) of the MTP (Amendment) Rules, 2021 refers to the timeline of three days for the medical board to either accept the request or reject it. Moreover, Rule 3A(b)(iii) ensures that the termination procedure, when advised by the medical board, is carried out with all safety precautions along with appropriate counseling within five days of the receipt of the request for the medical termination of pregnancy under subsection (2b) of section 3.

MTP (Amendment) Rules, 2021 – Rule 3A(b)

- The functions of the Medical Board shall be the following, namely (i) to examine the woman and her reports, who may approach for medical termination of pregnancy under subsection (2b) of section 3; (ii) to provide the opinion of Medical Board in Form D with regard to the termination of pregnancy or rejection of request for termination within three days of receiving the request for medical termination of pregnancy under sub-section (2b) of section 3; (iii) to ensure that the termination procedure, when advised by the Medical Board, is carried out with all safety precautions along with appropriate counselling within five days of the receipt of the request for medical termination of pregnancy under subsection (2b) of section 3.

Previously, medical boards were created by the court while dealing with the writ petitions seeking permission for termination. The decision of the court was based on the medical board's report, among other factors. Now, under section 3(2C) of the Amendment Act, the medical boards are established by the state government or union territory.

The Amendment Act also expands the grounds for abortion to include any 'woman or her partner' in place of only 'married woman or her husband' under section 3(2). In *X v. Principal Secretary, Health and Family Welfare Department, Govt. of NCT of Delhi,*[9] the Supreme Court ruled that all women are entitled to safe and legal abortion, and the distinction between married and unmarried women is unconstitutional. The change in this provision empowers single women, particularly those from marginalized groups such as sex workers. It can also decrease the plethora of health problems that were previously faced by single pregnant women.

However, the phrase 'women and her partner' suggests that women will continue to be required to cite relational reasons when seeking an abortion. Since the legal procedure to get permission is still cumbersome, women are likely to initially face the social stigma surrounding unwed mothers. Section 3(2)(b) of the Amendment Act and Rule 3B of the MTP Rules still exclude unmarried women from their ambit.

The Act continues to allow abortion on the ground of contraceptive failure as a token gesture. But it does not have any guidelines to verify the proof of contraceptive failure. Thus, a majority of women furnish contraceptive failure as the reason for their pregnancy when they approach doctors for abortion in public hospitals. Moreover, the evaluation of the degree of mental injury of the pregnant woman is very subjective. In order to terminate the pregnancy solely of their own volition, the woman may be forced to lie or plead with the doctor. Thus, pregnant women are subjected to additional mental stress as well as the financial burden associated with obtaining a doctor's approval.

Notably, the Amendment Act and Rules still use the term 'woman.' Thus, it is unclear whether a transgender, intersex, or gender-diverse individual is legally covered under the provisions. Transgender persons have been recognized as an additional gender in India under the Transgender Persons (Protection and Rights) Act, 2019. Certain medical studies have indicated that transgender individuals (and not women) may become pregnant even after receiving hormone therapy to transition from

---

9 SLP (C) No 12612 of 2022, Decided on 29th September 2022.

female to male. Such probability necessitates legal termination services for them as well.[10]

The Amendment Act requires authorization for abortions after 24 weeks from the medical board. This third-party authorization requirement compels individuals to obtain consent from a party beyond their healthcare provider, such as a parent, spouse, or a judge. This can delay women and girls' access to abortion services while they seek the necessary approvals. It might also result in denial of access altogether. As a result, women and girls may be forced to opt for unsafe abortion services. The WHO acknowledges that the third-party authorization requirements undermine women's autonomous decision-making and urges countries to remove such requirements from health laws and policies. It specifically states that third-party authorization requirement creates a significant barrier that can deter women from accessing abortion services.[11]

As per the Amendment Act, the board is comprised of at least five experts under Section 3(2D).

MTP (Amendment) Act, 2021 – Section 3(2D)

- **Section 3(2D):** The Medical Board shall consist of the following, namely (a) a Gynaecologist; (b) a Paediatrician; (c) a Radiologist or Sonologist; and (d) such other number of members as may be notified in the Official Gazette by the State Government or Union territory, as the case may be.

The majority of medical experts reside in urban areas. As a result, seeking authorization from these boards incurs significant costs and delays for marginalized individuals, particularly those living in rural areas. This places a disproportionate burden on groups such as Dalits and Adivasis who already face multiple barriers in accessing quality healthcare.

Further, the confidentiality clause under section 5A permits disclosure of a pregnant person's information to persons authorized by law. This clause violates the pregnant woman's right to privacy and contributes little to the advancement of her rights or recognition of her personhood.

In *Puttaswamy*,[12] the Supreme Court held that reproductive choice should be interpreted within the context of the right to personal liberty

---

[10] A. Light et al., "Transgender Men Who Experienced Pregnancy After Female-to-Male Gender Transitioning", 124(6), *Obstetrics and Gynaecology*, 1120–1127 (2014).

[11] WHO, Safe Abortion Guide, page 68, 86, and 94.

[12] *K.S. Puttaswamy v. Union of India* (2017), 10 SCC 1.

under Article 21. The MTP Act, 2021 was enacted with the aim of upholding this ideal and ensuring "dignity, autonomy, and justice for women seeking to terminate a pregnancy." However, the amendment makes no reference to women's decision-making capacity. It fails to transfer the power from the physician to the woman seeking an abortion. Rather, it vests the decision-making power in the State through the statutory boards.

A number of hurdles continue to prevent full access to safe and legal abortions. These barriers include insufficient infrastructural facilities, a lack of awareness, social stigma, and failure to ensure confidential care. Unmarried women face specific barriers due to gender stereotypes about women's sexual autonomy outside marriage. Such barriers may contribute to a delay in accessing abortion services or a complete denial of such services, consequently negating women's right to reproductive autonomy.[13]

Thus, it is essential to develop a rights-based legal framework for abortion that is consistent with India's constitutional values and international human rights conventions. The most fundamental right that a woman enjoys is reproductive autonomy and self-determination. The demand is for such a legislation that guarantees access to safe abortions and completely decriminalizes abortion. The law protects people's rights to equality, autonomy, bodily integrity, and privacy. The demand is for such laws that transform the social space in which people can exercise the full spectrum of their reproductive rights.

---

13 *X v. The Principal Secretary, Health and Family Welfare Department*, Govt. of NCT of Delhi & Anr., SLP (C) No 12612 of 2022, decided on 29th September, 2022.

SEVEN

Judicial Recognition of Reproductive Rights in India

Reproductive Rights fall under the purview of the Right to Privacy, previous precedents on reproductive autonomy as well as the various aspects of Human Rights law.

– K.S. Puttaswamy and Anr. v. Union of India[1]

In the past five decades, the judiciary in India has steadily progressed toward recognizing the reproductive rights of women as part of their fundamental human rights. The conceptual understanding and legal framework for abortion rights have been dealt with extensively in the previous chapters of this book. This chapter discusses various judgments given by constitutional courts recognizing various aspects of reproductive rights of women in India.

The landmark judgment by the US Supreme Court in *Roe v. Wade*[2] profoundly impacted abortion laws in India. It sparked an inevitable debate on State interference and the right to privacy of citizens. *Roe* recognized the right to privacy and its supremacy over State action and surveillance. In India, *Roe's* judgment has been relied upon to hold that although the right to privacy is not absolute, other rights such as the right to choose are covered under the term 'privacy.' Any unwarranted interference with such rights by the State amounts to a violation of the citizen's constitutional rights. Since its announcement around 50 years ago, the *Roe* judgment has strongly influenced the progressive change in abortion laws in India.

Constitutionality of the Medical Termination of Pregnancy Act, 1971

Though the Medical Termination of Pregnancy Act was passed in 1971, pregnant women still had trouble availing appropriate health services,

[1] (2017) 10 SCC 1.

[2] (1973) 410 U.S. 113.

even though the courts partially recognized women's right to reproductive autonomy. The Supreme Court, in 1994, made it clear in *Jacob George v. the State of Kerala*[3] that the MTP Act takes precedence over the miscarriage provisions of the Indian Penal Code.

The constitutionality of the MTP Act was challenged in *Nand Kishore Sharma v. Union of India.*[4] The petitioner argued that the MTP Act is unconstitutional because it threatens the life of an unborn child. It was further argued that section 3 was unethical and in violation of Article 21 of the Indian Constitution. The Rajasthan High Court held the MTP Act to be valid as its objectives were consistent with Article 21 of the Constitution.

Women's right to reproductive autonomy was diminished in *Javed v. the State of Haryana*[5] and *Samar Ghosh v. Jaya Ghosh.*[6] In *Javed v. the State of Haryana*, the Supreme Court considered the constitutionality of a law prohibiting anyone with more than two living children from holding certain public offices in Haryana. The court held the said law to be non-arbitrary as its purpose was population control and the law was covered under the constitutional exception of "public order, morality, and health." Activists criticized the judgment and argued that the court overlooked significant barriers to contraceptive information and services, particularly for marginalized women. The court also rejected numerous submissions highlighting how women's limited reproductive autonomy would further decline due to the provision of the said law. Through this case, the court justified the denial of reproductive autonomy to subserve population control purposes. In the *Samar Ghosh* case, when a married woman terminated her pregnancy without her husband's permission, her husband filed a divorce petition on the ground of mental cruelty. The Supreme Court held that terminating a pregnancy unilaterally constituted cruelty and granted the divorce.

Fundamental Rights as the Foundation of the Right to Abortion

In the landmark case of *Suchita Srivastava v. Chandigarh Administration,*[7] the Supreme Court upheld a woman's right to reproductive autonomy,

3 (1994) 3 SCC 430.

4 AIR 2006 Raj. 166.

5 AIR 2003 SC 3057.

6 (2007) 4 SCC 511.

7 (2009) 9 SCC 1.

including the freedom to decide whether or not to have children. A 20-year-old woman with mild to moderate intellectual disabilities got raped and became pregnant while residing in a government-run welfare institution. The right of women to survive pregnancy and childbirth was recognized as a fundamental right by the court. It also held that 'personal liberty' under Article 21 also includes the right of a woman to make her own decisions regarding her reproductive health.

In *Sandesh Bansal v. Union of India and others,*[8] the Madhya Pradesh High Court recognized women's inability to survive pregnancy and childbirth as a violation of the right to life under Article 21. The PIL was filed against the Government of Madhya Pradesh over the lack of implementation of maternal health schemes in the state. This landmark judgment proved to be a great step forward for women's health in India. Consequently, a growing number of High Courts began to recognize reproductive rights as fundamental rights. The judgment also led to the setting up of a blood bank and construction of a water tank to improve the condition of public health centers. In *Hallo Bi v. State of Madhya Pradesh,*[9] a woman who was awaiting trial filed a petition in the Madhya Pradesh High Court requesting authorization to terminate her forced prostitution-led pregnancy of 12 weeks. The chief judicial magistrate declined the request initially. The High Court, following the *Suchita* judgement, held that a woman's reproductive choices are necessary for the exercise of her fundamental right to personal liberty. The High Court allowed her to terminate her pregnancy. The Court observed that 'forced prostitution' is a form of rape and thus falls under Section 3(2) of the MTP Act.

In *Devika Biswas v. Union of India,*[10] the Supreme Court ruled that coercive and sub-standard sterilization procedures used by public healthcare professionals violated women's reproductive rights. Beyond the legal framework, the court recognized women's autonomy and gender equality as essential components of women's reproductive rights. In this case, the Supreme Court reiterated that women's reproductive rights are protected under constitutional provisions.

In *High Court on its Own Motion v. State of Maharashtra,*[11] the Bombay High Court highlighted gender discrimination in the abortion rights debate, emphasizing that the burden of an unintended or accidental

[8] 2016 SCC OnLine MP 3287.

[9] 2013 Cri.L.J. 2868 (MP).

[10] (2016) 10 SCC 726.

[11] (2016) SCC Online Bom 8426.

pregnancy falls disproportionately on women. The court observed that an 'unborn fetus' lacks human rights but a pregnant woman retains sole control over her pregnancy. The court reaffirmed *Suchita's* judgment and held that Section 3 of the MTP Act endows a pregnant woman with a priceless right to say no to motherhood. Further, the court directed all jail authorities in the state to ensure that imprisoned women receive effective medical care.[12]

On August 24, 2017, the Supreme Court took a step forward in *K.S. Puttaswamy v. Union of India,*[13] by stating that "it is established beyond a reasonable doubt that privacy is a component of fundamental rights." The bench held that dignity cannot exist in the absence of privacy as both are rooted in the inalienable values of life, liberty, and freedom recognized by the Constitution. The court also observed that "privacy is a fundamental constitutional value that cuts across the spectrum of fundamental rights and safeguards the individual's zone of choice and self-determination." The majority opinion said that "women's intimate personal choices, such as those governing reproduction, are protected by decisional privacy." The concurring opinion stated that "the right to abort a fetus falls under the category of privacy interests." On the same lines, the second concurring opinion stated that "a woman's freedom of choice regarding whether to bear a child or terminate her pregnancy are areas that fall under the category of privacy."

Puttaswamy's judgment affirmed three fundamental aspects of privacy rights: (i) protection from invasion of an individual's physical body, (ii) informational privacy, and (iii) choice of privacy. The right to privacy protects personal information and prohibits the State from making unauthorized use of such information. However, privacy is not an absolute right. The State can pass through a person's privacy if needed in the public interest. In that case, the action of the State must meet certain prerequisites; (i) it must be legal, (ii) it must have a legitimate purpose, and (iii) it must be fair.

Post the *Puttaswamy* judgment, there have been several cases in which courts permitted abortions on the basis of privacy, autonomy, and dignity. For example, in *State v. S,*[14] where the pregnant minor was a rape survivor,

---

12 Dipika Jain, "Time to Rethink Criminalisation of Abortion? Towards a Gender Justice Approach", 12 *N.U.J.S.L. Rev.* 2 (2019).

13 (2017) 10 SCC 1.

14 *State of Rajasthan v. S, Rajasthan High Court,* Division Bench Special Appeal Writ No. 1344 of 2019.

the Rajasthan High Court observed that "the right of a child rape victim to terminate the fetus significantly outweighs the right of the child in the womb to be born, even when the pregnancy is advanced." In *Surekha Gautam v. State of NCT of Delhi*,[15] the petitioner cited the *Puttaswamy* judgment to get a minor girl's 26-week pregnancy terminated. The abortion was approved by the Delhi High Court.

In 2015, the Convention on the Elimination of all Forms of Discrimination (CEDAW) urged countries to eliminate barriers to access to abortion (such as spousal permission).[16] In line with this and to further expand the reproductive rights of women, the Parliament of India enacted the Medical Termination of Pregnancy (Amendment) Act, 2021, which came into force on September 24, 2021. The amendment raised the upper gestation limit from 20 to 24 weeks for particular groups of women, which include rape survivors, incest victims, and other vulnerable women. It aimed to broaden the scope of safe abortion services available to women. Most importantly, it intended to ensure dignity, autonomy, secrecy, and justice for women who need to end their pregnancies.

Historically, men have controlled the reproductive rights of women. While India has been aspiring to broaden women's reproductive autonomy and access to safe abortion, the US Supreme Court overturned the same intrinsic right in *Dobbs v. Jackson Women's Health Organisation*.[17] In *Dobbs*, the US Supreme Court ruled that a woman's right to abortion is not constitutionally protected in the country. It held that "the Constitution does not confer a right to abortion" and "the authority to regulate abortion is returned to the elected representatives of the States." It also stated that any purposeful reading of the 'Due Process' clause in the Fourteenth Amendment to the US Constitution must be deeply rooted in the nation's history and tradition.[18]

This judgment overruled the landmark decision of *Roe v. Wade*[19] wherein the US Supreme Court had allowed women a qualified right to abortion by recognizing it within the domain of individual privacy. Subsequently, the decision of *Roe* was modified in *Planned Parenthood of Southeastern Pennsylvania v. Casey*.[20] In *Casey*, the Supreme Court held

---

[15] Delhi High Court Writ Petition (Criminal) No. 69 of 2021.

[16] CEDAW, General Recommendation No. 33 on Women's Access to Justice (2015).

[17] 597 U.S 33 (2022).

[18] 597 U.S 33 (2022).

[19] 1973 SCC OnLine US SC 20.

[20] 1994 SCC OnLine US SC 11.

that abortion can be regulated without causing an "undue burden" on women.

The Supreme Court of India often refers to US Supreme Court while deliberating any important question on constitutional principles. After *Dobbs*, the US Supreme Court may not be seen as a torchbearer of constitutional rights.

Puttaswamy,[21] *Navtej Johar,*[22] *and Joseph Shine*[23] paved the way for an equality-based expansion of reproductive rights in India. Such landmark cases demonstrate great promise in addressing social barriers in order to ensure reproductive autonomy for all individuals, even the most marginalized. While both the privacy and equality arguments for reproductive rights have limitations, the cases decided by the constitutional courts demonstrate innovative ways to reconcile these arguments.

The *Navtej Johar* and *Joseph Shine* cases demonstrate that assessment of the right to privacy must include a comprehensive understanding of the State's interest. In terms of reproductive rights, it is important to understand how restrictions on abortion and reproductive autonomy are part of maintaining patriarchal power structures through reproductive control.

In a recent verdict by Justice Swarana Kanta Sharma, the Delhi High Court observed that denying a woman the right to medical termination of pregnancy in sexual assault cases and imposing the responsibility of motherhood on her would amount to "denying her the human right to live with dignity." The court held that the woman has a right in relation to her body, including the right to say 'yes or no' to being a mother. It also emphasized on both aspects of physical injury and mental agony caused to the pregnant woman.[24]

Scope of the Right to Abortion Under the MTP Act

Right to Abortion for All Categories of Women

On July 21, 2022, in *X v. Principal Secretary, Health and Family Welfare Department, Govt. of NCT of Delhi,*[25] the Supreme Court allowed an

---

[21] (2017) 10 SCC 1.

[22] (2016) 3 SCC (CRI) 221.

[23] (2018) SCC OnLine SC 1676.

[24] *Minor R v. State* (NCT of Delhi), WP (Crl) No. 221 of 2023, decided on 25-1-2023 (Del).

[25] SLP (Civil) No. 12612 of 2022, decided on 21-7-2022.

unmarried woman to terminate her unwanted pregnancy. A 25-year-old unmarried woman approached the Delhi High Court seeking termination of 23 weeks of pregnancy. She stated that her pregnancy arose out of a consensual relationship, but since the partner refused to marry her, she could not give birth to the child as an unwed mother. A division bench of the Delhi High Court refused interim relief to her. She then approached the Supreme Court. The Supreme Court allowed her to abort the pregnancy and held that the expression "change in marital status" under Rule 3B(c) must be given a 'purposive interpretation.' The bench took into account the MTP Amendment Act, 2021, which substituted the word 'husband' in Explanation 1 of section 3(2) with the word 'partner.'

The court observed that "section 3(2)(b) aims to allow women to undergo abortion between 20–24 weeks. Therefore, including only married and excluding unmarried women will be violative of Article 14 of the Constitution." It stated that "there is no basis to deny unmarried women the right to medically terminate the pregnancy when the same choice is available to other categories of women." Therefore, the decision to terminate is firmly rooted in the right to bodily autonomy. If the State forces a woman to carry an unwanted pregnancy to the full term, it will amount to her indignity.

MTP Rules, 2021 – Section 3B(c)

- The categories of women mentioned in Rule 3B of the MTP Rules framed by the Central Government are: (a) survivors of sexual assault or rape or incest; (b) minors; (c) change of marital status during the ongoing pregnancy (widowhood and divorce); (d) women with physical disabilities [major disability as per criteria laid down under the Rights of Persons with Disabilities Act, 2016 (49 of 2016)]; (e) mentally ill women including mental retardation; (f) the foetal malformation that has substantial risk of being incompatible with life or if the child is born it may suffer from such physical or mental abnormalities to be seriously handicapped; and (g) women with pregnancy in humanitarian settings or disaster or emergency situations as may be declared by the Government.

These categories were added in the MTP Rules by the central government following the 2021 amendment to the MTP Act, which raised the ceiling limit for termination of pregnancy.In the above-mentioned case, the Supreme Court also held that rape includes 'marital rape' for the purposes of the MTP Act. A wife conceiving out of forced sex can also seek an abortion. The court explained that Rule 3B(a) is based on the reality that survivors of sexual assault, rape, or incest may face immense stigma if and when they are assaulted by others, including family members. A woman may become pregnant as a result of non-consensual sexual intercourse performed upon her by her husband. The court observed that, if the woman is in an abusive relationship, she may face great difficulty in accessing medical resources or consulting doctors. Thus, in order to avail the benefit of Rule 3B(a), the woman need not necessarily seek recourse to formal legal proceedings to prove the factum of sexual assault or rape. Further, there is no requirement that an FIR must be registered before it can be considered true for the purposes of the MTP Act. Such requirements would be contrary to the object and purpose of the MTP Act.

In *Aryamol P.S. v. Union of India*,[26] the Kerala High Court established a new angle and observed that strain in a marriage can also constitute a valid ground to seek abortion within the gestation period of up to 24 weeks. The drastic changes in the matrimonial life of a pregnant woman is sufficient ground to fulfill the condition of "change of marital status" in Rule 3B of the Medical Termination of Pregnancy Rules, 2003. The court further held that even though the woman might not be legally divorced, her husband's permission would not constitute an essential requisite for undergoing medical termination of pregnancy.

Strictly Construed Statutory Duration of Pregnancy (20 Weeks Before 2021)

In 2008, the verdict in *Dr. Nikhil Dattar & Ors. v. Union of India*[27] (the *Nikita Mehta case*) sparked an intense debate on the MTP Act. The central issue was whether the statutory time limit for abortion should be increased from 20 weeks to 24 weeks. The issue involved law, medical science as well as morality. In this case, the gestational period had progressed significantly beyond the prescribed limit of 20 weeks under the MTP Act. The petitioners argued that the fetal heart blockage was detected too late and expressed their inability to bear the emotional stress and financial burden associated with giving birth to such a child. The Mumbai High Court denied medical termination of the pregnancy, reasoning that no categorical expert opinion had been received stating that the child would

---

26 WP (C) No. 29402 of 2022, decided on 26-9-2022 (Ker HC).

27 (2008) 110 Bom. L.R. 3293.

be born with severe handicaps. The court observed that terminating the life of a viable unborn child on the grounds of potential handicap was comparable to mercy killing. The argument was that the negative consequences of giving birth to handicapped children can be mitigated by establishing effective State mechanisms to provide adequate financial and non-financial support to such children and families. The court stated that even if the petition had been filed prior to the 20-week gestation period, it would not have decided in favor of the petitioners because the requirements of section 3(2)(ii) read with section 3(2)(b) of the Act were not followed.

In *Suchita Srivastava*, the Supreme Court laid down the 'best interests test' and 'substituted judgment test.' The 'best interests test' requires the court to ascertain the course of action that would serve the best interests of the person in question and not those of the guardians or society in general. The 'substituted judgment test' requires the court to step into the shoes of a person who is considered to be mentally incapable. In such cases, the court attempts to make the decision that the said person would have made if she was competent to do so. The apex court made a distinction between those who are 'mentally ill' and those who suffer from 'mild mental retardation' in this case.

In *Savita Sachin Patil v. Union of India*,[28] a 37-year-old woman approached the Supreme Court to seek judicial intervention because the law prohibited abortion after 20 weeks of pregnancy. The court denied her request to terminate her 26-week-old fetus who had 'Down syndrome' as per the medical report. The medical report also observed that intelligence among people with Down syndrome is variable. Thus, Down syndrome does not directly indicate mental retardation. In this case, the court cited the board's recommendation against abortion and concluded that there was no danger to the woman's health. The bench later sympathized that it was very sad for a mother to raise a mentally retarded child and regrettable that women lack reproductive autonomy.

In *Sheetal Shankar Salvi v. Union of India*,[29] the Supreme Court, on the basis of the report of the medical board, declined to grant permission to a woman to undergo medical termination. The petitioner was 27 weeks pregnant. As per the report, the fetus had severe physical anomalies and the child would have severe physical and mental morbidity on birth. It

---

[28] (2017) 13 SCC 436.

[29] 2018 11 SCC 606.

was not possible for the medical board to determine the period of time for which the baby was likely to survive. The report reasoned that "since there is no danger to the mother's life and there is the likelihood that the baby may be born alive and may survive for a variable period of time," abortion was not justified.

After 2021, the statutory limit for the exercise of abortion increased from 20 to 24 weeks. The courts exercise discretion to allow abortions beyond 24 weeks, after taking into consideration medical opinions. In November 2021, the Calcutta High Court denied the plea of a woman who sought medical termination of her 32-week-old fetus due to a rare congenital heart defect. The medical board report observed that the termination could not be allowed due to the advanced stage of pregnancy. The court upheld the recommendation of the board.

But in February 2022, the Calcutta High Court in *Smt. Nivedita Basu v. State of West Bengal & Ors.*[30] permitted a woman to terminate her 34-week-old fetus due to medical complications. The medical board report stated that the likelihood of a healthy child being born out of this pregnancy is remote. If the child is born, the chances of survival are doubtful and the mother shall suffer mental injury if the pregnancy is continued. The medical board categorically arrived at a conclusion that pregnancy should be allowed to be terminated after 20 weeks in such cases. Similarly, the Delhi High Court in *Mrs. Pooja Kumar v. GNCTD and Another*[31] allowed the petitioner to undergo the procedure for medical termination at 33 weeks under the supervision of a properly constituted medical team.

In *N. v. Secy. Health and Family Welfare Dept.*,[32] the Delhi High Court discussed two contradicting provisions – section 19(1) of the POCSO Act 2012, which mandates the reporting of child sexual offences to the special juvenile police unit, and section 3 of the MTP Act, which allows medical termination of pregnancy and also provides for confidentiality to be maintained. The Court directed the Delhi government to issue a circular stating that the identity of a minor girl who is seeking medical termination of her pregnancy and her family shall not be disclosed in the report prepared by medical practitioners to the police.

---

30 WPA 2513/2022, decided on 17th February, 2022.

31 W.P.(C) 16607/ 2022, decided on 6th Dec. 2022.

32 2023 SCC OnLine Del 376.

Healthcare and Benefits Under Government-funded Schemes

In 2008, before the *Suchita* judgment, an NGO named Human Rights Law Network had filed petitions in several High Courts demanding accountability for pregnancy-related deaths. The *Niketa Mehta* case set the precedent. A number of these petitions resulted in judicial recognition of women's fundamental right to survive pregnancy and childbirth.

The Delhi High Court decided two such petitions, *Jaitun v. Janpura Maternity Home*[33] and *Laxmi Mandal v. Deen Dayal Harinagar Hospital,*[34] simultaneously. The petitions were concerning deficiencies in the implementation of government-funded schemes aimed at reducing infant and maternal mortality.

The *Laxmi Mandal* case involved Shanti Devi, who – seven months into her fifth pregnancy – had severe oedema, anemia, and fever, and had also fallen on the stairs of a building. She saw a midwife and was referred to Faridabad Hospital. Due to insufficient finances, Shanti Devi was unable to attend the hospital for two weeks. The hospital advised that Shanti Devi had miscarried the child and referred her to Sanjay Gandhi Hospital. Sanjay Gandhi Hospital then referred Shanti Devi to Saroj Hospital due to insufficient facilities for the removal of the fetus. Despite providing the relevant BPL documentation on arrival, Saroj Hospital refused treatment on the ground that Shanti Devi was not below the poverty line (BPL patients in urgent need of medical attention can obtain treatment at no cost). They further referred her to Deen Dayal Hospital, where she was diagnosed with platelet derangement due to a lack of protein during pregnancy and the fetus was finally removed. One year later, Shanti Devi became pregnant for the sixth time and died giving birth to a premature baby at home without the presence of a skilled birth attendant. A maternal audit of the death of Shanti Devi was conducted and the report concluded that the primary cause of Shanti Devi's death was postpartum hemorrhage due to retained placenta.

In the *Jaitun* case, Fatema visited a maternity home for vaccination and to inquire about the cash benefits she could avail for delivery. She visited the place twice during her pregnancy but received no assistance from the authorities. Fatema lived under a tree in Janpura, Delhi and suffered from epilepsy. Consequently, she delivered her daughter under the tree without access to skilled healthcare and medical guidance. Despite being informed

---

[33] 2010(172) DLT 9.

[34] 2010(172) DLT 9.

of the delivery, no visit was made by the hospital staff. Five days after the birth, Fatema took the baby to the maternity home for her vaccination. The baby was not examined and Fatema was not given any advice. The hospital just issued a discharge slip so that she could get a birth certificate for the baby and cash assistance under a particular government scheme. Through the intervention of a social activist, Fatema was able to get Rs. 550 from the maternity hospital. Fatema and the baby did not receive any nutrition or healthcare under the relevant schemes and thus their health deteriorated.

Unfortunately, in neither of the two cases of *Fatema* and *Shanti Devi,* the substantive benefits under particular schemes were made available. The schemes envisage that assistance has to be provided to pregnant women even for home deliveries. In both these cases, the Delhi High Court followed the directives of the Convention on the Elimination of All Forms of Discrimination Against Women (CEDAW) and the International Covenant on Economic, Social, and Cultural Rights (ICESCR) and held that "no woman, particularly a pregnant woman, should be denied treatment at any stage, regardless of her social or economic circumstances." The court recognized that the right to health includes women's rights to survive pregnancy and childbirth and have access to reproductive healthcare.[35] It also reinforced that there cannot be a situation where a pregnant woman has been turned away from government health facilities only on the ground that she was unable to prove her BPL status. In addition, the court noted that the government, both central and state, in operationalizing the schemes should ensure that a maximum number of people derive benefits. The burden on persons 'below the poverty line' to prove that they are persons in need of urgent medical assistance constitutes a major barrier to their access to the services.

Opinion of Medical Practitioners/Medical Board

In *X v. Principal Secretary, Health, and Family Welfare Department, Govt. of NCT of Delhi,*[36] the Supreme Court allowed an unmarried woman to terminate her 23-week unwanted pregnancy. The Supreme Court relied on the medical board's report concluding that the fetus could be aborted without risk to the life of the woman. The ruling also indicates that sexual autonomy is increasingly gaining ground in abortion law jurisprudence.

---

[35] *Laxmi Mandal v. Deen Dayal Harinagar Hospital* (2010) 172 DLT 9.

[36] SLP (Civil) No. 12612 of 2022, Decided on 21-7-2022.

In *ABC v. State of Maharashtra*,[37] the Bombay High Court allowed the termination of a pregnancy of 32 weeks. The petitioner sought the termination due to the inability to afford the expenses of an infant born with multiple anomalies. The medical board's report read "deformity being correctable free of cost at government hospitals, and considering the advanced gestational age, the medical termination of pregnancy is not recommended." The court did not find the medical board's recommendations appealing as they totally overlooked the fact that there was no prospect for the baby being born normal. The court further referred to the National Institute of Neurological Disorders and Stroke (NINDS) to get into the depths of fetus' condition in the case. The report from the NINDS stated that the abnormality may result in the infant's head's size being underdeveloped, which may be life-threatening as well. Considering the petitioner's socio-economic condition and serious fetal abnormalities, the court relied on the Supreme Court's broader interpretation of the MTP Act in *X v. Health & Family Welfare Department*.[38] This judgment made it clear that it is no more the ultimate decision of the medical practitioner, rather it is the women's sole decision to terminate her pregnancy. In the end, the court stated that "the right to choose lies with the petitioner and not the medical board."

Risk to the Pregnant Woman from Continuing with the Pregnancy

In *High Court on its Own Motion v. the State of Maharashtra*,[39] the Bombay High Court ruled that if a woman carries an unwanted pregnancy to term, it "violates the woman's bodily integrity and aggravates her mental trauma, which is detrimental to her mental health." However, after the twentieth week of pregnancy, the majority of cases require a medical opinion on the risks of continuing the pregnancy to determine if the pregnancy poses a threat to the life of the pregnant woman.

In *Meera Santosh Pal v. Union of India*,[40] a woman who was carrying a 24-week fetus approached the Supreme Court with the plea to undergo medical termination of pregnancy. The court directed a medical board to be set up and the board was of the opinion that continuation of the pregnancy would not only result in grave injury to the physical and mental health of the woman, but the fetus would not be able to survive

---

[37] *ABC v. State of Maharashtra*, WP (ST) No. 1357 of 2023, decided on 20-1-2023.

[38] 2022 SCC OnLine SC 1321.

[39] 2016 SCC OnLine Bom 4448.

[40] 2017 SCC OnLine SC 39.

'extra-uterine life' due to abnormalities. The court permitted the woman to undergo abortion as per the provisions of the MTP Act and emphasized upon women's right to reproductive autonomy and bodily integrity, which includes the right to take all measures necessary to preserve her own life.

Risk to the Pregnant Woman from Termination

The courts routinely seek a medical opinion on the likeliness of risk to the pregnant woman's life in case of abortion. For example, the Rajasthan High Court in *Jamana Suthar v. State of Rajasthan*[41] disallowed termination of pregnancy as the medical board's report stated that it was likely to endanger the life of the minor rape survivor.

In *Kavita v. State of Haryana*,[42] the appellant's daughter was a 12-year-old minor girl who had been subjected to repeated sexual assaults and got burdened with a pregnancy of about 34 weeks. The medical board opined that "the termination of pregnancy at 34 weeks of gestation carries a higher risk to the girl than allowing the pregnancy to continue with regular pregnancy check-ups." The report emphasized that termination of pregnancy at that stage had the likelihood to result in the birth of a live baby. The court ordered a regular psychological assessment of the girl owning to the sensitive nature of the issue and her age. To look after the food and medicine of the victim, the court also directed the State of Haryana to release Rs. 2 lakhs to the appellant.

In *Alakh Alok Srivastava v. Union of India*,[43] the Supreme Court heavily relied on the medical board's opinion concerning the risks involved in the termination of pregnancy without making an explicit reference to section 3 or 5 of the MTP Act. The medical board opined that the risk of terminating the pregnancy was higher than the risk of carrying the pregnancy to term. Thus, the court declined the permission to abort over the 20-week limit. However, in *Murugan Nayakkar v. Union of India*[44] and *Chanchala Kumari v. Union of India*,[45] the respective medical boards were of the opinion that the risk of terminating the pregnancy was less than the risk of carrying the pregnancy to term. The Supreme Court accordingly permitted the abortion in both cases.

---

[41] 2009 SCC OnLine Raj 3468.

[42] 2018 SCC OnLine SC 1532.

[43] 2018 (7) SCALE 88.

[44] 2017 SCC OnLine SC 1906.

[45] 2018 SCC OnLine Del 12891.

Fetal Impairment and Disability

In *Meera Santosh Pal v. Union of India*[46] and *X v. Union of India*,[47] the Supreme Court stressed that a pregnant woman has the right to preserve her own life. The medical opinion noted that the pregnant woman's mental and physical health would be at risk if she carried the pregnancy to term and there were fatal fetal abnormalities in both cases.

The Supreme Court of India allowed abortions after the twentieth week of pregnancy in *Mamta Verma v. Union of India*[48] and *X v. Union of India*,[49] on the grounds that the fetus' disabilities made survival outside the womb impossible. The court gave serious consideration to the possibility of psychological harm to the pregnant woman in both cases.

In *Tapasya Umesh Pisal v. Union of India*,[50] the Court permitted termination of a 25-week pregnancy solely on the basis that the fetal impairment was associated with a high probability of death at birth. Referring to section 3(2)(b)(ii) of the MTP Act, the court determined that because this case falls within the scope of this section, except for the gestational limit, it would be in the public interest to permit the abortion.

In *Shaikh Ayesha Khatoon v. Union of India*,[51] considering the multiple fetal abnormalities and the low likelihood of independent survival of the fetus after birth, the court allowed the termination of a 27-week pregnancy. The court held that the conditions for medical termination of pregnancy under section 3(2)(b)(i) & (ii) should be read with section 5(1).

Risk to the Mental Health of Women

Under section 3(4)(a) of the principal Act, the word 'lunatic' got substituted with the words 'mentally ill person' by the MTP (Amendment) Act, 2002. As per Section 2(i)(b) of the 2002 amendment Act, a 'mentally ill person' means a person who needs treatment by reason of any mental disorder other than mental retardation.

Therefore, under the new provisions, while the consent of the guardian to make decisions on behalf of a 'mentally ill person' as per section 3(4)(a) of the MTP Act is mandatory, the same is not required on

---

46 (2017) 3 SCC 462.

47 (2017) 3 SCC 458.

48 2017 SCC OnLine SC 1150.

49 (2016) 14 SCC 382.

50 (2018) 12 SCC 57.

51 (2018) SCC OnLine Bom 11.

behalf of a person who is in a condition of mental retardation.[52] This was seen as a progressive change as those who suffer from 'mental retardation' are capable of making their own choices with respect to termination of pregnancy.

In *Sarmishtha Chakrabortty v. Union of India,*[53] the Supreme Court permitted the termination of pregnancy for a 26-week pregnant woman. The court relied on the medical board's report that revealed the threat of severe mental injury to the woman and multiple complex issues with the child if born alive.

In *Sonali Sandeep Jadhav v. Union of India,*[54] the petitioner's pregnancy was of 22 weeks with a substantial risk of mortality and morbidity in the fetus if born alive. The medical board report stated that the petitioner had submitted a letter demanding the termination of pregnancy. The board held that the continuation of pregnancy shall pose severe mental injury to her. The Supreme Court granted her permission as per the demand.

The Bombay High Court in *Priti Mahendra Singh Rawal v. Union of India*[55] and the Himachal Pradesh High Court in *Geeta Devi v. State of Himachal Pradesh*[56] allowed medical termination of pregnancy as the woman's mental health was at risk in case the pregnancy continued.

In the matter of *Mrs. X. v. Union of India & Ors.*,[57] the Kerela High Court relied on the case of *Sarmishtha Chakrabortty* and allowed the writ petition seeking termination of pregnancy of a minor rape victim. The High Court observed that under section 5, the termination of pregnancy is permissible even in cases where the period of gestation has been exceeded as per sections 3 and 4 of the MTP Act. It added that "the Registry and all concerned, shall maintain absolute privacy with respect to the identity of the petitioner while issuing the certified copy of the judgment or otherwise."

---

[52] MTP Amendment Act, 2021 – Section 3(4): (a) No pregnancy of a woman, who has not attained the age of eighteen years, or, who having attained the age of eighteen years, is a mentally ill person, shall be terminated except with the consent in writing of her guardian. (b) Save as otherwise provided in clause (a), no pregnancy shall be terminated except with the consent of the pregnant woman.

[53] (2018) 13 SCC 339.

[54] 2022 SCC OnLine SC 1813.

[55] 2017 SCC OnLine Bom 10209.

[56] 2017 SCC OnLine HP 1574.

[57] 2020 SCC OnLine Raj 860.

Pregnancy Resulting from Rape

In *Suchita Srivastava v. Chandigarh Administration,*[58] the Supreme Court considered the women's 'best interests' and not those of her guardian or society at large. An orphaned woman living in a government-run welfare institution in Chandigarh, who had the mental capacity of a nine-year old, was raped. She subsequently became pregnant. Upon this discovery, the Chandigarh Administration filed a criminal case under Sections 376 and 120B of the Indian Penal Code, 1860 and constituted a medical board to evaluate the mental status of the woman. The medical board opined that the woman suffered from 'mild mental retardation' and that the pregnancy should be terminated. However, the Supreme Court held that abortion should be independent of the woman's understanding of the sexual act or any reservations there may be about her ability to carry the pregnancy to term or discharge her maternal responsibilities. Though the *Suchita* case did not address abortion for minors directly, High Courts have relied on this decision and applied the 'best interest' standard in determining that abortion for minors is permissible.

In *Ashaben v. State of Gujarat,*[59] the Gujarat High Court permitted the termination of a 27-week fetus of a rape victim. The court applied a strict interpretation of section 5 of the MTP Act, holding that it permitted termination of pregnancies longer than 20 weeks if continuing the pregnancy would jeopardize the pregnant woman's life.

In *Bashir Khan v. State of Punjab*[60] and *Kamla Devi v. State of Haryana,*[61] the Punjab and Haryana High Court recognized the physical and psychological harm caused to rape survivors by a delay in terminating the pregnancy. The courts directed the states to assist rape survivors seeking abortion in obtaining the necessary medical opinion and services.

The Gujarat High Court allowed medical termination of pregnancy in *Bhavikaben v. State of Gujarat,*[62] citing the rape survivor's young age and health and the grave mental injury caused by the unwanted pregnancy. Similarly, in *Madhuben Arvindbhai Nimavat v. State of Gujarat*[63] and

---

[58] (2009) 9 SCC 1.

[59] AIR 2015 SC 3387.

[60] AIR 2014 P&H 150.

[61] CWP No 2007 of 2015, decided on Feb. 9, 2015 (P & H).

[62] 47 (2016) 3 RCR (Cri) 362.

[63] 2016 SCC OnLine Guj 662.

Pujaben Subedar Yadav v. State of Gujarat,[64] the High Court delegated the discretion to allow pregnancy termination to medical practitioners if they believed that it was in the 'best interests' of the minor rape victim.

In *R v. State of Haryana,*[65] the Punjab and Haryana High Court applied the 'best interest test' and considered the grave injury to the minor rape survivor's physical and mental health. The court looked into the social and emotional consequences of continuing the pregnancy. However, because the medical board recommended against terminating the pregnancy on the grounds that it exceeded the legal 20-week limit, the court felt unable to permit such termination. The court emphasized on amending the law to increase the time limit in order to permit abortions beyond 20 weeks. It also cautioned that doctors acting in good faith, to prevent grave injury to rape survivors' physical or mental health, should not be prosecuted unnecessarily.

In *Alakh Alok Srivastava v. Union of India,*[66] the Court refused a 10-year-old, 32-week pregnant rape victim to abort. The medical board concluded that allowing the pregnancy to continue was less dangerous than terminating it at that stage. The court directed the central government to establish permanent medical boards to expeditiously examine termination requests after 20 weeks of pregnancy. The Centre issued instructions for the state governments to do the needful.

In *Murugan Nayakkar v. Union of India & Ors.,*[67] the Supreme Court allowed the termination of a 13-year-old rape victim's 32-week-old pregnancy. The Court observed that "considering the petitioner's age, the trauma she has suffered as a result of the sexual abuse, the agony she is currently experiencing, and as per the report of the medical board, it is appropriate to allow termination of pregnancy."

In *Anusha Ravindra v. Union of India,*[68] the Supreme Court acknowledged the importance of framing appropriate medico-legal guidelines for establishing a permanent mechanism for safe abortions. The court issued directions to frame guidelines for expeditious termination of pregnancies beyond 20 weeks in cases involving rape survivors and fetal impairment.

---

[64] 2017 Cri. L.J. (NOC 719) 225.

[65] 2016 SCC OnLine P&H 18369.

[66] 2018 (7) SCALE 88.

[67] 2017 SCC OnLine SC 1906.

[68] W.P. (C) 934 / 2017 SC.

In *X (since minor through her mother) v. Union of India*,[69] the Bombay High Court permitted a deaf and mute minor rape survivor diagnosed with Down syndrome to abort. Apart from the physical danger posed by the pregnancy's continuation, the court considered the psychological trauma caused by the unwanted pregnancy.

In *Bhatou Boro v. State of Assam*,[70] the medical board refused to issue an opinion on the termination of a minor rape survivor's pregnancy as it had progressed beyond 20 weeks. The Gauhati High Court directed the medical board to re-examine the case in light of the unwanted pregnancy's impact on the petitioner's mental health. The court also cited the precedents wherein permission for termination was granted without undue regard to the legal limitations.

In *Pramod A. Solanke v. Dean of B.J. Govt. Medical College & Sasoon Hospital, Pune*,[71] the court stated that "where continuation of the pregnancy causes grave harm to the mother's physical and mental health, she cannot be compelled to continue the pregnancy simply because it had exceeded 20 weeks. This would constitute a grave violation of the pregnant mother's fundamental rights to reproduction and mental health." The division bench held that in such cases, the court may grant permission for medical termination of pregnancy despite the gestation period being above 20 weeks.

In January 2023, the Delhi High Court in *Minor R Through Mother H v. State NCT of Delhi & Anr.*[72] held that denying a woman the right to medical termination of pregnancy in sexual assault cases and imposing the responsibility of motherhood on her would amount to "denying her the human right to live with dignity." The woman has a right in relation to her body, including the right to say 'yes or no' to being a mother.

Spousal Consent for Medical Termination of Pregnancy

Section 3(4)(b) requires only a woman's consent to terminate her pregnancy, granted she is above 18 years with a sound mind. It means that the husband's consent is not needed for the termination of the pregnancy of an adult woman.

---

[69] 2017 SCC OnLine Bom 9334.

[70] (2018) 2 Gau. LR 577.

[71] 2020 SCC OnLine Bom. 639.

[72] W.P. (Crl) 221/2023.

In *Samar Ghosh v. Jaya Ghosh*,[73] a married woman terminated her pregnancy without her husband's permission. Her husband later filed a divorce petition on the ground of mental cruelty. The Supreme Court held that terminating a pregnancy unilaterally constitutes cruelty and granted the divorce. However, since then, the reproductive rights discourse has undergone several significant progressive shifts in India.[74]

In *Dr. Mangla Dogra and others v. Anil Kumar Malhotra and others*,[75] the Punjab and Haryana High Court ruled that a woman does not need her husband's consent to have an abortion. The husband cannot force his wife to continue a pregnancy. The High Courts dismissed the petition filed by the husband against his wife and doctors. In *Anil Kumar Malhotra v. Ajay Pasricha*,[76] the Supreme Court dismissed an appeal against the decision.

In *Nirav Anupambhai Tarkas v. State of Gujarat*,[77] the High Court dismissed a criminal complaint filed by a husband against his wife and her family for terminating her pregnancy despite his opposition. The dismissal was based on the interpretation of section 3(4)(b).

In *X v. Principal Secretary, Health and Family Welfare Department, Govt. of NCT of Delhi*,[78] the apex court observed that a woman seeking legal abortion cannot be required to seek consent from her family. It is only the woman's consent (or her guardian's consent if she is a minor or mentally ill) that is material. The court noted that it is a common practice for registered medical practitioners (RMPs) to insist on compliance with extra-legal conditions such as consent from the woman's family, documentary proofs, or judicial authorization. In case, the woman fails to comply with these additional requirements, RMPs frequently decline to provide their services in conducting legal abortions. The court stated that "these extra-legal requirements have no basis in law. RMPs only need to ensure that the provisions of the MTP Act (along with the accompanying rules and regulations) are complied with." This is a huge step forward in the domain of the evolving feminist jurisprudence in India as the marital status of women will no longer determine the availability of rights.

---

[73] (2007) 4 SCC 511.

[74] Aparna Chandra & Mrinal Satish, "Securing Reproductive Justice in Indian Courts: A Casebook", *Ctr. for Reproductive Rights*, 3–11 (2019).

[75] CR No. 6337 and 6017 of 2011 (P & H).

[76] Civil Appeal No. 4704 of 2013, Supreme Court, decided on 27-10-2017.

[77] (2011) SCC OnLine Guj 5577.

[78] SLP (Civil) No. 12612 of 2022, decided on 21-7-2022.

Right to Abortion of Women in Prison

In *Sunil Batra v. Delhi Administration,*[79] the Supreme Court held that a prisoner's fundamental rights "do not dissipate at the prison's gates." Throughout the years, the court has reaffirmed this approach and defended prisoners' rights. The reproductive rights of imprisoned women have also gained prominence through cases that have been brought before the courts.

In *High Court on Its Own Motion v. State of Maharashtra,*[80] the court observed that pregnant women include pregnant women prisoners. Under Article 21, all pregnant women have a right to reproductive health and the right to terminate their pregnancy. The court directed that upon admission to the prison, every woman of reproductive age should undergo the pregnancy test. If she is found to be pregnant, the medical officer should inform her about the right to terminate her pregnancy. The court held that once a pregnant prisoner expresses a desire to terminate her pregnancy, she should immediately be referred to a hospital. To support this, it cited international human rights laws under which women's bodily autonomy has been recognized.

In *R. D. Upadhyay v. State of Andhra Pradesh,*[81] the Supreme Court issued guidelines regarding the treatment of pregnant women in prisons. The guidelines include provisions for their medical care, dietary needs of pregnant women and their children, measures taken at childbirth (the woman should be released on bail for delivery outside the prison), and child custody.

In *State of Gujarat v. Jadav @ Jatin Bhagvanbhai Prajapati & Ors.,*[82] the Gujarat High Court applied one of the guidelines issued in *R.D. Upadhyay*[83] regarding pregnant women receiving bail to deliver their children outside the prison. After convicting the accused woman, the court suspended her sentence and granted her bail for eleven months upon learning of her pregnancy. Thus, she was allowed to not only deliver her baby outside the prison environment but also care for the child during the initial months. The court directed jail authorities to allow women to keep children in prison until they reach the specified age under the specified Jail Manual.

---

[79] (1978) 4 SCC 409.

[80] (2007) 15 SCC 337.

[81] AIR 2006 SC 1946.

[82] (2015) Cri LJ 2282 (P&H).

[83] Writ Petition (civil) 559 of 1994. Decided on 13-4-2006.

Imprisoned women have been demanding the recognition and enforcement of their conjugal rights. In *Jasvir Singh v. State of Punjab,*[84] a couple filed a petition in the Punjab and Haryana High Court to seek their right to conjugal life. The husband had been sentenced to death, while the wife had been sentenced to life in prison. The court concluded that the right to procreation and conjugal visits is a component of the right to live with dignity. It held that imprisonment does not affect the right to procreation. The court also observed that reasonable restrictions apply to the right to conjugal visits or procreation. The restrictions could be imposed in accordance with legislative procedures. The court directed the State of Punjab to establish a jail reforms committee to formulate a scheme for upholding the conjugal rights of inmates.

In Safoora Zargar v. State,[85] a woman from Kashmir was pregnant at the time of her arrest. She got arrested by the Delhi Police under the Unlawful Activities (Prevention) Act for opposing the Citizenship Amendment Act, 2019. The Sessions Court rejected her bail application, finding prima facie evidence of a conspiracy to blockades. Safoora approached the Delhi High Court seeking relief, which was granted on humanitarian grounds due to her 23-week pregnancy. In granting bail to Safoora Zargar, the Delhi High Court followed the American precedent of *Roe v. Wade.*[86] The right to reproductive justice was reiterated in the *Safoora Zargar* case in line with *Puttaswamy*, *Navtej Johar, the Independent Thought*, and *Joseph Shine* case decisions.

Right to Abortion of Women with Disability

The Parliament enacted the Rights of Persons with Disabilities Act (RPD Act) in 2016, ensuring a range of rights for people with disabilities, including reproductive autonomy.[87] According to section 3(4)(b) of the MTP Act, 1971, no pregnancy can be terminated without the pregnant woman's consent. The RPD Act, 2016 reinforces this further in the context of women with disabilities.

In the *Suchita Srivastava* case, the Supreme Court had observed that states are required to ensure that women with mental retardation have their reproductive choices respected as per the Convention on the Rights of Persons with Disabilities.

[84] (2018) SCC OnLine Mad 278.

[85] 2020 SCC OnLine Del 664.

[86] 1973 U.S. LEXIS 159.

[87] Rights of Persons with Disabilities Act, 2016, Section 10.

The Supreme Court in *Z v. State of Bihar & Ors.*[88] emphasized a woman's right to bodily integrity and autonomy, while cautioning against placing excess importance on the concept of a guardian. In this case, a woman with mild mental retardation was denied abortion due to a lack of guardian and spousal consent. The court criticized the requirement for guardian's consent when (i) the woman was a major and did not suffer from mental illness; (ii) she had been raped and desired to terminate her pregnancy; and (iii) her medical report indicated no risk to her life from termination of pregnancy. The court awarded the woman with compensation under the Victim Compensation Scheme. The scheme was introduced under the Code of Criminal Procedure, 1973 to attempt to compensate for the grave mental injury caused by having to carry a pregnancy resulting from rape due to the State authorities' laxity.

The foregoing cases indicate a positive trajectory for reproductive rights, specifically abortion, upheld by courts in India. The physiological and psychological changes that occur during pregnancy have far-reaching effects on the expectant mother's health and quality of life. Therefore, each woman should be able to make her own decisions about her body, fertility, and motherhood.

The legal approach articulated by the judiciary serves as a strong call to continue defending and upholding women's reproductive rights, including reproductive health and autonomy. The following cases reflect the safeguards established by constitutional courts on various aspects of reproductive rights in India.

Prosecution for Contravention of the MTP Act, 1971

Pregnancy termination without the consent of the woman is a non-bailable offence under Section 313 of the IPC. Courts have taken a strict stance when considering bail applications or petitions for revocation of criminal prosecution filed in such cases.

In *Surendra Chauhan v. State of M.P.*,[89] the Supreme Court upheld the Madhya Pradesh High Court's decision convicting the accused of causing a woman's miscarriage. The accused had 'illicit relations' with the woman, which resulted in pregnancy, and then brought her to a clinic that did not meet the requirements of the MTP Act and Rules. Both the doctor and the defendant were convicted under Section 314 of the Indian Penal Code.

---

[88] (2018) 11 SCC 572.

[89] AIR 2000 SC 1436.

In *Raj Bokaria v. Medical Council of India,*[90] the court emphasized the importance of documenting the medical opinion on pregnancy termination pursuant to section 5(1) in the manner prescribed by the MTP Regulations, 2003. Due to the absence of such a record, the court upheld the action taken by the Medical Council of India's Ethics Committee against the doctor, who terminated a woman's pregnancy after 20 weeks in order to save her life.

In *Sushil Kumar v. Govt. of NCT of Delhi,*[91] the Delhi High Court denied an anticipatory bail application filed by a husband and his family. The offence was grave. The defendant was charged under Section 313 for inducing his wife to consume abortion pills. In *Dr Saraswati v. State of Maharashtra,*[92] the abortion performed in violation of the MTP Act resulted in the death of the pregnant woman. The Bombay High Court denied the bail application, finding a strong prima facie case that the doctor's actions resulted in the woman's death.

In *Binod Bihari Naik v. State of Orissa,*[93] the Orissa High Court dismissed a doctor's plea to quash criminal charges against him for allegedly terminating a pregnancy without the woman's consent. The High Court held that a prima facie case had been established against the doctor.

Inadequate Implementation of the Pre-conception and Pre-natal Diagnostic Techniques (Prohibition of Sex Selection) Act, 1994

The Supreme Court and High Courts have been approached frequently for issuing directions to the appropriate authorities regarding the effective implementation of the PCPNDT Act, 1994. The Act was enacted in 1994, amended and effectively implemented in 2003, and strictly amended in 2011.

The Supreme Court noted in *Centre for Enquiry into Health and Allied Themes (CEHAT) v. Union of India*[94] that the PCPNDT Act had not been implemented well after five years of its enactment. Consequently, the court issued directions to the central and state governments and other authorities working under the PCPNDT Act to ensure its proper implementation and examine the necessity of any amendment in light of the technologies used

---

[90] (2010) SCC OnLine Del 4125.

[91] (2013) SCC OnLine Del 2068.

[92] (2013) SCC OnLine Bom 1014.

[93] (2018) Cri LJ 2676.

[94] (2001) 5 SCC 577.

by violators. The court also directed the governments to increase public awareness about the act through advertisements and electronic media.

In numerous cases, High Courts have discussed the constitutional validity of different provisions of the PCPNDT Act. In *Vinod Soni v. Union of India,*[95] the petitioner claimed that the PCPDNT Act violated their personal liberty to determine the nature of their family. The Bombay High Court held that Article 21 does not include a right to choose the sex of one's baby. The PCPNDT Act aims to promote the right of every child, regardless of gender, to attain full development as guaranteed by Article 21 of the Indian Constitution.

In *Vijay Sharma v. Union of India,*[96] the petitioners argued that the PCPNDT Act violated Article 14 because it failed to consider the mental agony suffered by prospective mothers carrying an unwanted female fetus. The Bombay High Court upheld the PCPNDT Act's constitutionality. The Court observed that both the PCPNDT Act and MTP Act operate in distinct spheres and have distinct objectives. It was held that sex selection violates women's collective rights to life and dignity. The mothers who wish to choose the sex of their offspring fall into a different category than those seeking abortion on specified grounds under the MTP Act.

In *Voluntary Health Association of Punjab v. Union of India,*[97] the Supreme Court heard a writ petition highlighting the continued malpractice of sex selection and the decline in the female sex ratio in several states. While the court dismissed this writ petition,[98] it issued directions addressing the non-implementation of its *CEHAT* case orders. The court took note of the failure to supervise diagnostic centers and seize violators' ultrasound machines by the concerned authorities. The directives included 'fast-tracking' PCPNDT cases, establishing a judicial committee for periodic monitoring, and imparting trainings to sensitize the judicial officers. The court also emphasized the importance of increasing public awareness of the PCPNDT Act.

In *Amy Antoinette McGregor & Anr. v. Directorate of Family Welfare Govt. of NCT of Delhi,*[99] an Australian couple seeking to have a male and female child via surrogacy filed a petition in the Delhi High Court. The

95 (2005) Cri LJ 3408 (Bom).

96 AIR 2008 Bom 29.

97 (2013) 4 SCC 1.

98 (2016) 19 SCC 275.

99 (2013) 205 DLT 96.

petition argued that the PCPNDT Act was ultra vires to the surrogacy process. The High Court dismissed the petition and concluded that the court cannot treat the parents desiring to balance their family through surrogacy differently from others.

In *Saksham Foundation Charitable Society v. Union of India,*[100] provisions prohibiting disclosure of the fetus' sex and prohibiting sex determination were challenged. The petitioner argued that the PCPNDT Act violated Articles 14 and 21 of the Indian Constitution, and the disclosure of the fetus' sex shall be made mandatory on the grounds that such measures would prevent sex selection. The court dismissed the writ petition, holding that the PCPNDT Act did not violate Articles 14 and 21, and the statute's purpose was to prevent diagnostic techniques from being used for sex determination and selection.

In *Sabu Mathew George v. Union of India,*[101] a writ petition was filed by the appellant to ban advertisements relating to pre-natal sex determination from search engines in India. Advertisements for pre-conception and pre-natal sex determination are prohibited under section 22 of the PCPNDT Act. The Supreme Court issued an order to block all websites and online advertisements promoting gender-based sex selection. The court directed the establishment of a nodal agency to monitor and report violations to search engines for removal.

The cases discussed above demonstrate the critical and evolving role that the judiciary is playing in India in addressing the legal and practical barriers that women and girls face in exercising their reproductive rights. Constitutional courts have clearly and firmly recognized reproductive rights as fundamental rights. Consequently, this has created a mandate for the government to prioritize women's rights to dignity, autonomy, and bodily integrity in abortion laws. While the judiciary has almost consistently upheld the right to reproductive autonomy, gaps persist as a result of the complex legal framework regulating abortion. The courts have clearly highlighted this right within the framework of life and personal liberty, but are yet to address abortion or reproductive autonomy as a matter of equality and non-discrimination.[102]

---

[100] (2014) 5 All LJ 496.

[101] (2018) 3 SCC 229.

[102] (2017) 10 SCC 1.

EIGHT

Right to Abortion and Contemporary Issues in India

These extra-legal requirements have no basis in law. As noted above, it is only the woman's consent (or her guardian's consent if she is a minor or mentally ill) which is material.

– *X v. Principal Secretary, Health and Family Welfare Department*, Govt. of NCT of Delhi[1]

Reproductive rights have been recognized as a component of human rights, and the two are no longer mutually exclusive. Bodily autonomy, sexual health, access to maternal healthcare, freedom from sexual violence and torture, access to contraception and birth control, and access to safe and sanitary abortion services are all part of it. However, the interface between the reproductive health sector and women reveals various forms of social discrimination that line the formulation and implementation of biased health policies. Women, particularly those from marginalized groups, are frequently treated inadequately, indifferently, and callously in public health facilities, which robs them of their dignity and agency.

This chapter focuses on the various challenges that women face while exercising their reproductive rights, such as inadequate infrastructure, which lead to a high rate of unintended pregnancies, unsafe abortions, and injury during childbirth. It also looks at harmful traditional practices and various forms of violence (such as marital rape) that contribute to discrimination against women, thereby diminishing their reproductive health, well-being, and social status. In addition, the chapter addresses the critical issue of lack of knowledge and access to contraception. Sexual/obstetric offence is another challenge. Lastly, it addresses a fundamental concern pertaining to vulnerable and excluded women with disabilities and diverse sexual orientations.

---

[1] SLP (C) No 12612 of 2022, decided on 29th September 2022.

The theoretical aspect of the contemporary issues in India has been discussed below:

Absence of Reproductive Autonomy

Reproductive autonomy is defined as the right of women to choose whether or not to have children, and if they do, the right to determine the number of children, when, and with whom as well as the freedom to choose the means and methods by which they exercise their fertility. Access to sex education, contraceptives, reproductive and maternal healthcare, safe abortion services, and economic resources are some of the most critical determinants of the degree of reproductive autonomy exercised by women within a legal system.

The right to reproductive autonomy has also been recognized as a constitutionally protected fundamental right by the judiciary in India. From the 1990s when the Supreme Court refused to comment on women's right to abort an unwanted pregnancy in *Jacob George v. the State of Kerala*[2] to the Delhi High Court's decision in *Laxmi Mandal v. Deen Dayal Harinagar Hospital*,[3] the judicial attitude toward the right to abortion has shifted significantly. In 1996, in *Paschim Banga Khet Majdoor Samiti v. State of West Bengal*,[4] the Supreme Court recognized the right to health suggesting the development of a legal structure complying with international instruments to strengthen women's rights.

Further, in *Suchita Srivastava & Anr. v. Chandigarh Administration*,[5] the right of a woman to choose her reproductive prospects got recognized as a facet of personal liberty under Article 21 of the Constitution. Since it was determined that a woman's right to privacy, dignity, and bodily integrity is paramount, restrictions on the exercise of reproductive choices cannot be imposed. Women, as part of their reproductive rights, can opt for birth control methods such as sterilization as well as carry a pregnancy to term and deliver and nurture a child.

However, the comprehensive realization of reproductive rights in India becomes difficult as abortion is considered taboo. Though married women in the country have the legal right to abortion, they still face

---

[2] (2) SCALE 563.

[3] 172 (2010) DLT 9.

[4] (1996) 4 SCC 37.

[5] (2009) 9 SCC 1.

significant obstacles. The traditional schools of thinking consider abortion violative of divine laws, which instill a sense of shame and stigma around pre-marital sex and abortion. This stigma stems from intrinsic gender discrimination, according to which the worth of a woman is determined by her role as a 'pure' wife and mother only.

The stance on abortion has always been divisive; there is a collision between the two ethically separate pro-life and pro-choice ideologies. Autonomy and dignity are critical components of a person's reproductive rights. Autonomy and abortion can be considered mutually reinforcing concepts. According to the principle of autonomy, an individual has the right and competence to make decisions about their health and would do so following their moral standards. Abortion may be viewed as a matter of a pregnant women's autonomy if her freedom to choose is recognized. Thus, the practice of restricting abortion choice, thereby impinging on the woman's autonomy, is problematic. The final decision must be made by the mother alone.

Moving to the legislative sphere, it can be observed that while the MTP (Amendment) Act, 2021 provides women with a broad range of abortion rights in principle, they are limited in practice. Women are denied an abortion for reasons other than those expressly specified in the legislation. As a result, in reality, abortion is not a 'free choice' for women. At one level, the State apparatus is expected to support this partial choice, while at another, it is subordinated to patriarchal interests and authority. Thus, abortion becomes a family decision, and pregnancy and abortion are rarely considered to be exclusive female issues.

In addition to the MTP Act's ineffective implementation, which limits women's ability to exercise their reproductive rights, its failure to extend the rights to minor girls and mentally retarded women is disappointing. As per the MTP Act, a juvenile girl cannot have her pregnancy terminated without her guardian's written authorization.

Thus, it can be noted that legalization still has a long way to go in advancing women's freedom of making choices and improving their overall health in India. The argument that reproductive autonomy is an inherent civil right allows anti-abortionists to immediately contextualize the rights of the unborn child with that of the woman's right to freedom of choice.[6]

---

[6] S. Chandrasekhar, *Abortion in a crowded world: The problem of abortion with special reference to India*, 42 (Allen and Unwin, London, 1974).

Abortion and Ethics

During the early stages of the shaping of the abortion policy, western civilizations objected to the practice of abortion. For many years, the ethical debate about the legal stance on preventing unwanted pregnancies went on across the world. By the nineteenth century, several countries had passed laws prohibiting abortion. It was not until the late twentieth century that women's rights were given legal recognition followed by a few awareness campaigns, and some countries, including the United States of America, proceeded to legalize abortion.

Despite legislative and judicial control, ethical controversies surrounding medical termination of pregnancy persisted in India. Apart from the general society, which believed that abortion was immoral, some judicial pronouncements also cast a question on the ethics of women's abortion rights. The Supreme Court in *Suman Kapur v. Sudhir Kapur*[7] held that an abortion performed by a woman without her husband's consent constitutes mental cruelty and a ground for divorce. It observed that "mental cruelty is a state of mind. The feeling of deep anguish, disappointment, and frustration in one spouse caused by the conduct of the other for a long time may lead to mental cruelty."

On the subject of ethical termination, the International Federation of Gynaecology and Obstetrics (FIGO) holds that women should be able to terminate a severely malformed fetus.[8] The FIGO emphasizes that the decision to terminate a pregnancy should rest primarily with the parents in such cases. Many countries allow legal abortion throughout pregnancy in cases of fetal impairment to protect a pregnant woman's health.

Maternal Mortality

In India, unsound maternal health continues to be a big concern. Maternal mortality is a leading measure of a country's maternal health status, and while the rate of maternal fatalities has decreased globally in recent years, it remains extraordinarily high in India. Maternal healthcare continues to be fragmented and focused on encouraging in-facility deliveries. The State often overlooks the inadequate care provided to pregnant women, the lack of information, inadequate infrastructure, and obstetric violence. All

---

[7] AIR 2009 SC 589.

[8] International Federation of Obstetricians and Gyneocologists, "Recommendations on Ethical Issues in Obstetrics and Gynecology", 58, *Committee for the Study of Ethical Aspects of Human Reproduction and Women's Health* (2009).

these barriers contribute to a limited understanding of the comprehensive framework of sexual and reproductive rights.

According to United Nations (UN) agencies, over 117,004 maternal fatalities occur in India each year, accounting for nearly one-quarter of all maternal deaths globally.[9] Unsafe abortions are considered to account for 9% to 13% of the country's maternal death rate. This figure can go up to 50% in some districts of India.[10] The lack of appropriate facilities and the dearth of educated and licensed doctors create significant barriers for those seeking an abortion. The incompetent healthcare providers also fail to give adequate information regarding the MTP Act to women, frequently jeopardizing abortion rights, particularly for those from vulnerable groups.

Maternal mortality is a significant indicator of the systematic inequalities and prejudice women face as a result of their reproductive potential. Governments are obligated under an international treaty to safeguard basic human rights without discrimination of any kind.[11] The CEDAW expressly outlaws' discrimination against women in all spheres of life, including healthcare.[12] It imposes a clear responsibility on member states to enact particular protective measures for pregnant women and expressly specifies that "measures aimed at protecting maternity shall not be regarded as discriminatory."

In India, stratified society is mainly based on gender and patrilineal descent, in which women's say in terms of decision-making, movement, and access to and control over resources is severely limited.[13] Gender equity is inextricably linked to reproductive health, female literacy, education, and decision-making authority.[14] It is sometimes assumed

[9] UNFPA, Maternal Mortality Declining in Middle-income Countries.

[10] Mary Philip Sebastian, M.E. Khan and Daliya Sebastian (2013). "Unintended Pregnancy and Abortion in India with Focus on Bihar, Madhya Pradesh and Odisha" (Population Council, New Delhi, India).

[11] Convention for the Protection of Human Rights and Fundamental Freedoms, Nov. 4, 1950, Art. 2, Europ. T.S. No. 5, Art. 14.

[12] Convention on the Elimination of Discrimination Against Women, adopted Dec. 18, 1979, G.A, Res. 34/180, UN GAOR 34th Sess., Supp. No. 46, Art. 1, U.N. Doc. A/34/46. 1249 U.N.T.S. 13.

[13] S. Jejeebhoy, Z. Sathar., "Women's Autonomy in India and Pakistan: The Influence of Religion and Region", 27, *PDR*, 687–712 (2001).

[14] A. Sen, "Gender Equity and The Population Problem", 31, *IJHS*, 469–74 (2001).

that low economic position and gender bias are connected[15] and affect women's access to contraceptives, abortion, and healthcare-seeking behavior throughout pregnancy and delivery.[16] Both urban slum dwellers and rural poor have less maternal and reproductive healthcare access than non-poor residents in the same locations.

There is also a correlation between education and maternal reproductive health connected to family planning. Women with less education are more likely to have an unmet need for contraception and be sterilized (resultantly) than women with higher education.[17]

There is no single panacea for reducing maternal mortality. Additional legislation and regulations are required to comprehend how economic status, gender, caste, and education contribute to unequal access to maternal health rights in India.

Pro-life and Pro-choice Dissension

One of the most controversial issues in modern medicine, science, and law is the question of when does human life begin and whether the fetus is a person. Intelligence, self-awareness, self-control, and other characteristics are among the necessary conditions for being a person. The infrastructure for those abilities is housed in the cortex, which gets fully developed by the thirtieth week of pregnancy. From this perspective, every neonate or fetus in the third trimester of pregnancy is a person. At birth, the human being becomes a legal person with rights.

In this regard, the abortion debate is made more emotional by the idea that a fetus is a person with its own rights. On the other hand, a woman has a unique and unchangeable right to her body and her ability to have children. Taken together, these perspectives lead to an impasse. As a solution, one school of thought maintains that the rights of the mother should not be pitted against the rights of the unborn. It is necessary to examine the issue from the point of view of both the woman and the fetus once the fetus has reached the point where it can survive outside of the womb. It holds that a human being ceases to exist as a legal person upon

---

15 G. Sen, A. Iyer, "Who Gains, Who Loses and How: Leveraging Gender and Class Intersections to Secure Health Entitlements", 74, *SSM*, 1802–11 (2012).

16 A. Iyer, G. Sen, A. George, "The Dynamics of Gender and Class in Access to Health Care: Evidence from Rural Karnataka, India", 37, *IJHS*, 537–54 (2007).

17 N. Singh, G. Kaur, J. Singh, "The Use of Contraceptives and Unmet Need For Family Planning In A Rural Area Of Patiala District", 55, *JFW*, 34–8 (2009).

death and does not become a fully independent legal person until after birth.

Through a series of decisions, the Supreme Court has recognized various rights under Article 21, namely the right to free enjoyment, the right to human dignity, the right to access justice, and the right to privacy. The judgments reflect that no law or person can morally compel a woman to carry on a pregnancy forcefully. When a pregnancy has already progressed to the point where the fetus is viable, the situation must be judged from both the woman's and the fetus' perspectives.

Further, with the decision in *Suchita Srivastava v. Chandigarh Administration,*[18] the Supreme Court recognized a woman's right to make reproductive choices, including the choice to procreate or abstain from procreating, as part of her personal liberty under Article 21.[19] In *the High Court on its Own Motion v. State of Maharashtra,*[20] the Bombay High Court reiterated the same position as stated in the *Suchita Srivastava* case.

Another outlook on the case of abortion is that women's rights outweigh any potential future rights of the fetus. It is illegitimate to prioritize the rights of a fetus over the rights of a real woman with real needs and desires. The biased treatment against women's rights to autonomy and decision-making reflects broader gender inequality practiced in political and social circles. There should no longer be a debate preferring the rights of the fetus over those of the individual woman and her physical, mental, and reproductive health.

Sex-selective Abortion

The issue of sex selection is of international importance. 12.5 million incidences of female feticide have been registered in India in the last three decades, while unofficial sources estimate the figure to be 30 million. The practice of sex selection goes against the spirit of the Universal Declaration of Human Rights (UNHR), 1948. In the context of population control, "sex selection" refers to the targeted elimination of a specific demographic, in this case, female infants and unborn children. It is a form of gender cleansing disguised as medical practice, a crime against humanity committed in times of peace, and a form of genocide, according to the United Nations Convention on the Prevention and Punishment of the

---

[18] (2009) 9 SCC 1.

[19] *Puttaswamy v. Union of India* (2017), 10 SCC 1.

[20] 2017 Cri LJ 218.

Crime of Genocide, 1948. In Indian law, the practice is often downplayed as a "sociological crime." Recognizing sex selection as a crime against humanity and genocide would be a welcome and encouraging step for women-specific legislations.

Gender discrimination against women is an expression of patriarchal social structures that favor men. Sons are expected to work in the family business, earn higher wages, and support their parents in their old age but the daughters leave their parents' homes and serve their husband's family after marriage. Daughters are viewed as an economic liability to their parents due to the large dowry they need to give to the groom's family upon their marriage. The purpose of having sons stems from a mindset that only a son can perform religious rituals. According to Hindu belief, the soul of a deceased parent can attain heaven if they have a son to light the funeral pyre.

Even though the government implemented the PCPNDT Act, 1994 and initiated various programs, the problem of sex-selective abortions still persists. To stop this trend, the government must monitor the implementation of the existing laws prohibiting sex-selective abortion. This must be accompanied by an effective cultural transformation that recognizes women's equal rights and the right to life of every unborn child, regardless of the child's gender, disability status, or any perceived socioeconomic burden that such a child would place on the family. Public awareness programs must not just attack son preference and inequitable gender views, but also strive to target those most vulnerable to sex selection and directly abolish the practice of sex-selective abortions.[21]

Forced Sterilization

There is a perception in India that women are less likely to protest sterilization procedures than men. Consequently, it is the females on whom sterilization is performed, even though sterilizations are easier to execute on men, according to specialists.

Between the years 2009 and 2012, 700 people died as a result of failed sterilization procedures. During 2013–2014, up to 4 million sterilizations were performed in India, yet less than 1% of these procedures were

[21] Jonathan Abbamonte, "Sex-Selective Abortion in India – Estimates on the Occurrence of Sex-Selective Abortion in India and Some Possible Solutions to Eliminate the Practice", *Population Research Institute* (2019),

performed on men.[22] In 2014, a case in Chhattisgarh exposed a sterilization center's continued deplorable conditions. Eleven women died as a result of tubal ligations performed at a government-run health camp. According to witnesses, 83 women were operated on in just six hours by a doctor and his helper. The women were all from impoverished households and received a $20 stipend. The surviving women were then treated at three separate hospitals.[23] It remains true that males are not as involved in family planning programs as they should be.

It is critical to transform the story around family planning in general as well as the prejudices that become defining narratives. Additionally, more effort should be made to recruit men, whether as patients or educators, into these programs.

Unsafe Abortion

The leading cause of maternal mortality is unsafe abortions. Medically, a woman is unlikely to suffer serious medical complications after undergoing an abortion. Abortions that are conducted erroneously are the ones that kill women.[24]

Reproductive tract infections, many of which are sexually transmitted, account for a significant proportion of the morbidity experienced by women in India, according to a recent study.[25] The 'culture of silence' that surrounds these diseases and the lack of healthcare for these illnesses make them invisible to women, who are often unable to seek treatment. These infections are notoriously difficult to diagnose and treat, as recent efforts to put in place a comprehensive set of reproductive health services have shown.

---

[22] Ministry of Statistics and Programme Implementation, "Selected Socio-Economic Indicators for India Statistics" 2017.

[23] Jan Swasthya Abhiyan, Sama Resource Group for Women and Health and National Alliance for Maternal Health and Human Rights, 2014; Camp of Wrongs: The Mourning Afterwards – A Fact-Finding Report on Sterilisation Deaths in Bilaspur, 16–18 November 2014.

[24] Melissa Stillman, Jennifer J. Frost, Susheela Singh et al., "Abortion in India: A Literature Review", *The Guttmacher Institute* (2014). Available at: https://www.guttmacher.org/sites/default/files/report_pdf/abortion-india-lit-review.pdf.

[25] N. Chaudhary, R. Kalyan, M. Singh, J. Agarwal et al., "Prevalence of Reproductive Tract Infections in Women Attending a Tertiary Care Centre in Northern India with Special Focus on Associated Risk Factors", *Indian J Sex Transm Dis* (2019).

Unwanted pregnancies can be avoided by using effective contraception, which reduces the need for abortions. The significant maternal mortality and morbidity associated with unsafe methods of terminating undesired pregnancies will persist in the absence of safe contraceptive backup.

Women, particularly those living in rural regions, continue to face difficulties in obtaining safe abortion services. Unsafe abortions are harmful to public health, and the same scientific, objective approach needs to be applied for solving this problem that is employed while addressing other public health issues. Even though treatments are readily available and inexpensive, the governments in underdeveloped countries often lack the political will to implement them. Safe abortions will benefit not just women, but also their families, communities, and society in the present and future.[26]

Obstetric Violence

The phrase 'obstetric violence' has been used to refer to healthcare providers' mistreatment, disregard, and assault of women during childbirth. Obstetric violence also includes the erroneous use of equipment and movements that are known to be dangerous. The inaccurate use of forceps or vacuum extraction can result in the death of the mother or infant.

In India, 'obstetric violence' was shown to be connected with socio-demographic characteristics, with lower-status women facing higher levels of abuse. Further, obstetric violence is not exclusive to rural areas or towns; it also occurs in urban areas. In 2013, an intern sparked outrage when he posted on social media that "at a government hospital, giving birth to a child is not a unit less than third-degree torture in prison in India." Sensitization about gender and the impartation of soft skills - such as how to communicate with patients - must be included in HCP training, but incidentally and regrettably, there is no such training.[27]

The report titled "Disrespectful and abusive treatment during childbirth in facilities" published by the WHO in 2014, included the following behaviors as obstetric violence: physical abuse, profound

---

[26] P. Stephenson, M. Wagner, M. Badea, F. Serbanescu, "Commentary: The Public Health Consequences of Restricted Induced Abortion—Lessons from Romania", 82, *Am J Public Health*, 1328–311(992).

[27] N.A. Riyami, F.A. Shezawi, Al-Ruheli, Al-Dughaishi T. et al., "Perinatal Outcome in Pregnancies with Extreme Preterm Premature Rupture of Membranes (Midtrimester PROM)", 13(1), *SQUMJ*, 51–6 (2013).

humiliation and verbal abuse, coercive or unconsented medical procedures (including sterilization), lack of confidentiality, failure to get fully informed consent, refusal to give pain medication, gross violations of privacy, refusal of admission to health facilities, neglecting women during childbirth - leading them to suffer life-threatening, avoidable complications, and detention of women and their newborn in facilities after childbirth due to an inability to pay for the medical services.[28]

In 2016, nurses at a Delhi hospital threatened to smack a pregnant mother if she yelled during labor and brought her the stillborn baby's dirty body in a plastic bag. The HRLN - Human Rights Legal Network - filed a complaint in the Delhi High Court, which ordered the government to pay the mother Rs. 10,000 as an interim measure and scheduled the case for further hearing.[29]

As per a survey[30] done on institutional birth, a pregnant woman was requested by hospital workers to clean up her blood and then turned away for fear of 'spreading coronavirus.' Following this heinous treatment, the victim wrote to the Chief Minister, claiming that she was beaten because she was Muslim and that the ordeal culminated in the death of her baby. This is a particular and normalized kind of violence toward women during labor, variably referred to as disrespect, abuse, mistreatment, and obstetric violence. It is a worldwide naturalized phenomenon that occurs in conjunction with institutional birth in an over-medicalized environment, which relies on power hierarchies between the patient and provider.

The health sector regularly witnesses substantial budget cuts at the central level and underspending at the state level, resulting in the shrinkage of the public health sector and an ongoing scarcity of doctors. Schemes such as the Janani Suraksha Yojana, which compensates pregnant women and health professionals for delivering babies in health facilities, have increased institutional deliveries from 40% to over 80%. The Madhya Pradesh High Court rendered a ground-breaking decision,[31]

[28] World Health Organization (2015). The prevention and elimination of disrespect and abuse during facility-based childbirth.

[29] The Human Right Law Network, *Women Justice*, available at https://hrln.org/initiative/women-s-justice-initiative.

[30] Meghan A. Bohren, Hedieh Mehrtash, Bukola Fawole, "How Women are Treated during Facility-Based Childbirth in Four Countries: A Cross-Sectional Study eith Labour Observations and Community-based Surveys", *The Lancet* (2019).

[31] *Sandesh Bansal v. Union of India and Others* (PIL) W.P. No. 9061/2008.

acknowledging that a woman's right to survive pregnancy and childbirth is a basic right protected by Article 21 of the Constitution of India.[32] If the issue of abuse is not addressed, the deliveries at home may be preferred which, while riskier, provide a more compassionate setting.[33]

Obstetric violence is a violation of women's rights. However, a majority of women are unaware that such actions can be reported to authorities. It is important that women who have endured this mistreatment raise their collective voices in opposition to this injustice; otherwise, it will continue to stay undocumented and rarely discussed. Further, a rights-based, multi-pronged strategy is needed to deal with the social, political, and structural factors that lead to obstetric violence in the country.[34]

Obstetric violence is not confined to India; it affects women worldwide. Serena Williams, the tennis champion, has been working to increase awareness of obstetric violence faced by black women.[35] The WHO issued a statement emphasizing the importance of avoiding and eliminating disrespect and abuse during childbirth. The body directed public health staff to view delivery care as a duty.

Intersex, Transgenders, and Gender-diverse Persons

Individuals belonging to the LGBTQIA community face significant barriers in accessing sexual and reproductive health information. When they do obtain assistance, they may withhold information about their sexual orientation or gender identity from their healthcare practitioners, preventing them from receiving the necessary information and care.[36]

Since the queer theory has questioned the basic formation of the gender binary, implying that the categories of 'woman' and 'man' are no

---

[32] White Ribbon Alliance, "Respectful Maternity Care: The Universal Rights of Childbearing Women" (White Ribbon Alliance Washington, DC2011). Available at http://whiteribbonalliance.org/wpcontent/uploads/2013/10/Final_RMC_Charter.pdf.

[33] S. Bhattacharya, Ravindran, Sundari "T.K. Silent Voices: Institutional Disrespect and Abuse During Delivery Among Women of Varanasi District, Northern India", 18, *BMC Pregnancy Childbirth*, 338 (2018).

[34] S. Shrivastava, & M. Sivakami, "Evidence of Obstetric Violence in India: An Integrative Review", 52(4), *Journal of Biosocial Science*, 610–628 (2020).

[35] P.R. Lockhart, "What Serena Williams's Scary Childbirth Story Says about Medical Treatment of Black Women", *Vox* (2018).

[36] Hannah Brooks, Carrie D. Llewellyn, Tom Nadarzynski, Fernando Castilho Pelloso, Felipe De Souza Guilherme, Alex Pollard and Christina J Jones, *British Journal of General Practice* 2018, 68 (668): e187–e196.

longer permanent, calls for 'queer/transgender abortion rights advocacy' have increased. The apex court of India in *National Legal Services Authority v. Union of India*[37] established that transgender people have the right to self-determination and legal recognition of their gender identity as well as the right to enjoy all other fundamental rights. The Delhi High Court had inserted the right to reproductive healthcare under Article 21 in *Laxmi Mandal v. Deen Dayal Harinagar Hospital.*[38] Thus, activists argue that all provisions relating to the right to abortion and the right to reproductive healthcare services must be considered equally applicable to gender-diverse individuals along with women.

While discussing legal reforms affecting reproductive rights in India, it is critical that all stakeholders' voices are heard, including those from the disability rights movement, the anti-caste movement, indigenous peoples' movements, and transgender, gender-diverse, and intersex persons' organizations.

Disabled Women

People with disabilities have had limited access to reproductive and sexual rights in India. Apart from cultural and societal exclusion, the barriers to the realization of these rights include high specialized healthcare costs, indifferent attitude of nursing staff, communication difficulties, and lack of inclusive healthcare facilities.

Disabled women frequently face exclusion from reproductive health information, care, and treatment; sexual non-heteronormative unions; prospects for parenthood; etc. Additionally, the quality of services and care provided to individuals with psycho-social disabilities in hospitals and other social welfare institutions often violate their reproductive rights. The 'care' extended to them is characterized by coercive measures such as the absence of informed consent, forced sterilization and hysterectomy, and forced medical examination following sexual assault (despite having established protocols and guidelines). Certain healthcare practitioners have indicated that they administer general anesthesia to survivors with psycho-social disabilities with their consent to finish the medico-legal processes of abortion. The medical process must respect individual autonomy and dignity and must not violate the human rights of disabled people.

---

[37] (2014) 5 SCC 438.

[38] 2010 SCC OnLine Del 2234.

With the enactment of the Rights of Persons with Disabilities Act, 2017 (RPWD Act) and the Mental Healthcare Act, 2017 (MH Act), the Indian legislative framework governing disability underwent a substantial transformation. The RPWD Act takes a 'twin-track' strategy by including special protections for disabled women. The law also confronts their vulnerabilities in the areas of discrimination, social welfare, healthcare, and sexual offences.

The MTP Act does not protect mentally retarded (MR) women because it fails to distinguish between MR and mental illness. The Act also ignores the fact that both groups of women are disproportionately poor, which adds another layer of complexity to guardianship decisions.

Even though the United Nations Convention[39] on the Rights of Persons with Disabilities mandates that the State develop comprehensive policies for MR women, the Supreme Court has rarely addressed support mechanisms for these women. Therefore, a substantial legal overhaul is required to bring the system into line with international norms.

Difficulties Faced by Rural Women

Over 200 million women, many of them poor and living in remote areas, do not have access to government family planning centers. The cost of raising a child has always been prohibitive for rural families. Abortion facilities and providers are dispersed unevenly across the country, posing a barrier to women in remote areas who need them. Rural women cannot afford the high-quality healthcare available in large cities. Around 800 poor women die each day from complications related to pregnancy and childbirth.[40]

In India, the majority of the population is rural and illiterate or lives in difficult-to-reach places. They are unaware of the existence of the right of women to have a safe abortion. Consequently, hazardous abortions occur behind the scenes, which are neither reported to the authorities nor the public.

As per a recent research report, some women in Rajasthan were prevented from seeking medical care in a nearby metropolitan hospital because of societal obstacles. In the report, the literacy rate in the state was found to be as low as 48% and 62% of marriages were solemnized

---

[39] The UN Convention, Art. 12.

[40] Dr. Natalia Kanem, "Protecting Reproductive Rights of Rural Women: A Pathway to a More Equal World", *United Nation Population Fund* (2018).

before the age of 18 years.[41] Surprisingly, three-quarters of women were not permitted by their families to go alone to the market or hospital, or travel beyond their village or town area. Only 4.6% of couples used the modern method of contraception prior to the birth of their first child and 16.5% used it between the birth of their first and second child.[42] Unsafe abortions were observed to be a leading cause of death among pregnant women, with a maternal mortality rate of 254 deaths per 100,000 live births.

In remote areas of the country, women may not be able to easily access a health center due to a lack of transportation; thus, health providers should aim to minimize unnecessary visits. This might be done by offering women the option of having an abortion at their initial visit or using abortion pills at home. Under various healthcare programs, the centers send instructions about the abortion process through text messages on mobile phones but mobile phones have not yet reached the majority of rural women. To create appropriate awareness, women in low-resource settings should be provided with context-specific written materials and vocal instructions from the very beginning of their visits. If a woman owns a mobile phone, she should be sent reminders or additional instructions.[43]

There are very few qualified abortions service providers accessible to poor women living in rural areas, which increases the likelihood of them seeking an abortion from an unsafe source. Uncertified providers thrive in rural areas due to the lower cost of their services and their proximity to women's homes. Hence, the rate of unsafe abortions in rural areas is found to be significantly higher than that in urban areas. Further, rural women sometimes choose to take pills rather than risk being shamed at a government hospital by insensitive nurses and doctors. Abortion pills are often administered by women as instructed by their husbands or pharmacists. A higher rate of hospitalization for abortion-related

---

[41] K. Iyengar, S.D. Iyengar, "Improving Access to Safe Abortion in a Rural Primary Care Setting in India: Experience of a Service Delivery Intervention", 13, *Reproductive Health Matters*, 54 (2016).

[42] International Institute of Population Sciences, "Report of the National Family Health Survey-3 (NFHS-3), 2005-6 Rajasthan" (IIPS, Mumbai 2007).

[43] D. Constant, De Tolly K, J. Harries, L. Myer, "Mobile Phone Messages to Provide Support to Women during the Home Phase of Medical Abortion in South Africa: A Randomised Controlled Trial", 90(3), *Contraception*, 226–33 (2014).

complications has been observed for rural women, indicating that unsafe abortion is directly linked to high morbidity rather than mortality.[44]

Health centers serve as the primary point of contact for healthcare for rural people. Each health center is required to have one gynecologist, but there is a 76.3% shortage of obstetricians and gynecologists currently. Consequently, the responsibility of providing abortions has been transferred to public hospitals or community health centers.

Inadequate Awareness About the Use of Contraception

Due to unwanted pregnancies, women face a range of issues from unsafe abortions to long-term morbidity and maternal death.

According to the most recent National Family Health Survey (NFHS-5) conducted by the government between 2019 and 2021, the preference for males persists despite an improvement in the sex ratio. Women are more likely to use contraceptives if they already have a son, according to the survey.[45] 73.3% of men use contraception during intercourse with their spouses and 69.4% during intercourse with their live-in partners/girlfriends. 52.9% of unmarried males do not use contraception. The figures demonstrate that women lack an assertive voice for the safety of their bodies.[46]

In India, female sterilization is the most popular method of family planning, with a rate of 65.7%, which is very high as compared to other countries. One of the primary reasons for this, according to family planning experts, is the inadequate availability of contraceptive techniques in the public health sector. India has a contraceptive prevalence rate of 52.4% (consumption of contraceptives by sexually active couples). Abortion has become a 'proxy contraceptive' for sexually active young women from less affluent families, regardless of their education level. Since such women are unaware of precautions to avoid pregnancy and the risks associated with abortion, quacks are frequently their first choice for assistance to get the abortion done.

---

[44] WHO Unsafe abortion, "Report on the Global and Regional Estimates of the Incidence of Unsafe Abortion and Associated Mortality in 2008 Geneva" (WHO, 2008).

[45] National Family Health Survey (NFHS-5) 2019–21, available at: https://main.mohfw.gov.in/sites/default/files/NFHS-5_Phase-II_0.pdf.

[46] Population Matter, *Millions of Women have No Say Over What Happens to Their Bodies* (2020), available at: https://populationmatters.org/news/2020/04/millions-women-have-no-say-over-what-happens-their-bodies.

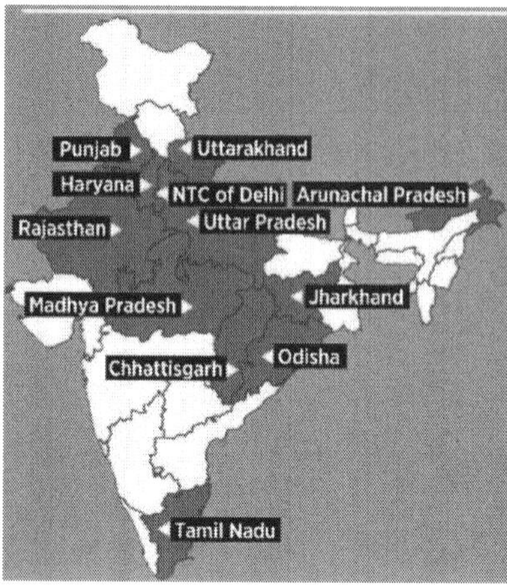

Phase II States from NFHS-5 (2019-21)	Women respondents who use contraception if at least 1 of their 2 children is a son (%)	Sex Ratio (no. of females per 1,000 males)
Uttar Pradesh	71	1,017
Tamil Nadu	86	1,088
Punjab	77	938
Rajasthan	84	1,009
Chhattisgarh	82	11,015
Madhya Pradesh	85	970
Odisha	86	1,063
Haryana	86	926
Jharkhand	74	1,050
Uttarakhand	83	1,016
Arunachal Pradesh	65	997
NCT of Delhi	86	913

Figure 1: The State of Contraceptive Use in India
Source: National Family Health Survey (NFHS-5) 2019-21[47]

The lack of information about contraception has been a significant barrier for both women and men. As per reports, 214 million women of reproductive age in developing regions (13% of women between 15 to 49 years of age) had an unmet demand for contraception, which means they wished to avoid pregnancy but were not using any modern method.[48] Access to information about safe contraception and services is vital for the realization of women's reproductive rights. The right to accurate and up-to-date information about contraception and access to safe, high-quality services is affirmed by several international human rights instruments.[49]

Contraceptive services of the highest quality are critical to enabling couples to have the number of children they desire when they desire and to avoid undesired pregnancies, unplanned births, and abortions. Women's use of contraceptive techniques is influenced by numerous factors, including personal, interpersonal, and partner-related aspects. The high proportion of unmet contraception needs can be attributed to a variety of factors, including a lack of access to effective family planning services, cultural and religious opposition, and anxiety over side effects. Women's empowerment through knowledge and adequate information about

---

[47] Available at: https://main.mohfw.gov.in/sites/default/files/NFHS-5_Phase-II_0.pdf.

[48] R. Jain & S. Muralidhar, "Contraceptive Methods: Needs, Options and Utilization", 61(6), *J Obstet Gynaecol India*, 626–634 (2011).

[49] World Health Organization, *The Right to Health*, Office of the United Nations High Commissioner for Human Rights, available at: https://www.ohchr.org/documents/publications/factsheet31.pdf.

contraception might lead to a progressive shift away from their forced sterilization.

Delay in Judicial Authorization and Issuance of Recommendations by the Medical Board

Indian courts have noted that additional layers of authorization have created barriers for women exercising their reproductive autonomy. They also hold that forcing pregnant people to continue with unwanted pregnancies due to pending third-party authorization (by courts or medical boards) is harmful to their physical and mental health. The requirement for third-party approval has also been criticized internationally. The UN Human Rights Special Procedures Working Group on the Issue of Discrimination against Women in Law and Practice stated in 2017 that abortion laws should not delay termination to the extent that the pregnancy becomes too far along.[50] Third-party authorization requirements undermine women's autonomy, according to the CEDAW[51] and WHO.[52]

Under the MTP Act, it is mandatory for each woman or girl seeking an abortion post 20 weeks (now 24 weeks) of pregnancy to file a petition in court to get her case referred to a medical board.[53] The medical board has a prescribed number of doctors and includes atleast one-woman physicians. When it comes to deciding whether or not to allow an abortion, courts have relied on the medical opinion of these boards.[54] The Centre for Reproductive Rights recently analyzed judicial orders in which women were obliged to obtain permission to have abortions. The analysis concluded that judicial and medical board authorization requirements jeopardize women's and girls' reproductive rights by causing delays, denials, public scrutiny, and trauma as well as leaving a chilling impact on access to abortion at the later stages of pregnancy.[55]

---

[50] U.N. Working Group on the Issue of Discrimination Against Women in Law and in Practice, Women's Autonomy, Equality and Reproductive Health in International Human Rights: Between Recognition, Backlash and Regressive Trends (2017).

[51] CEDAW General Recommendation 24 on Article 12 of the Convention (Women and Health) A/54/38/Rev.1, Chap. I (1999).

[52] WHO, Safe abortion: Technical & policy guidance for health systems (2015).

[53] *Meera Santosh Pal v. Union of India* (2017) SCC OnLine SC 39.

[54] *Ms X v. Union of India*, 2016 14 SCC 382.

[55] Payal Shaht, "Time to End Judicial Authorization for Abortion in India", *Centre of Reproductive Rights*, available at: https://reproductiverights.org/its-time-to-end-judicial-authorization-for-abortion-in-india/.

The Supreme Court has recognized women's right to reproductive choice, noting that reproductive decisions are protected under the right to privacy, as reiterated in the *Nikhil Datar* case[56] by the Bombay High Court. The higher courts in India have been doing a case-by-case investigation when dealing with petitions with a gestation period higher than 20 weeks (currently 24 weeks). At least 25 such incidents have occurred since 2015,[57] which involved pregnant women diagnosed with fetal impairment and pregnant adolescent victims of rape. However, the outcomes have been diverse, even in cases with similar facts and identical conditions, leading to confusion about the law and pointing to the necessity of reform.

In 2016, a 14-year-old rape survivor had to undergo three rounds of medical board examinations in addition to the initial post-rape exam. This was because the court gave the medical board specific instructions to ensure that it considered the mental health risks of forcing the woman to stay pregnant and did not deny the MTP merely because of the legal limit.[58] The court ordered another medical board in Delhi to review the case and inform the court about the actions taken in the best interest of the petitioner-victim. In the end, the court denied the abortion as the medical board's opinion did not endorse its performance.

Contradictory judgments have resulted in a lack of clarity regarding whether a woman or girl is legally authorized to terminate her pregnancy after the 20-week (now 24-week) mark. The courts have not provided clear guidelines on how to eliminate the requirement for judicial and medical board authorization or how to address a doctor's refusal to permit legal abortions. Numerous petitions have been filed in courts around the country asking for comprehensive legislation and policy reform. These petitions seek the following: to recognize the association between fetal impairment and a woman's physical and mental health; to create an exception on the basis of health of fetus that is the same as the exception for prolonging life, and to provide for an appeal for women who have been improperly denied abortions.

---

56 *Nikhil Datar v. Union of India* (2008) 110 Bom L.R. 3293.

57 The Centre for Reproductive Rights, "Report on the Reform to Address Women's and Girls' Need for Abortion after 20 Weeks in India" (*CRR*, 2018), available at: https://reproductiverights.org/sites/default/files/documents/Post-20-Week-Access-to-Abortion-India-0218.pdf.

58 *R v. State of Haryana*, W.P.(C), 6733 (2016), P&H High Court, Decided on 30-5-2017.

Lack of Awareness of Abortion Rights

The majority of Indians are either unaware or dismissive of reproductive health and rights. The stigma that surrounds sex and sexuality is at the base of many of the challenges that people, particularly women, experience daily. According to research conducted by the Family Planning Association (FPA) in 2019,[59] in India, 14% of pregnancies among women under the age of 20 were found unintended. As per the report, over 34% of adolescent married girls acknowledged experiencing physical, emotional, or sexual assault. 50% of maternal deaths among 15–19-years-old girls are the result of unsafe abortion practices.

Women who have completed high school are more aware of their right to abortion in the event of undesirable pregnancy and are less likely to postpone their abortion decision until the second trimester, reducing the risk of complications. On the other hand, a majority of unmarried and rural women are uninformed that they have the legal right to terminate an undesired pregnancy.[60] Thus, it is argued that to fully realize women's right to bodily autonomy and reduce maternal mortality, the State must make earnest efforts to raise knowledge of women's right to make autonomous and uninhibited reproductive choices.

The lack of awareness also stems from the shame associated with sexual rights, which are ignored and seen as moral dangers. It is frequently assumed that reproductive health encompasses sexual health; nevertheless, these are two distinct health spheres that must be handled independently but concurrently. Along with strengthening medical and therapeutic capabilities, it is necessary to establish and strengthen public health and community dialogue on sexual health. Everyone, including children and adolescents, should have access to comprehensive sexual education tailored to their age. India needs to recognize that sexual rights are just as important as the right to have children.

Lack of Trained Healthcare Providers

Under section 3(2C) of the MTP (Amendment) Act, each state and union territory shall be required to establish a medical board to decide

---

[59] Family Planning Association, youth dialogue: a perspective on FP (2020), available at: https://fpaindia.org/pdf/aspire-june-2019.pdf.

[60] Heidi Bart Johnston, "Abortion Practice in India: A Review of Literature", *Centre for Enquiry into Health and Allied Themes (CEHAT)*, available at: http://www.cehat.org/uploads/files/work1.pdf.

about the termination of pregnancies beyond 24 weeks in cases of fetal abnormalities. Under section 3(2D), the medical board shall be composed of a gynecologist, pediatrician, radiologist, and other such members as the state government or union territory may notify in the official gazette.

As per the findings of a study[61] undertaken in Haryana, medical professionals such as surgeons, gynecologists, pediatricians, and general practitioners were found to be underrepresented in some districts of the state. In 2019, only 3,880 positions out of 21,296 vacancies were filled, resulting in an 81.8% shortage.[62] Between 2015 and 2019, the gap in the shortage of doctors increased from 71% to 81.8%. It seems 'unfeasible' to form a panel of doctors to make decisions about abortions after 24 weeks under the MTP Act, 2021 because large number of medical posts remain vacant.

This shortage was even more pronounced in the north-eastern states, where Sikkim, Mizoram, and Manipur lacked gynecologists and pediatricians. Arunachal Pradesh and Meghalaya were reported to have no pediatricians.

Thus, the requirement for medical boards has proved to be draconian and invasive, robbing pregnant women of their autonomy. Even if the boards are established, pregnant women from rural areas have to pay exorbitant travel expenses to get assessed, adding to their financial burden. This legal change has made abortion more difficult for many people, particularly those from marginalized communities.

Reproductive autonomy is a necessary component in contemporary society, both in terms of human rights and women's health. A shift from restrictive to permissive law can pave the way for the realization of women's reproductive autonomy. To facilitate this, in addition to the law, public opinion must also be revised. The stigma associated with abortion and those seeking the procedure must be eliminated. To persuade legislators, the most progressive type of advocacy and activism is required.

---

[61] O.P. Jindal Law Global School, *Centre for Justice, Law and Society* (OPJLGS, Haryana, 2021).

[62] Dr. Dipika Jain, "Medical Boards for Access For Abortion To Untenable: Evidence From The Ground", *Centre for Justice, Law and Society (CJLS) JLGS* (2021).

NINE

Survey Research Methodology

Research is creating new knowledge."

– Neil Armstrong[1]

This chapter provides an outline of the research methodology used in the study. The present study is descriptive and empirical in nature. The primary data was collected through an empirical survey, which was conducted through a structured questionnaire. The questionnaire aimed to study the level of awareness about the reproductive rights of women and ascertain the scope of reproductive autonomy in India. The survey findings were analyzed to understand the issues and challenges faced by women in exercising the right to abortion.

Research Design

To conduct research, it is important to lay a roadmap guided by research objectives, research questions, existing knowledge, time span, availability of other resources, and researchers' philosophical underpinnings. This helps to decide the source of data collection; accessibility of data; and the time, location, and cost involved as well as address probable ethical, social, or political issues. The research can leverage both deductive and inductive approaches as they are not mutually exclusive. Some widely used research strategies include experiment, survey, case study, action research, grounded theory, ethnography, and archival analysis. This research study uses survey findings to meet its objectives. The survey method may use a variety of data collection methods, with the most common being questionnaires and interviews. It includes cross-sectional as well as longitudinal studies.

This study aimed to analyze the awareness of abortion laws and barriers faced by women in accessing their abortion rights in India. A cross-sectional sample was selected for the study. A random sampling

---

[1] Astronaut Neil Armstrong (1930–2012) is widely regarded as an American hero as he was the first human to set foot on the moon in 1969.

method was used to collect the responses from the respondents. The questionnaire was prepared in Google Forms/Docs and was electronically mailed to more than 500 women (who were above 18 years of age), out of which 238 responded.

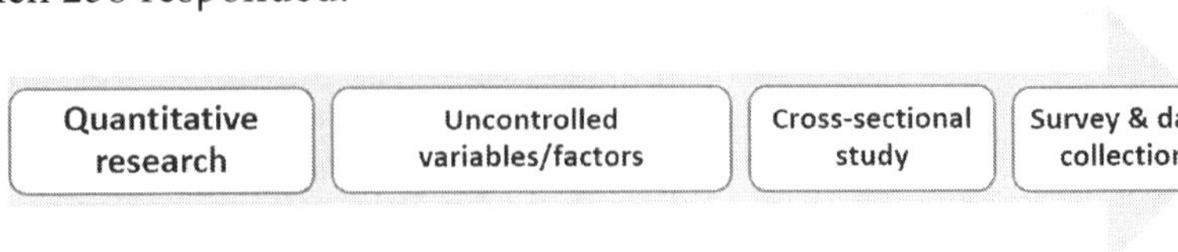

Figure 1: Steps of Research Methodology

Variables Considered for the Study

The independent and dependent variables considered in the study have been described briefly in the below mentioned figures.

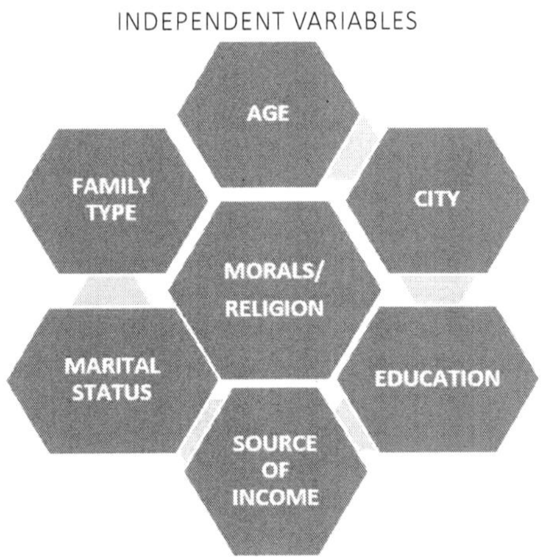

Figure 2: Considered Independent Variables

Table 1: Description of the Dependent Variables

S. No.	*Reproductive Autonomy in India*	*Barriers Faced by Women in Exercising their Right to Abortion*	*Implementation and Enforcement of the Laws*	*Awareness about the Reproductive Rights of Women in India*
1	Decision/choice of pregnancy in India	Sex-selective abortion is illegal	Preference of health providers during abortion	Awareness about abortion laws in India
2	The decision-making process is easy	Morality	Disallowed to abort the first child due to social stigma	Awareness of two-child norms

S. No.	*Reproductive Autonomy in India*	*Barriers Faced by Women in Exercising their Right to Abortion*	*Implementation and Enforcement of the Laws*	*Awareness about the Reproductive Rights of Women in India*
3	Dependency of an abortion decision	Religion	The necessity of court permission	Awareness about contraceptive pills
4	The procedure of abortion is painful for a woman	Acceptance of unmarried women's pregnancy	Delays in court approval	Women have undergone an abortion
5	Abortion at any stage of pregnancy	Sterilization after a male child	The only decision of the doctors	Right to Abortion in India
6	Circumstances in seeking abortion	Expensive abortion services in Delhi	Suggestive changes	Awareness of the MTP Act
7	Choice of health providers during the abortion	Availing of abortion services depends on affordability	—	Awareness of the PCPNDT Act
8	Forceful pregnancy for the male child	Lack of trained staff for abortion in hospitals	—	Abortion laws are favorable
9	Non-use of contraceptives results in abortion	Physical and mental trauma	—	—
10	—	Reason for not using contraceptive pills	—	—

Questionnaire Development

For this study, a survey instrument was developed based on an extensive literature review. This questionnaire had 43 questions addressing the variables considered for the study. Each of these items was then phrased into a statement measured on a 5-point Likert scale. The questionnaire had demographic questions in addition to valid and reliable research pointers. The purpose of the questionnaire was to understand the awareness level of the respondents about different aspects of the reproductive rights of women.

Statistical Tools and Techniques Used

A descriptive analysis of the responses was done by using SPSS 20.0. There are many types of graphs, such as bar graphs, histograms, and line graphs, that can be used to present the data. For this study, a simple bar chart was chosen.

Limitations of the Study

The following were the limitations of the study:

- Cultural barriers had not been considered while constructing the questionnaire.
- As the data was self-reported, it could not be objectively verified.
- Since the sample size was small, the results could not be generalized.
- Because the data was collected through an online platform (Google Forms), the not-so-tech-savvy respondents could not participate.
- As the area of research was sensitive, many respondents were not willing to share the information.

TEN

An Empirical Study of Abortion Rights

Seven Indian states have very high maternal mortality. These are Rajasthan, Uttar Pradesh, Madhya Pradesh, Chhattisgarh, Bihar, Odisha and Assam. 'Very high' MMR means 130 or more maternal deaths per 100,000 live births ... Unsafe abortion remains the third leading cause of maternal mortality in India, and close to 8 women die from causes related to unsafe abortion each day.

– A Study from Guttacmacher Institute (2018)[1]

This chapter scrutinises the range of contemporary issues that influence women's reproductive autonomy (gathered through survey findings). The purpose of the survey was to represent the lived realities of women regarding abortion rights in contemporary times. The analysis of the collected data highlights a variety of issues which are major obstacles for women seeking abortion and other reproductive rights.

Graphs have been used to present and classify the data on the basis of different independent variables like age, city, source of income, marital status, religion, education, and family type. For the quantitative representation (as the survey involved Likert scale questions), the SPSS software was used. The chapter includes a structured questionnaire that was prepared for the survey, which was taken by 231 respondents/women belonging to Delhi-NCR. The prior consent of the respondents was taken. The questionnaire was prepared in Google Forms. It had 43 questions. Each of these questions was then phrased into a statement measured on a 5-point Likert scale. There were 4 determinants/factors, i.e. social, economic, legal, and moral, and 7 variables, i.e. age, city, education, source of income, marital status, family type, and religion in the questionnaire. The questionnaire had demographic questions in addition to reliable research pointers. The random sampling method was used for response collection.

---

1 Singh S. et al., "Abortion and Unintended Pregnancy in Six Indian States: Findings and Implications for Policies and Programs", New York: Guttmacher Institute, 2018.

Following are the statements listed in the questionnaire and the responses of survey participants:

Women have the Choice to Decide on their Pregnancy

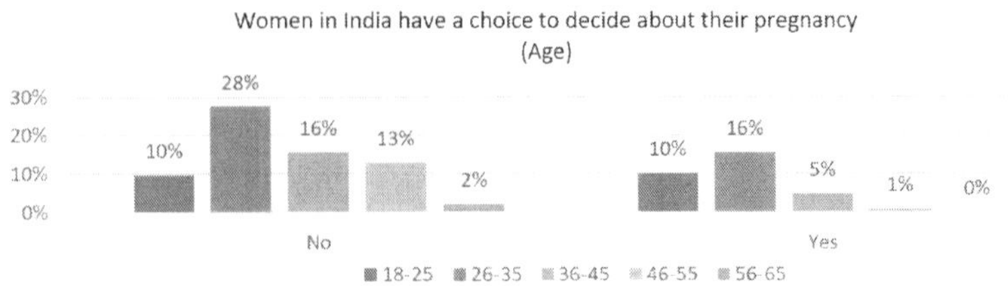

Figure 1: Age and Choice of Pregnancy

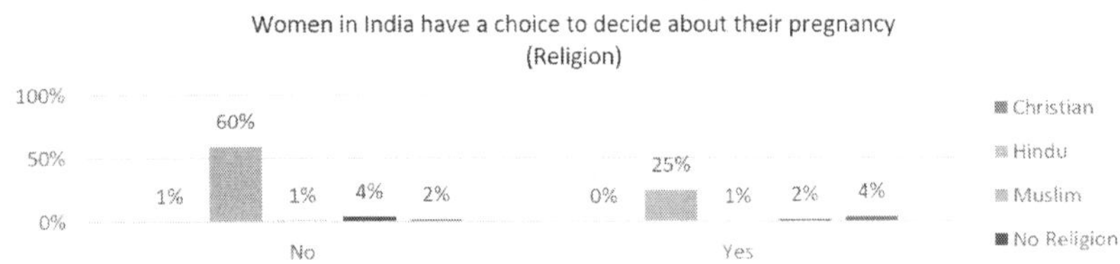

Figure 2: Religion and Choice of Pregnancy

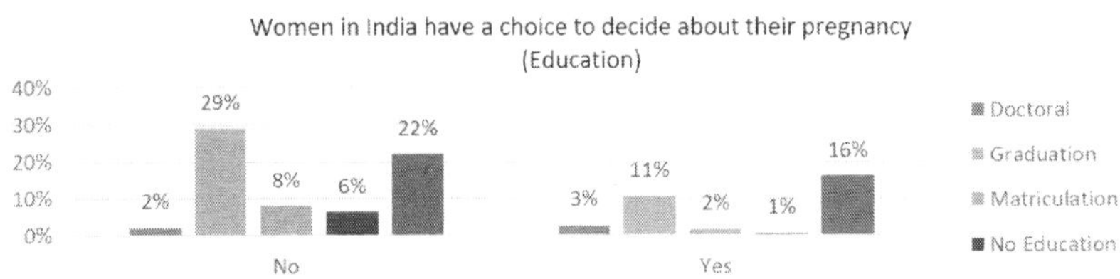

Figure 3: Education and Choice of Pregnancy

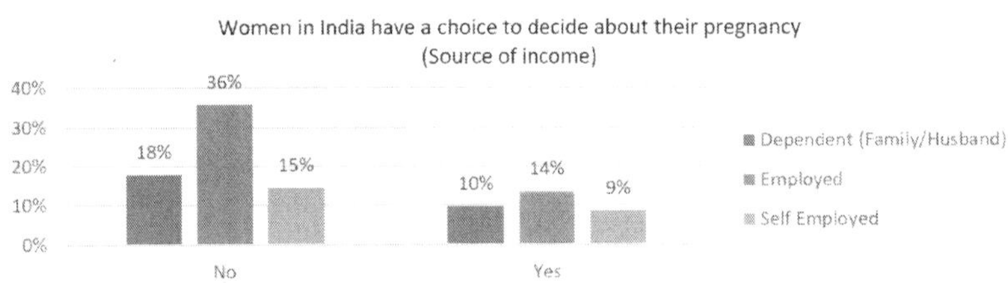

Figure 4: Source of Income and Choice of Pregnancy

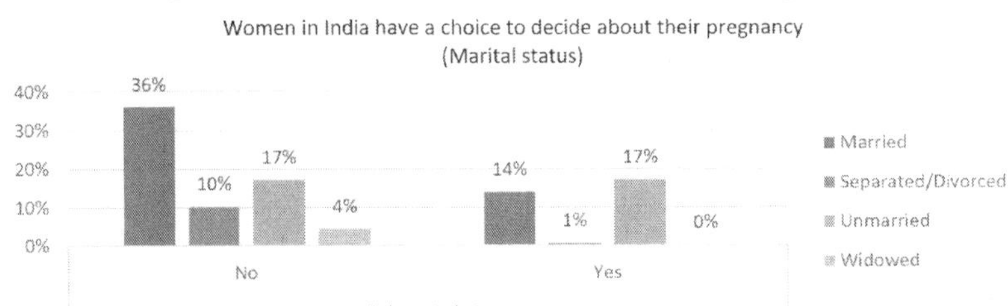

Figure 5: Marital Status and Choice of Pregnancy

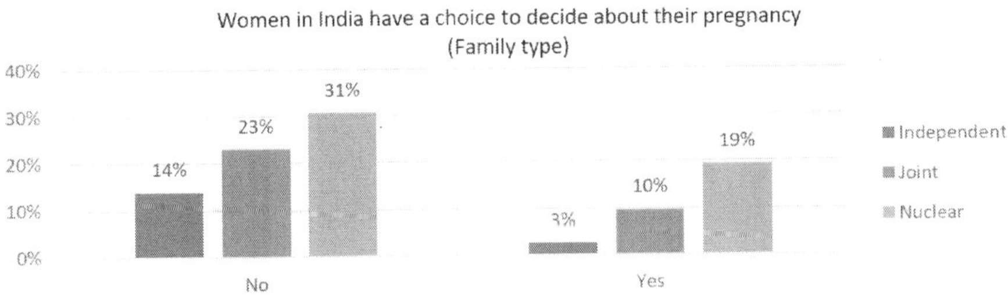

Figure 6: Family Type and Choice of Pregnancy

Analysis: Regarding Women having a Choice to Decide about their Pregnancy

- **Age:** 69% of women in the age group of 18–65 years agreed that they did not have the power/ choice to decide about their pregnancy.
- **Religion:** 60% of Hindu women respondents agreed that they had less freedom to decide about their pregnancy.
- **Education**: 67% of women respondents irrespective of their educational background still felt that decision-making did not rest in their hands.
- **Source of income:** 36% of employed women and 33% of dependent and self-employed women agreed that they did not take the decision about their pregnancy alone.
- **Marital status:** 36% of married, 14% of separated/divorced/widowed, and 17% of unmarried respondents believed that they did not have the decision-making power with regards to their pregnancy.
- **Family type:** The freedom to make pregnancy-related decisions is not found in 14% of independent and 54% of joint and nuclear families.

Thus, the data shows that women have low decision-making power when it comes to matters related to their pregnancy.

Ease of the Decision-Making Process for Abortion

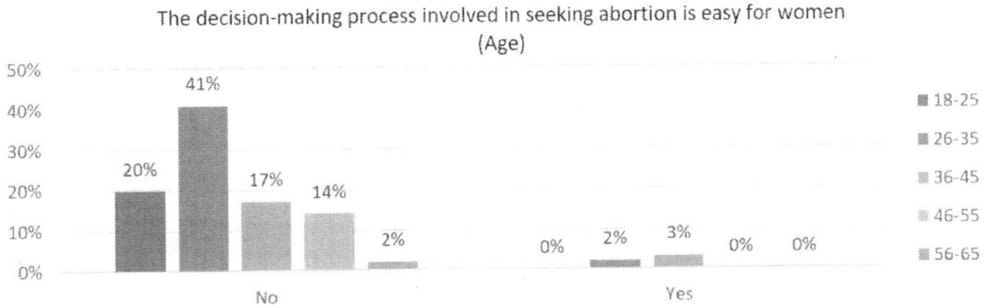

Figure 7: Age and Ease of Decision-Making Process

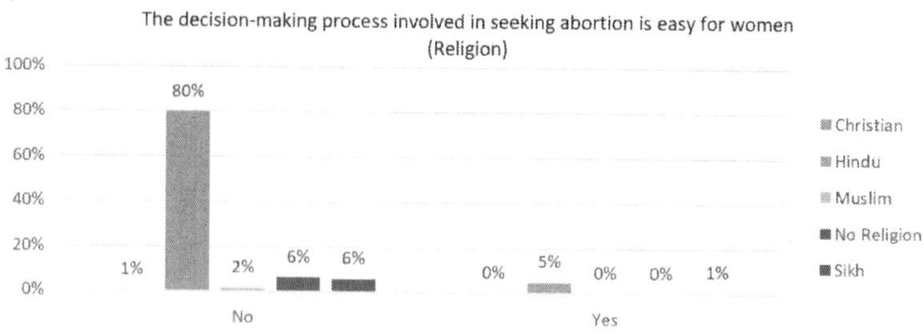

Figure 8: Religion and Ease of Decision-Making Process

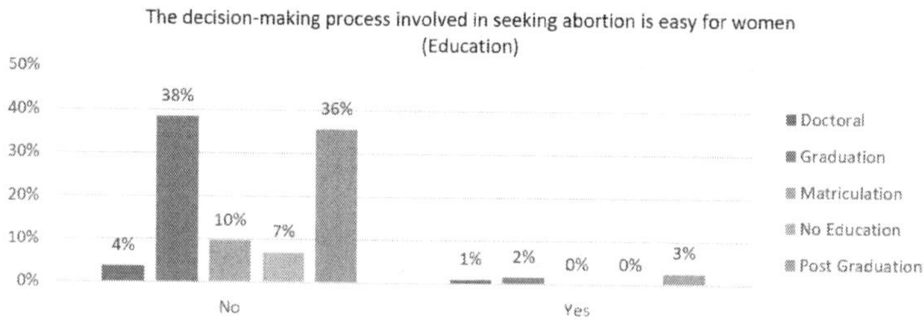

Figure 9: Education and Ease of Decision-Making Process

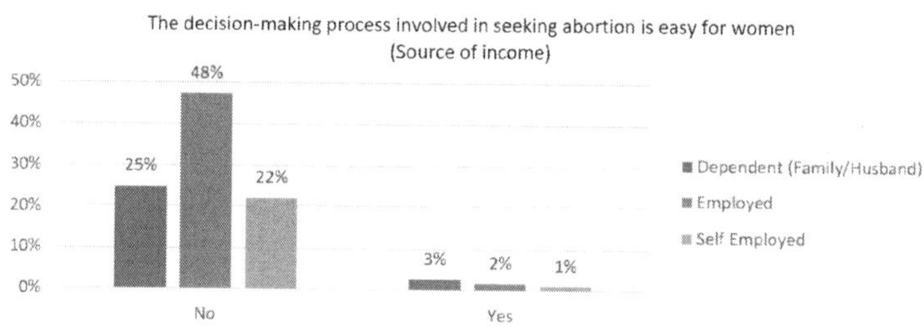

Figure 10: Source of Income and Ease of Decision-Making Process

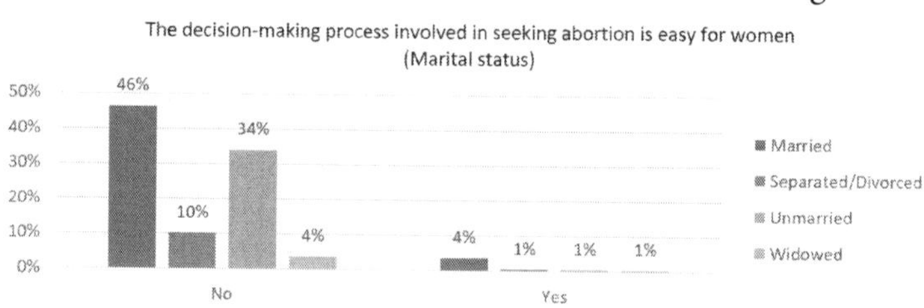

Figure 11: Marital Status and Ease of Decision-Making Process

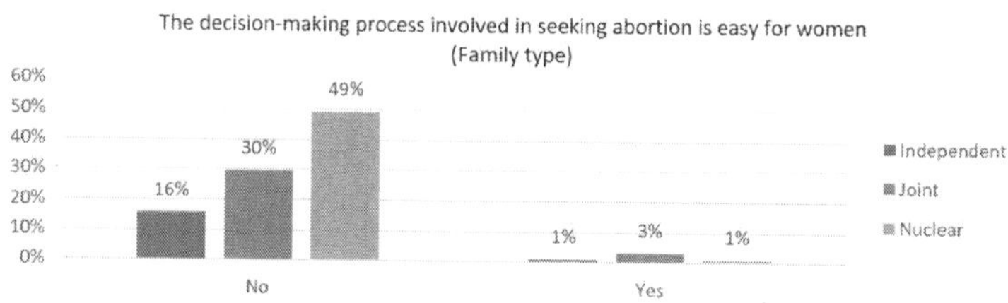

Figure 12: Family Type and Ease of Decision-Making Process

Analysis: Regarding the Ease of Decision-Making Process to Seek an Abortion for Women

- **Age:** 41% of women in the age group of 26–35 years, 17% in the age group of 36–45 years, 14% in the age group of 46–55 years, and 20% in the age group of 18–25 years found it difficult to decide about their abortion.
- **Religion**: 80% of Hindu women and 15% belonging to other religions also found it difficult to decide about abortion.
- **Education**: 36% of postgraduates, 38% of graduates, and 21% of respondents with other educational backgrounds believed that abortion-related decision-making was hard.
- **Source of income:** 22% of self-employed, 25% of unemployed/dependent, and 48% of employed respondents agreed that they had difficulty in making the decision for an abortion.
- **Marital status:** 34% of unmarried, 46% of married, and 14% of separated/divorced/widowed respondents found it difficult to make a decision for abortion.
- **Family type:** 30% of women living in joint families, 49% in nuclear families, and 16% in independent families found it challenging to exercise decisional autonomy.

Thus, women in Delhi-NCR, irrespective of their age, education, income, and familial structure, find it hard to make the decision to opt for an abortion.

Dependence on Others for Seeking Abortion

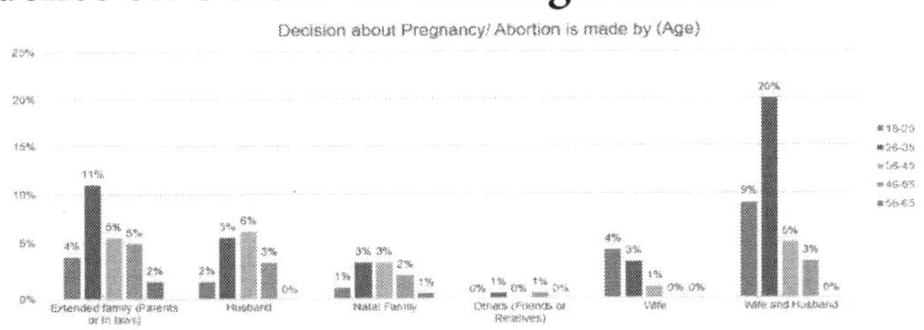

Figure 13: Age and Dependency for Abortion

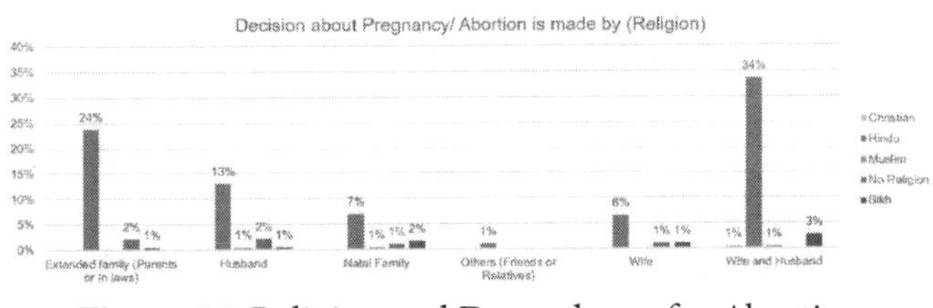

Figure 14: Religion and Dependency for Abortion

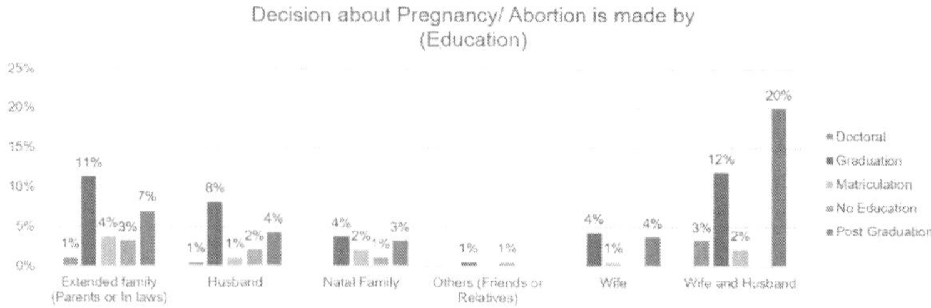

Figure 15: Education and Dependency for Abortion

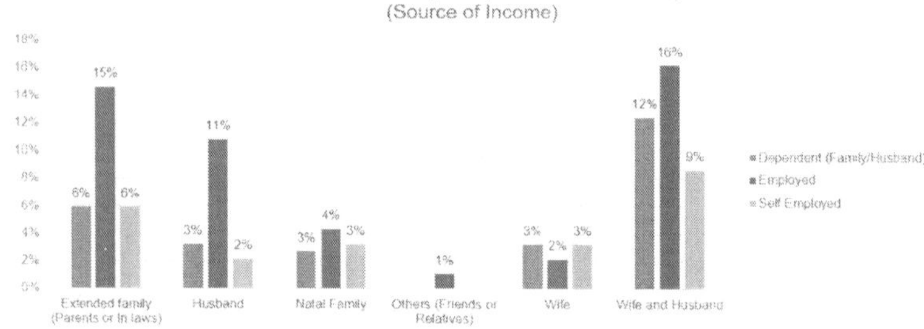

Figure 16: Source of Income and Dependency for Abortion

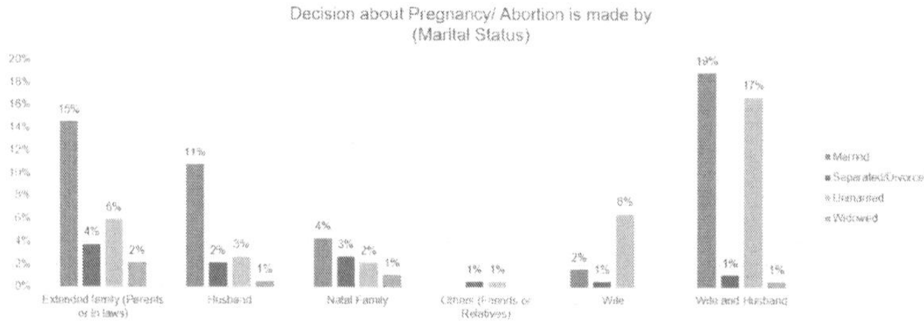

Figure 17: Marital Status and Dependency for Abortion

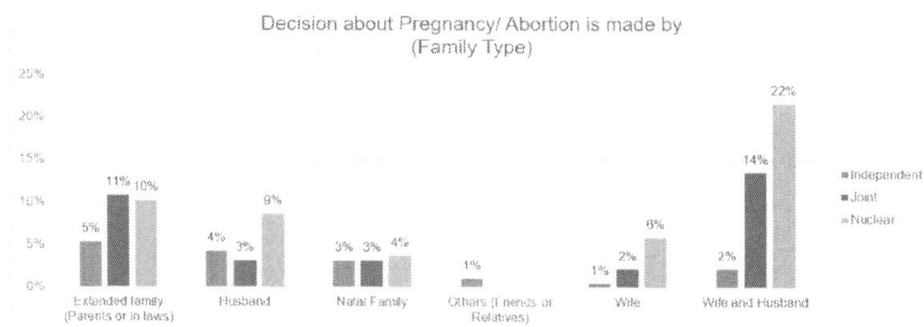

Figure 18: Familly Type and Dependency for Abortion

Analysis: Regarding Dependency on Others for Decisions about Pregnancy/Abortion

- **Age:** 37% of respondents in the age group of 18 to 65 years stated that they made a mutual decision for abortion with their husband, whereas 27% stated that their decision involved the opinions of the extended family as well. Only 8% of women responded that it was their sole decision.

- **Religion:** 34% of Hindu respondents stated that it was a mutual decision between the couple and 6% said that it was their sole decision. The responses appeared to be non-significant under the other religions' category.
- **Education:** 20% of postgraduates and 12% of graduates chose a "decision by husband and wife," whereas 9% chose the option "only wife." 11% of graduate and 7% of postgraduate respondents confirmed the involvement of the extended family in the decision-making process.
- **Source of income:** The majority of women i.e., 16% of employed, 12% of dependent, and 9% of self-employed chose the option "decision by husband and wife," while 15% of employed and the remaining 12% confirmed that the extended family was responsible for the decision for abortion. Only 8% stated that it was the sole decision of the wife.
- **Marital status:** 15% of married respondents chose the extended family option, whereas 19% chose the mutual decision option. Overall, 16% of respondents chose the option "only the husband" and 9% chose the "sole decision of wife" option irrespective of their marital status.
- **Family Type:** 16% of women from joint/independent families and 22% from nuclear families opted for the "decision by wife and husband." 9% of women respondents chose the "wife only" option and 16% chose the "husband only" option.

The data shows that the decision for abortion is usually made by both husband and wife or by the extended family. It is not the sole decision of the wife.

Social Stigma in Seeking Abortion

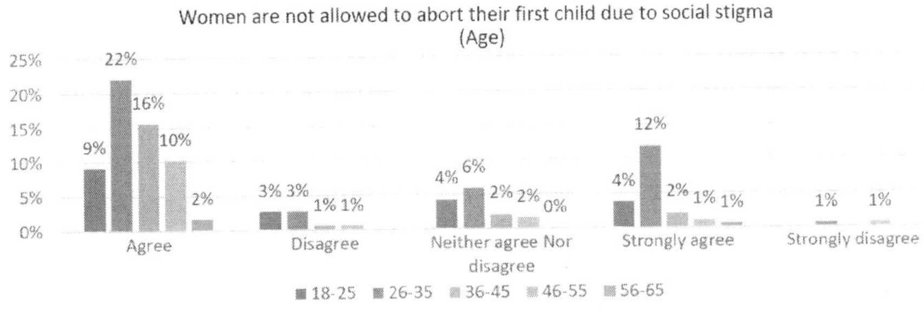

Figure 19: Age and Social Stigma about Abortion

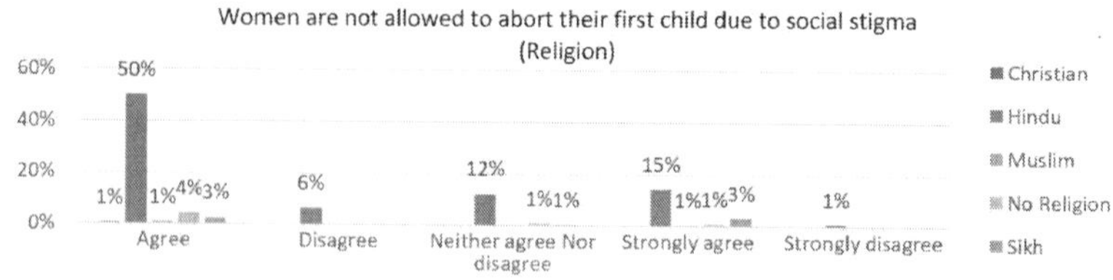

Figure 20: Religion and Social Stigma about Abortion

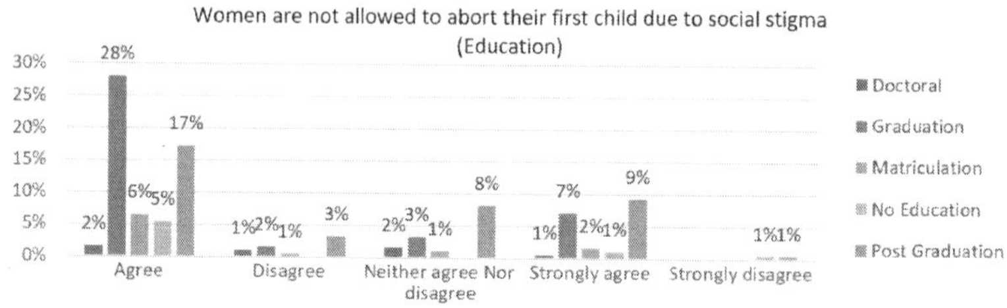

Figure 21: Education and Social Stigma about Abortion

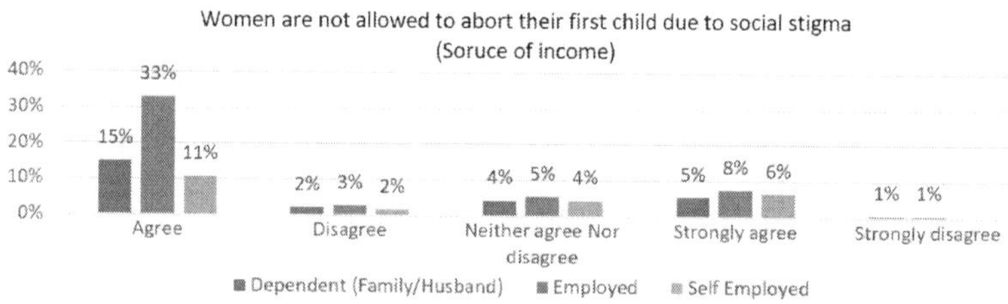

Figure 22: Source of Income and Social Stigma about Abortion

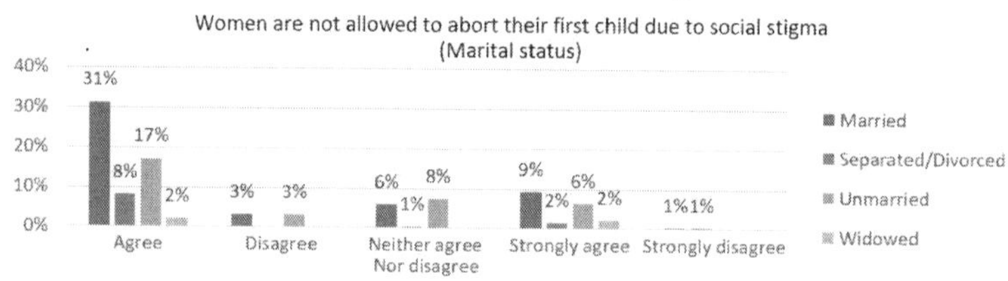

Figure 23: Marital Status and Social Stigma about Abortion

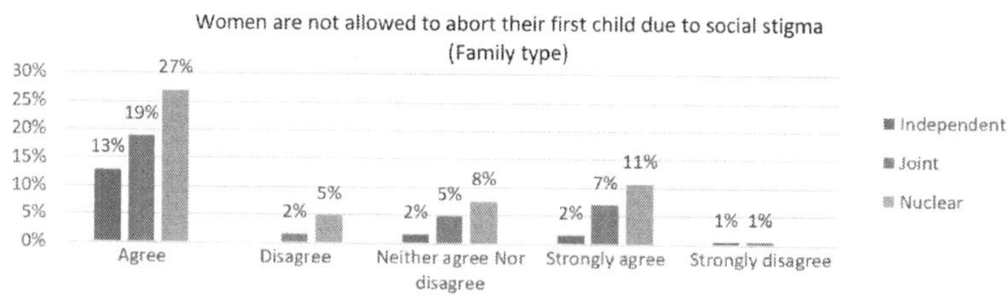

Figure 24: Family Type and Social Stigma about Abortion

Analysis: Regarding Abortion as a Social Stigma

- **Age:** 20% of respondents strongly agreed and 59% agreed that abortion is a social stigma.

- **Religion:** 65% of Hindu women believed that abortion is still a social stigma. 14% of women belonging to other religions also believed that there is a stigma attached to abortion.
- **Education:** 78% of respondents from various educational backgrounds agreed or strongly agreed with the premise (specifically 35% graduates and 26% postgraduates).
- **Source of income:** The majority of women from all income groups agreed that abortion is still a social stigma (41% employed, 20% dependent, and 17% unemployed women).
- **Marital status:** 40% of married, 23% of unmarried, and 14% of separated/divorced/widowed women responded in the same manner.
- **Family type:** 26% of respondents from joint families, 38% from nuclear families, and 15% from independent women agreed with the statement.

To conclude, abortion is still a social stigma in society.

Factors Associated with the Preference for Health Providers for Seeking Abortion

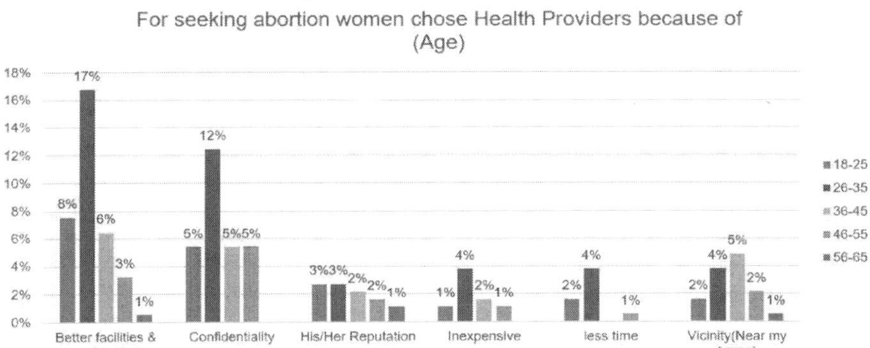

Figure 25: Age and Factors Behind Choosing Health Providers

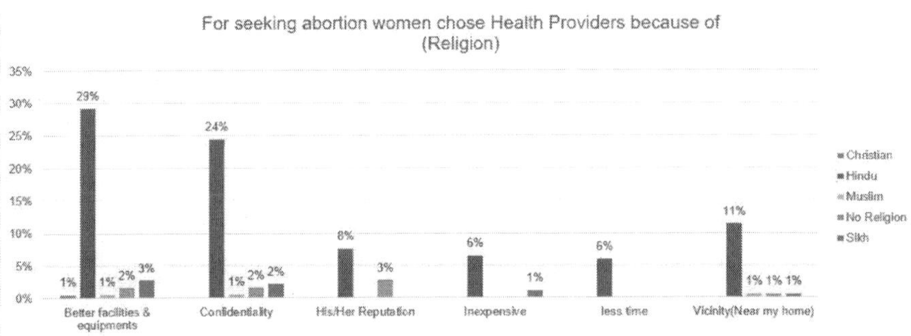

Figure 26: Religion and Factors Behind Choosing Health Providers

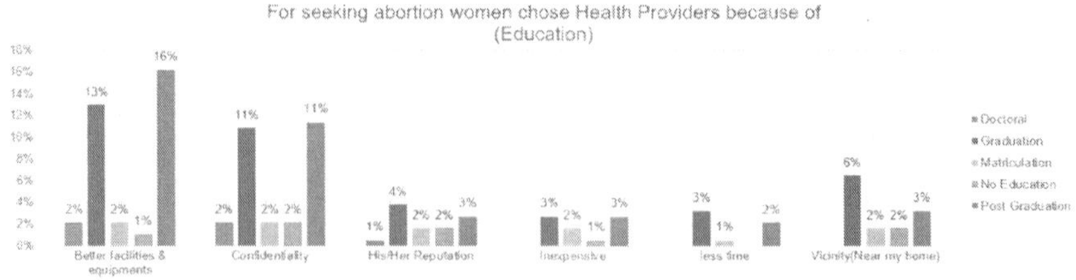

Figure 27: Education and Factors Behind Choosing Health Providers

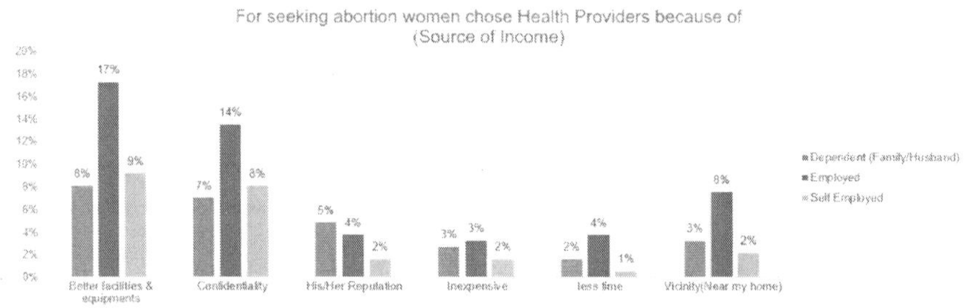

Figure 28: Source of Income and Factors Behind Choosing Health Providers

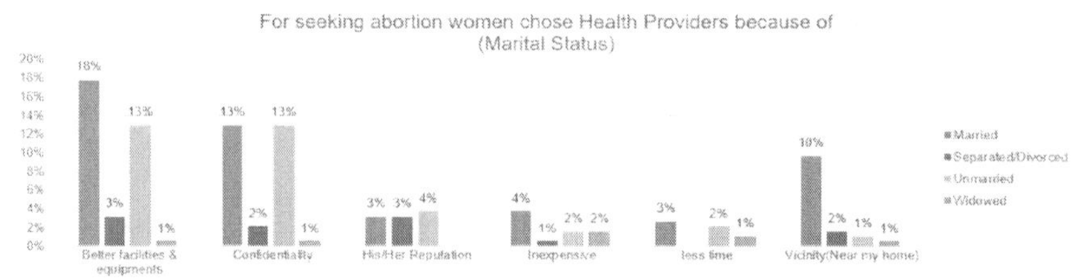

Figure 29: Marital Status and Factors Behind Choosing Health Providers

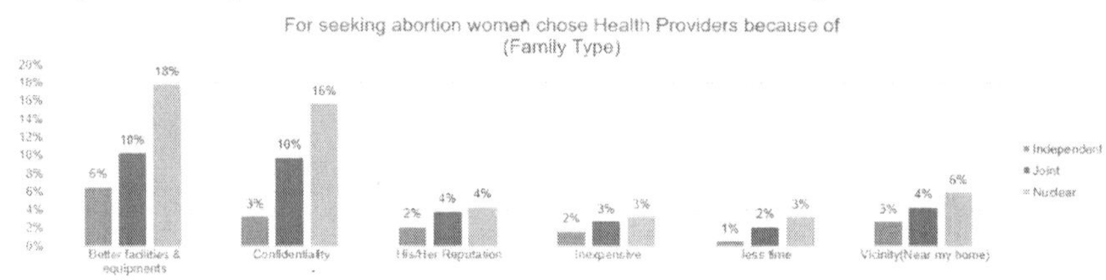

Figure 30: Family Type and Factors Behind Choosing Health Providers

Analysis: Regarding the Reasons Why Women Choose Health Providers for Abortion

- **Age:** 35% of women aged 18–65 years preferred health providers for better facilities and apparatus, 27% for confidentiality, and 14% for vicinity.
- **Religion:** 29% of Hindus and 7% of women belonging to other religions opted for health providers for better health facilities and equipment, while 29% of respondents opted for them for confidentiality purposes.

- **Education:** 34% of respondents from various educational backgrounds chose health providers due to better facilities and equipment, whereas 28% opted for them for confidentiality.
- **Marital status:** Collectively, 31% of unmarried and married women preferred health providers for abortion because of better facilities, 26% because of confidentiality, and 11% due to their vicinity.
- **Source of income:** Whether dependent, employed, or self-employed, 34% of respondents preferred health providers for better facilities and equipment and 29% for confidentiality. The overall preference of respondents varied as 11% opted for them because of their reputation, 8% due to inexpensiveness, 7% because of less time, and 13% due to vicinity.
- **Family type:** 34% of respondents from nuclear, independent, and joint families preferred health providers for abortion because of better facilities and equipment, 19% of respondents opted for them for confidentiality purposes, and 24% of respondents preferred them due to less time, inexpensiveness, and their reputation.

The data shows that there was a preference for health providers for abortion because they had better equipment with skilled doctors and most importantly could maintain confidentiality.

Forced Pregnancy for and in Case of a Male Child

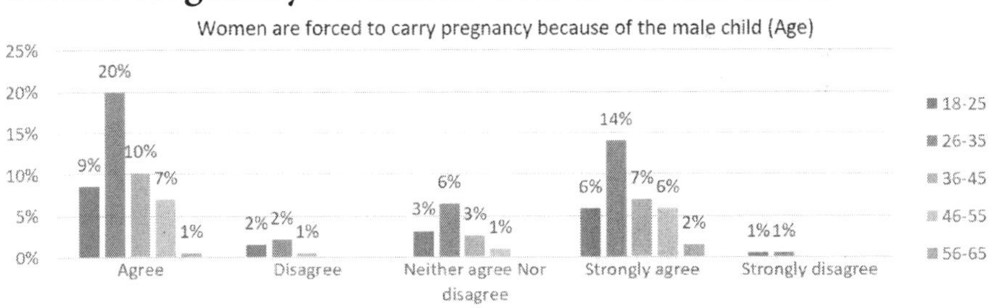

Figure 31: Age and Forced Male Child Pregnancy

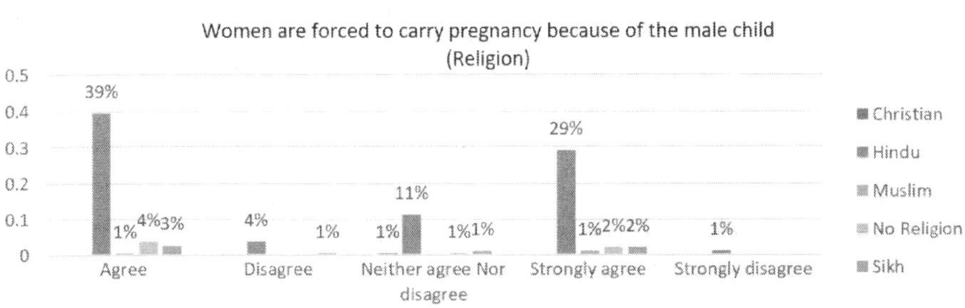

Figure 32: Religion and Forced Male Child Pregnancy

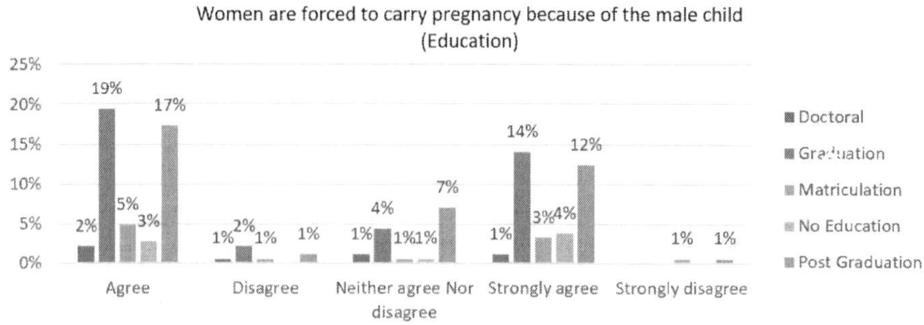

Figure 33: Education and Forced Male Child Pregnancy

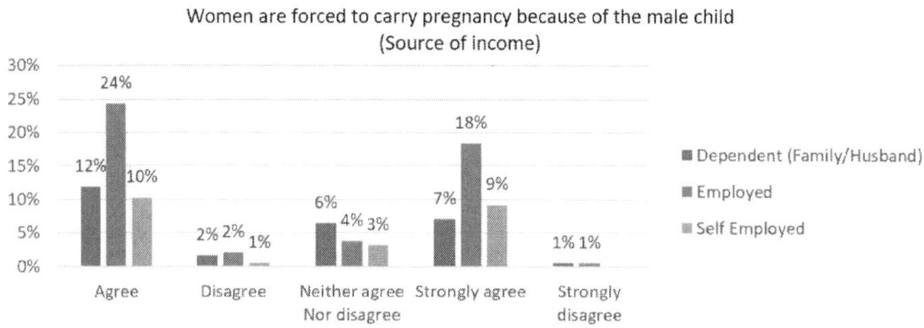

Figure 34: Source of Income and Forced Male Child Pregnancy

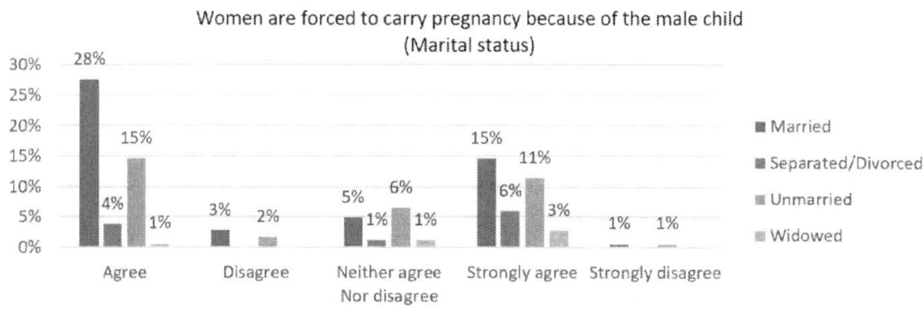

Figure 35: Marital Status and Forced Male Child Pregnancy

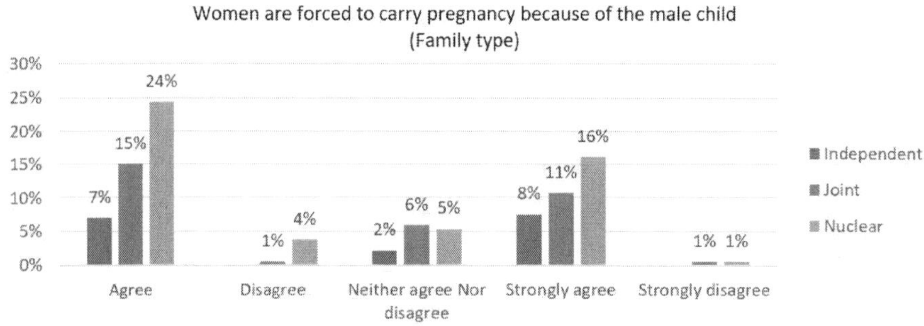

Figure 36: Family Type and Forced Male Child Pregnancy

Analysis: Regarding Whether Women are Forced to Carry a Pregnancy because of Preference for a Male Child

- **Age:** 47% of respondents agreed and 35% strongly agreed that women are forced to carry a pregnancy because of a male child, while 7% disagreed on the same.
- **Religion:** 81% of respondents belonging to various religions agreed and strongly agreed with the premise.
- **Education:** 33% of graduate women, 29% of postgraduate women, and 18% women from other educational backgrounds agreed or strongly agreed that women are forced to carry a pregnancy for a male child. Only 7% of the respondents disagreed with the same.
- **Source of income**: 42% of employed, 19% of dependent, and 19% of self-employed respondents believed that they were forced into pregnancy because of preference for a male child.
- **Marital status**: 43% of married, 26% of unmarried, and 14% of divorced/separated respondents confirmed the verity of the statement.
- **Family type:** Overall, 81% women agreed or strongly agreed on the same lines.

The data reflects a bias against women and strong preference for a male child due to the patriarchal mindset of the society.

Morality as an Impediment to the Exercise of the Right to Abortion

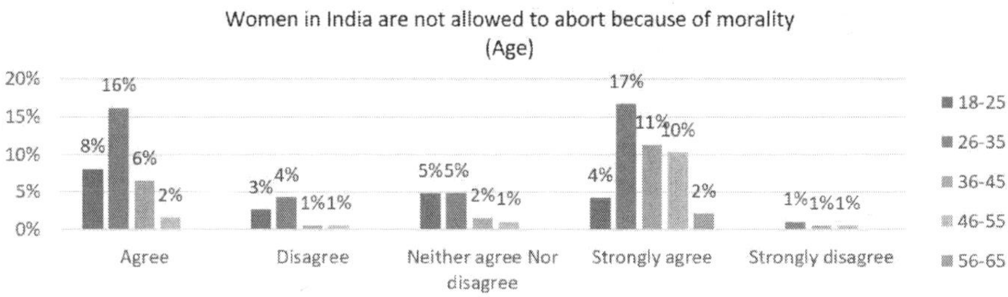

Figure 37: Age and Morality Influencing Abortion Decisions

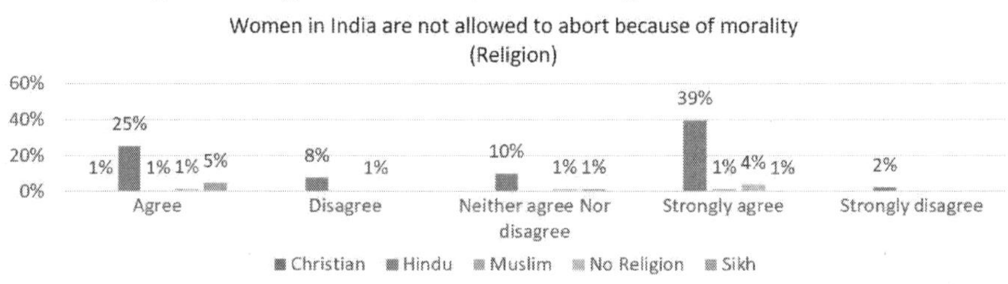

Figure 38: Religion and Morality Influencing Abortion Decisions

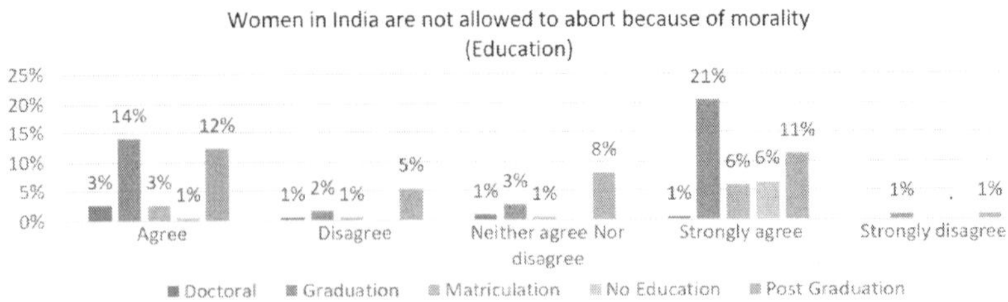

Figure 39: Education and Morality Influencing Abortion Decisions

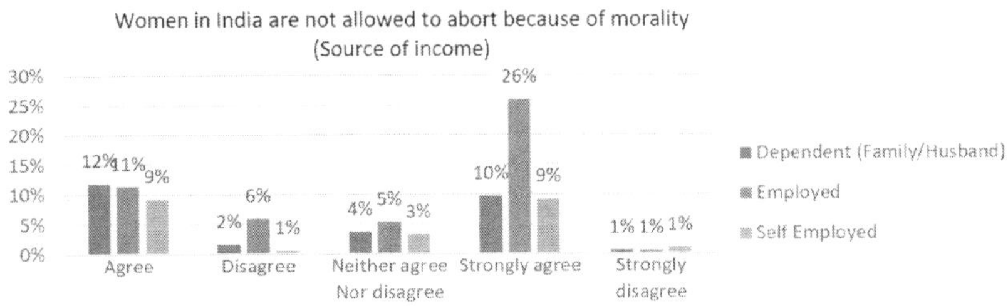

Figure 40: Source of Income and Morality Influencing Abortion Decisions

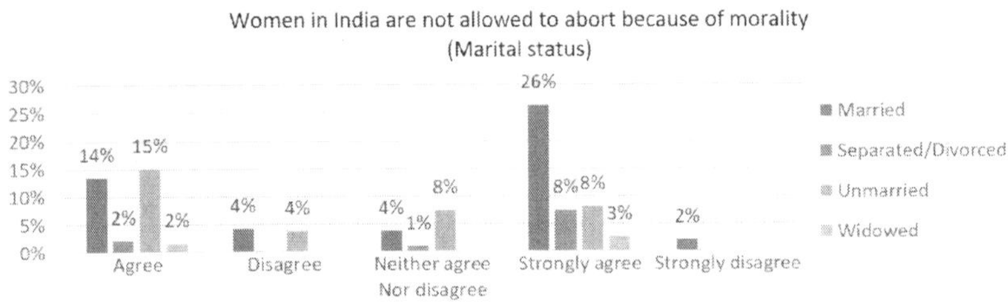

Figure 41: Marital Status and Morality Influencing Abortion Decisions

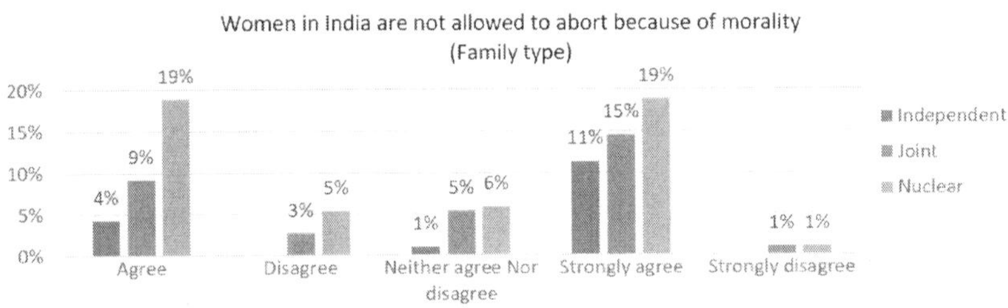

Figure 42: Family Type and Morality Influencing Abortion Decisions

Analysis: Regarding Inhibitions to Exercise the Right to Abortion on the Grounds of Morality

- **Age:** 76% of respondents from the age group of 18–65 years agreed or strongly agreed that morality was one of the reasons for the denial of abortion.
- **Place:** 80% of women from Delhi-NCR agreed, but 11% of women from the same city disagreed with the statement.

- **Religion**: 77% of respondents from the Hindu community confirmed that morality was one of the reasons for not opting for abortions, while 12% disagreed.
- **Education**: 35% of graduates, 23% of postgraduates, and 20% of women from other educational backgrounds agreed or strongly agreed with the same premise, whereas only 5% of uneducated women disagreed.
- **Source of income:** 77% of respondents believed that morality was among the reasons for not terminating the pregnancy, while only 12% disagreed with it.
- **Marital status:** 40% of married, 23% of unmarried, and 15% of divorced/separated/widowed women agreed/strongly agreed, while only 10% of the respondents disagreed with the question of morality as a barrier.
- **Family type:** 38% of women from nuclear families, 24% from joint families, and 15% living independently agreed on similar lines.

Thus, it is evident that morality is a far-reaching impediment to the free exercise of the right to abortion amongst women.

Non-acceptance of Pregnancy of Unmarried Women

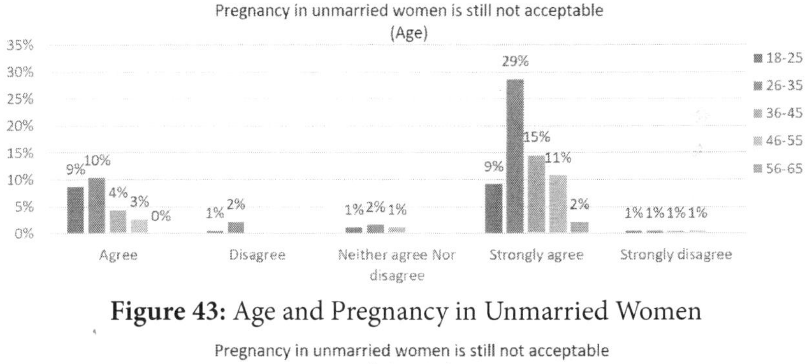

Figure 43: Age and Pregnancy in Unmarried Women

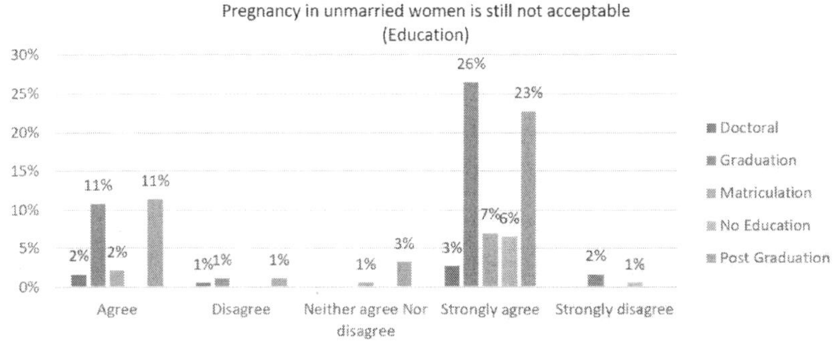

Figure 44: Education and Pregnancy in Unmarried Women

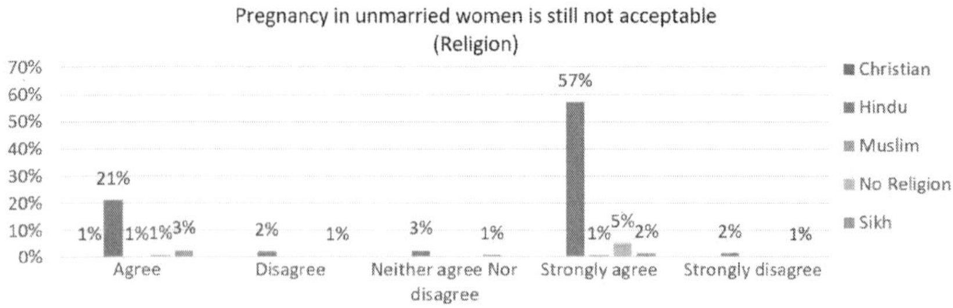

Figure 45: Religion and Pregnancy in Unmarried Women

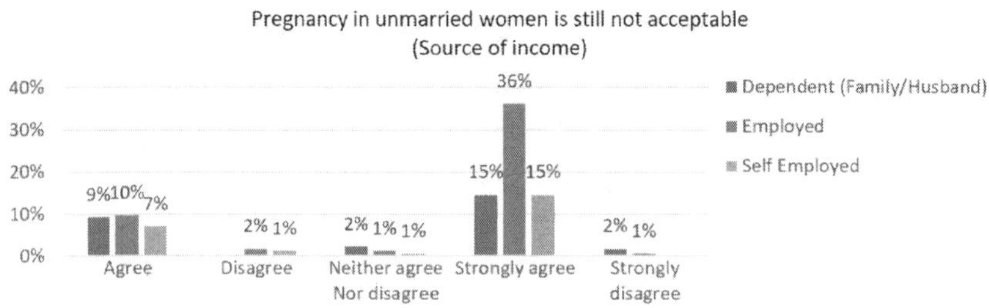

Figure 46: Source of Income and Pregnancy in Unmarried Women

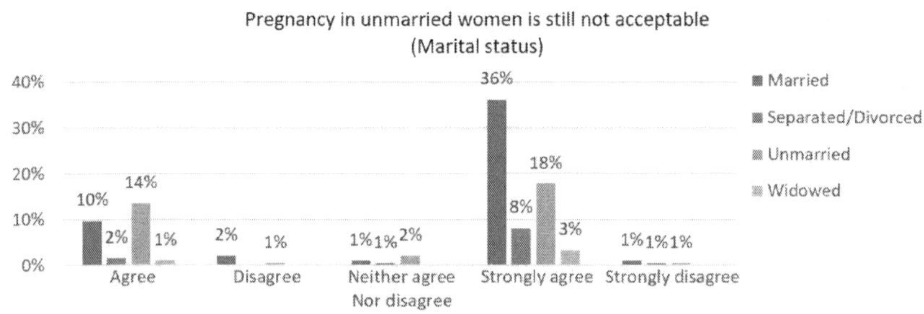

Figure 47: Marital Status and Pregnancy in Unmarried Women

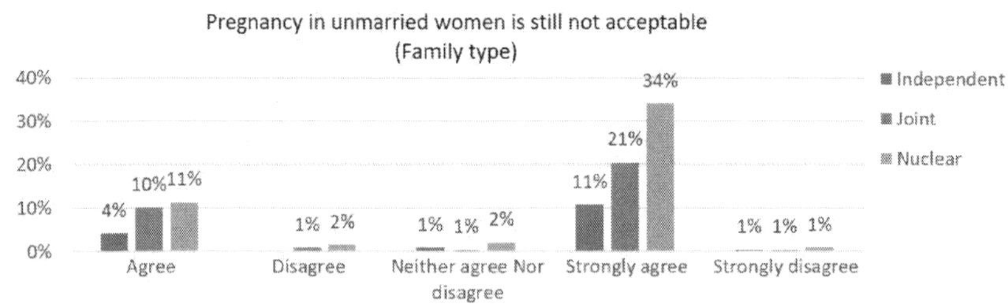

Figure 48: Family Type and Pregnancy in Unmarried Women

Analysis: Regarding the Non-acceptance of Pregnancy of Unmarried Women

- **Age:** 92% of respondents between 18 to 65 years of age agreed/strongly agreed with the premise that there is no acceptance for pregnancy of unmarried women in India.

- **Religion:** 92% of respondents, irrespective of their religions, strongly supported this notion.
- **Education:** 37% of graduates, 34% of postgraduates, and 20% of respondents from other educational backgrounds agreed/strongly agreed on the same.
- **Source of income:** 46% of employed women and 46% of both dependent and self-employed women strongly agreed that there is no acceptance for pregnancy of unmarried women.
- **Marital status**: 46% of married, 32% of unmarried, and 14% of widowed/separated/divorced women agreed to the viewpoint that pregnancy in unmarried women is still not acceptable in India.
- **Family type:** 45% of women from nuclear families, 31% from joint families, and 15% from independent setups agreed or strongly agreed with the premise.

Thus, it is clear that unmarried pregnant women are not accepted in Indian society.

Sterilization After a Male Child

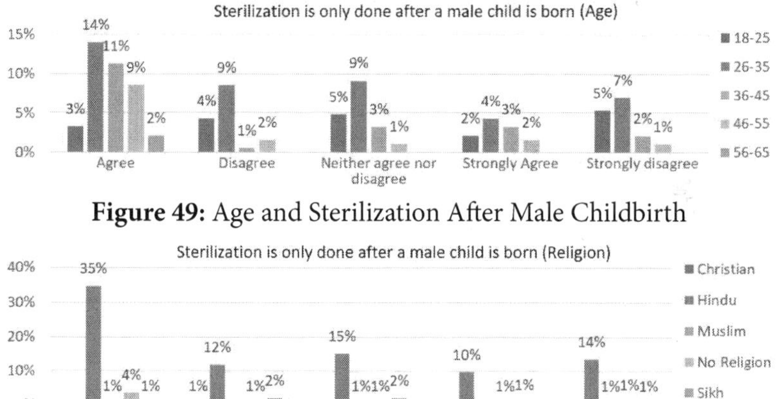

Figure 49: Age and Sterilization After Male Childbirth

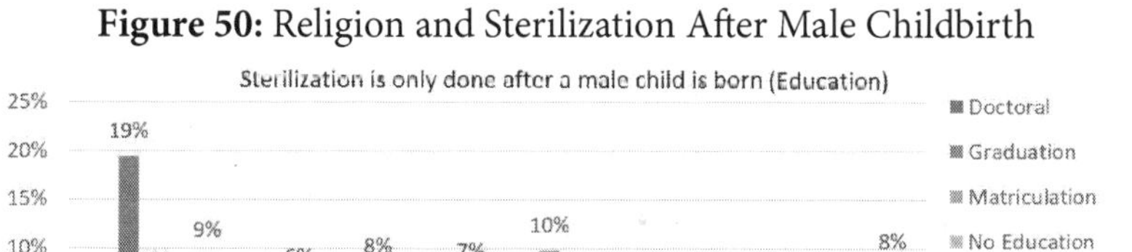

Figure 50: Religion and Sterilization After Male Childbirth

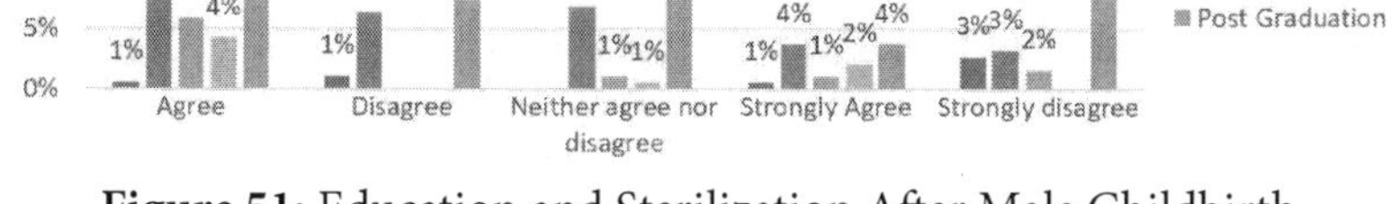

Figure 51: Education and Sterilization After Male Childbirth

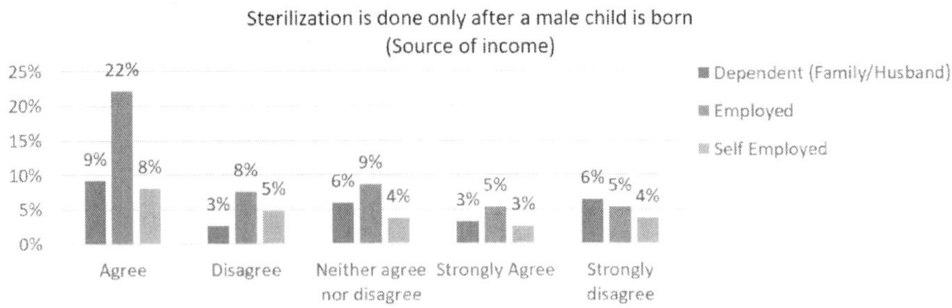

Figure 52: Source of Income and Sterilization After Male Childbirth

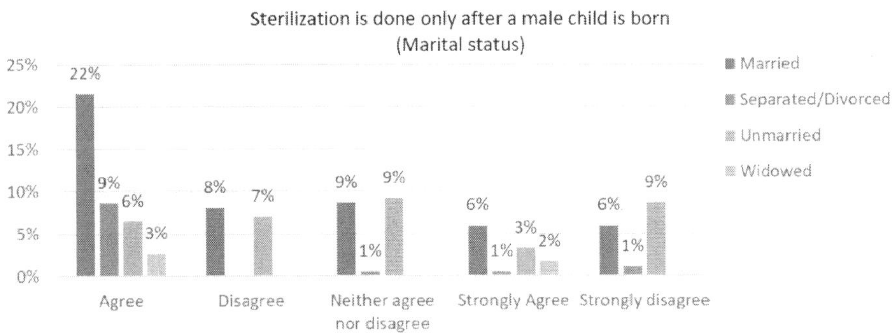

Figure 53: Marital Status and Sterilization After Male Childbirth

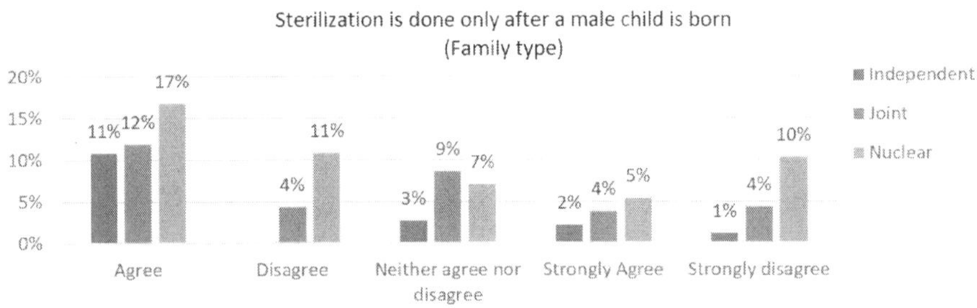

Figure 54: Family Type and Sterilization After Male Childbirth

Analysis: Regarding the Practice of Undergoing Sterilization After the Birth of a Male Child

- **Age:** 50% of women agreed/strongly agreed regarding the practice of undergoing sterilization after the birth of a male child. However, 31% of respondents disagreed and 18% remained neutral.
- **Religion**: 45% of Hindu respondents and 8% of respondents belonging to other religions agreed with the premise.
- **Education:** Overall, 51% of women from different educational backgrounds agreed that sterilization was usually performed after the birth of a male child, whereas 19% remained neutral.

- **Source of income**: 27% of employed and 23% of unemployed/ independent women believed that sterilization is performed after the birth of a male child.
- **Marital status:** 28% of married, 9% of unmarried, and 15% of separated/divorced/widowed women agreed with the premise.
- **Family type:** 22% of women from nuclear and 29% from joint and independent families also confirmed the same.

Thus, the data reflects that sterilization takes place only after the birth of a male child. This is not only a reflection of the patriarchal nature of society but also the cause of erosion of women's autonomy regarding childbirth and pregnancy.

Expensive/Unaffordable Abortion Services

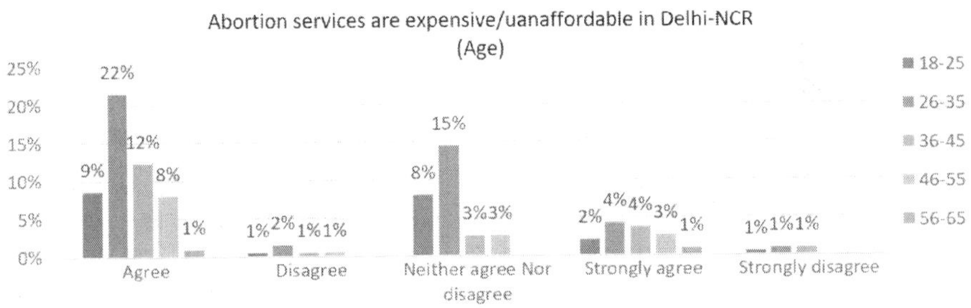

Figure 55: Age and Unaffordable Abortion Services

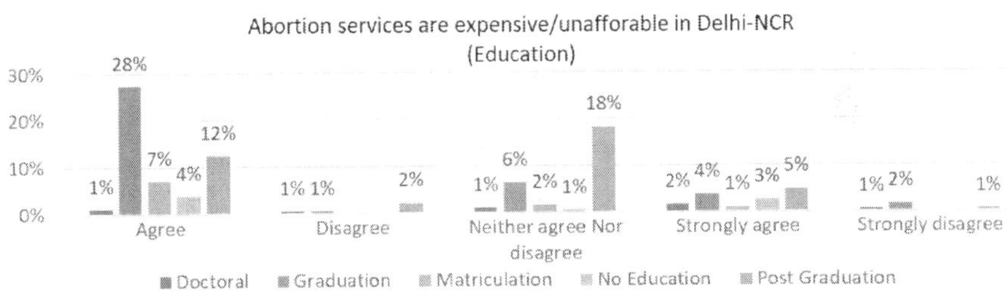

Figure 56: Education and Unaffordable Abortion Services

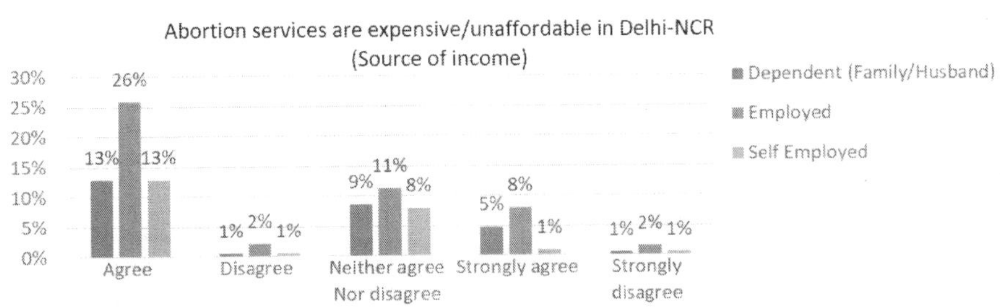

Figure 57: Source of Income and Unaffordable Abortion Services

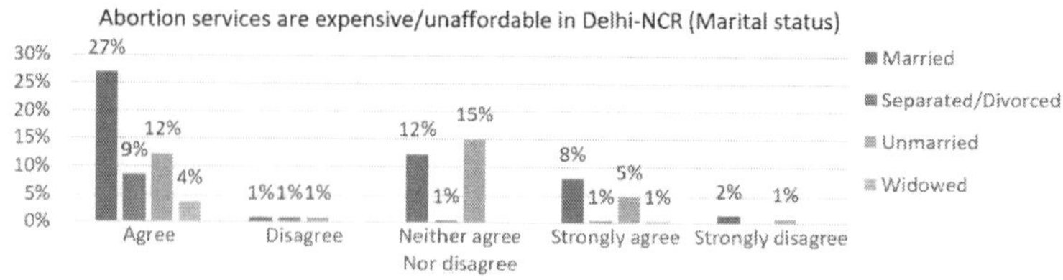

Figure 58: Marital Status and Unaffordable Abortion Services

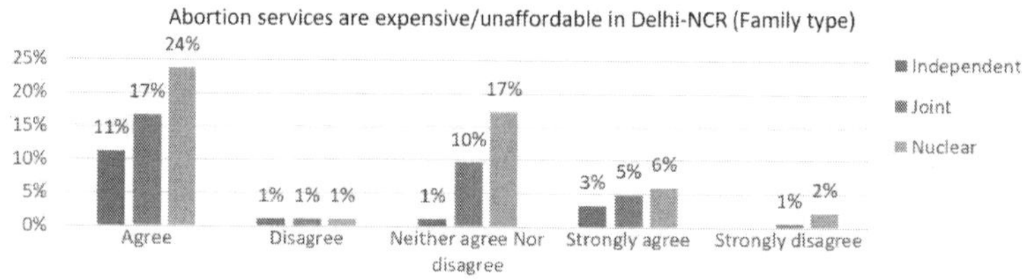

Figure 59: Family Type and Unaffordable Abortion Services

Analysis: Regarding Expensive/Unaffordable Abortion Services in Delhi-NCR

- **Age:** 66% of women of aged between 18 to 65 years agreed/strongly agreed that Delhi-NCR offers expensive abortion services.
- **Education:** 67% of educated and uneducated women believed that abortion services were unaffordable, while 28% of women from all educational backgrounds were neutral.
- **Source of income**: 48% of employed/self-employed and 18% of independent women believed that abortion services in the Delhi-NCR region were very expensive.
- **Marital status**: 35% of married and 32% of unmarried/separated/divorced women agreed or strongly agreed on the same lines.
- **Family type:** 30% of respondents from nuclear and 36% from joint and independent families stated that they could not afford safe abortion services in Delhi-NCR.

Thus, abortion services are expensive and unaffordable and resultantly the practice of unsafe abortion is still seeing an upward trend in society.

Unqualified/Inadequate Staff in Hospitals

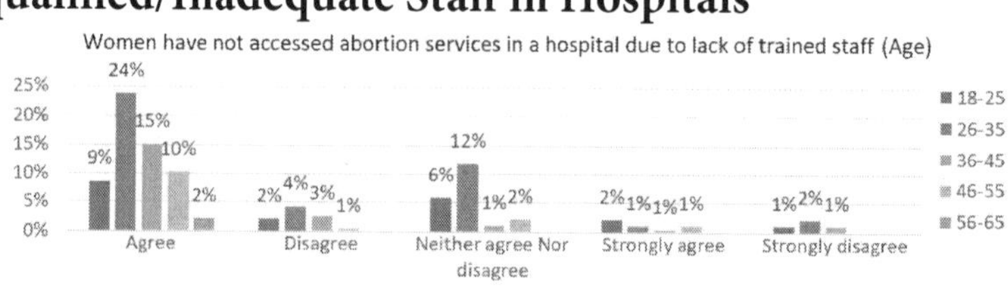

Figure 60: Age and Untrained Staff in Hospitals

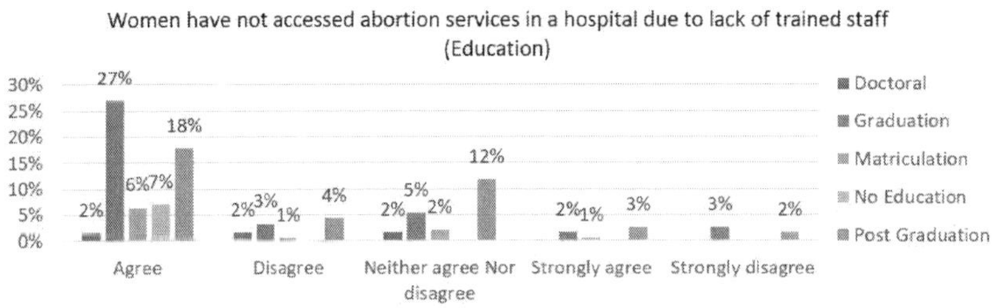

Figure 61: Education and Untrained Staff in Hospitals

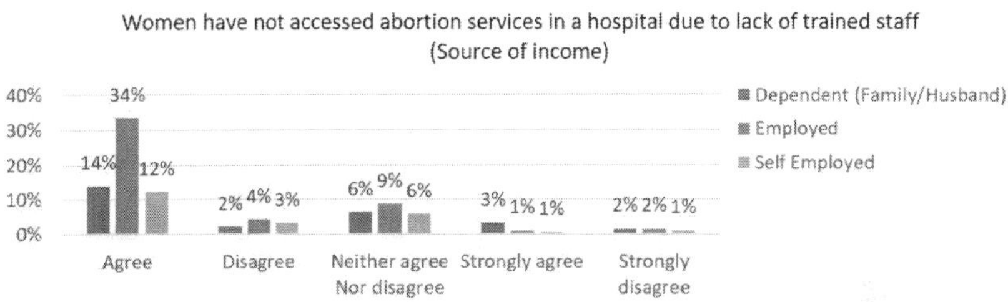

Figure 62: Source of Income and Untrained Staff in Hospitals

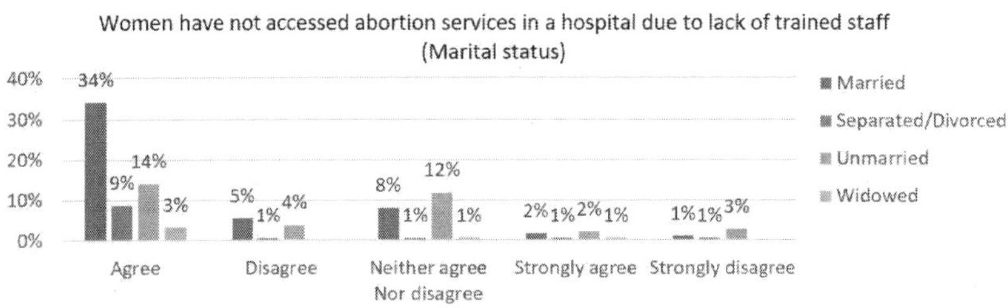

Figure 63: Marital Status and Untrained Staff in Hospitals

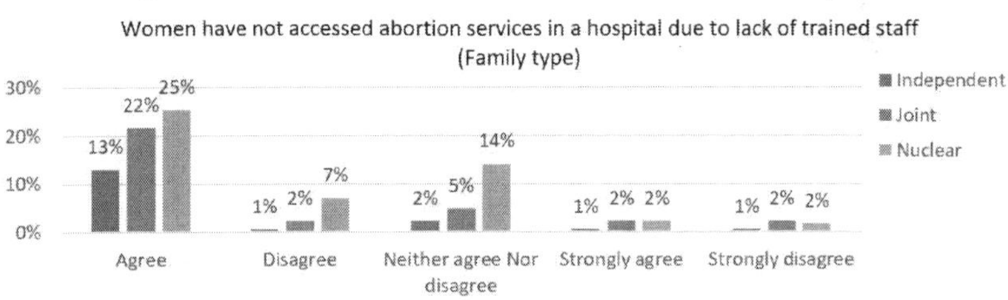

Figure 64: Family Type and Untrained Staff in Hospitals

Analysis: Regarding Inadequate Trained Staff in Hospitals

- **Age:** 65% of women agreed/strongly agreed that there was a lack of trained staff in hospitals to perform abortions.
- **Education:** 29% of graduate women agreed/strongly agreed with the viewpoint, and 37% of women from other educational backgrounds believed that women do not go to hospitals due to a lack of trained staff.

- **Source of income:** 35% of employed and 30% of unemployed and independent respondents agreed/strongly agreed with the premise.
- **Marital status:** 66% of respondents agreed/strongly agreed that they do not go to hospitals due to a lack of trained staff.
- **Family type**: 41% of women from nuclear families and independent setups and 24% from joint families agreed that hospitals did not have adequate and trained staff to perform abortions.

Thus, it was observed that there is a lack of trained staff in Delhi-NCR, which serves as a major barrier to access to safe abortions.

Preference for Health Providers for Seeking Abortion Services

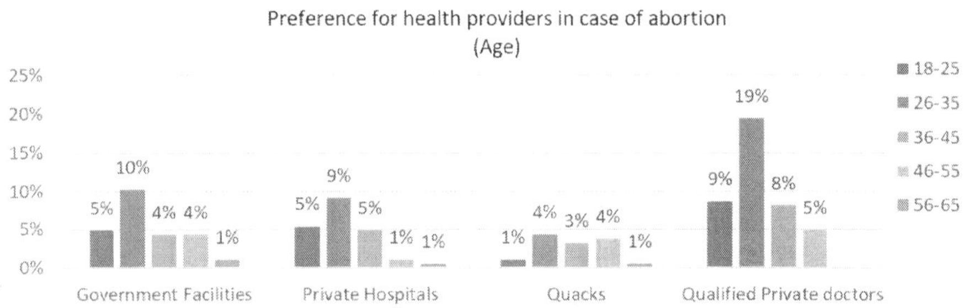

Figure 65: Age and Preference for Health Provider for Abortion

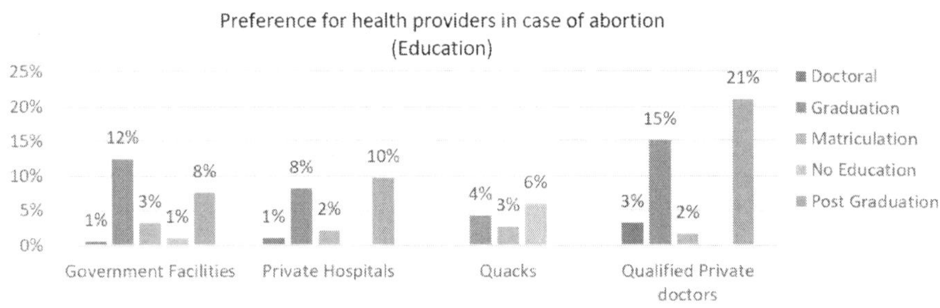

Figure 66: Education and Preference for Health Provider for Abortion

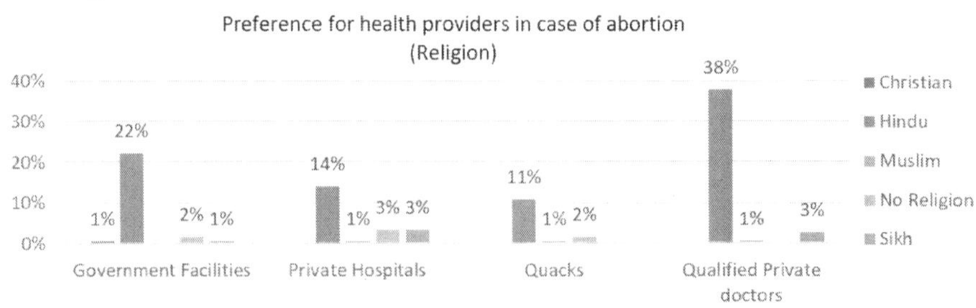

Figure 67: Religion and Preference for Health Provider for Abortion

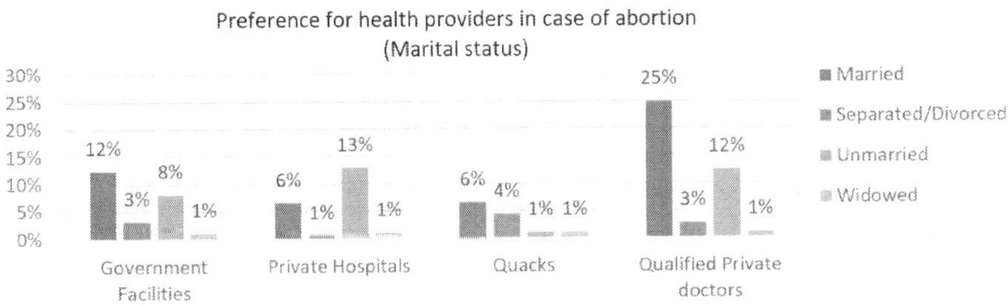

Figure 68: Marital Status and Preference for Health Provider for Abortion

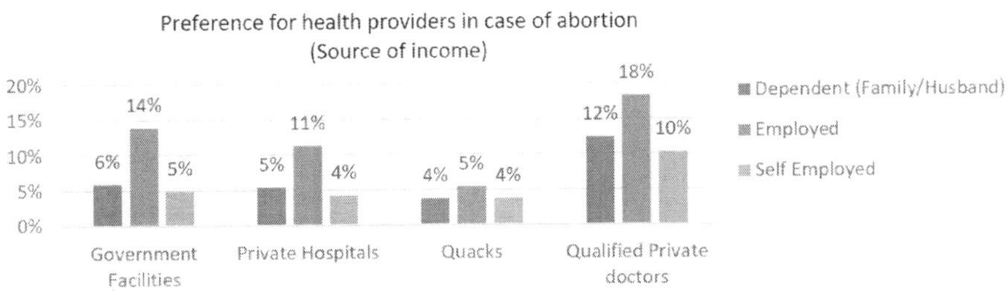

Figure 69: Source of Income and Preference for Health Provider for Abortion

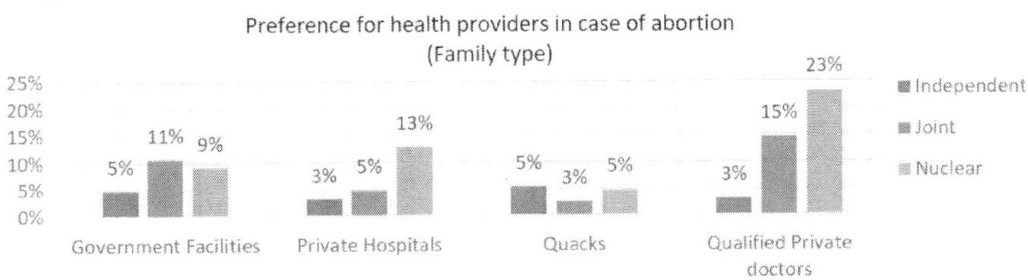

Figure 70: Family Type and Preference for Health Provider for Abortion

Analysis: Regarding the Preference for the Type of Health Provider for Availing Abortion Services

- **Age:** 41% of women preferred to visit qualified private doctors, 24% preferred government facilities, 21% preferred private hospitals, and 13% preferred to visit quacks for abortion services.
- **Education:** Irrespective of the educational background, 25% of respondents preferred government facilities, 21% preferred private hospitals, 41% preferred qualified doctors, and 13% went to quacks for abortion services.
- **Religion:** 42% of women belonging to various religions chose qualified private doctors and 26% preferred government facilities, whereas 14% preferred quacks for abortion services.
- **Marital status:** 25% of married and 12% of unmarried women preferred qualified private doctors, while 6% preferred private

hospitals. Overall, only 12% of respondents preferred quacks for services related to abortion.

- **Source of income:** 40% of women from various income groups preferred qualified private doctors, whereas 20% chose private hospitals, 25% opted for government hospitals, and 13% chose quacks for abortion services.
- **Family type:** 41% of women from different family types preferred a qualified private doctor for medical abortion services, whereas 25% went for government services. Only 5% of independent women sought advice from a quack.

The data shows that women choose the abortion service provider on the basis of their location, reasonability, methods, and sometimes legality. They depend on health providers' qualification, commitment, professional ethics, and accuracy.

Physical and Mental Trauma during Abortion

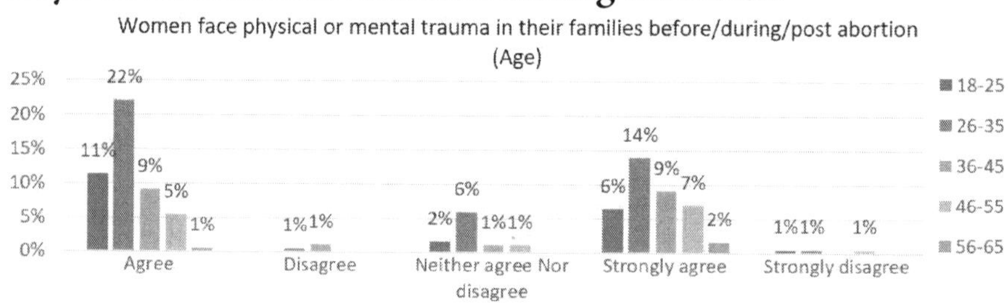

Figure 71: Age and Trauma during Abortion

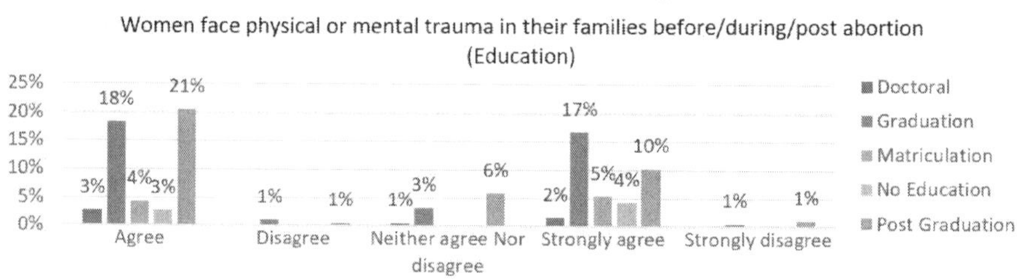

Figure 72: Education and Trauma during Abortion

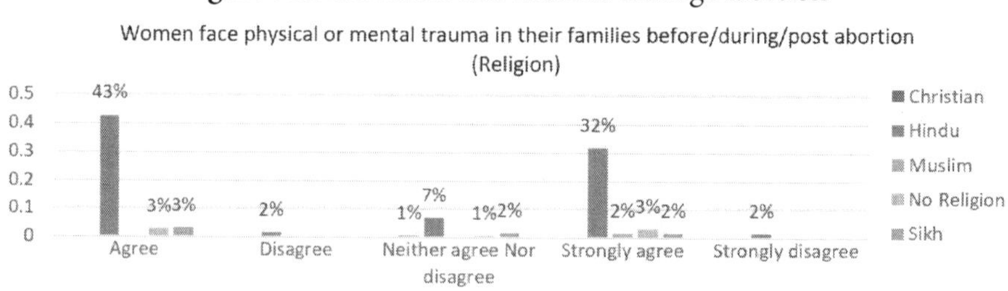

Figure 73: Religion and Trauma during Abortion

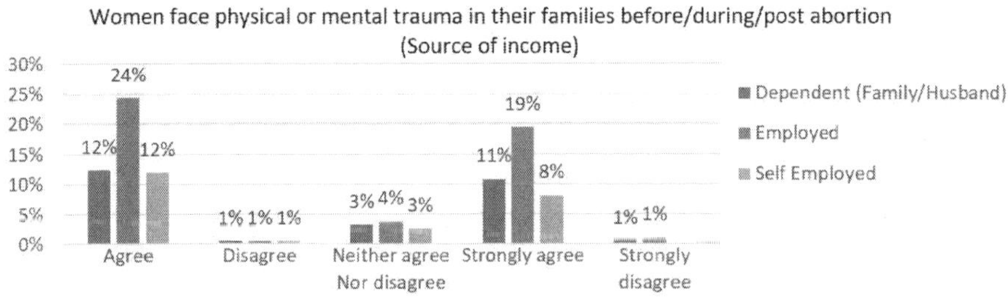

Figure 74: Source of Income and Trauma during Abortion

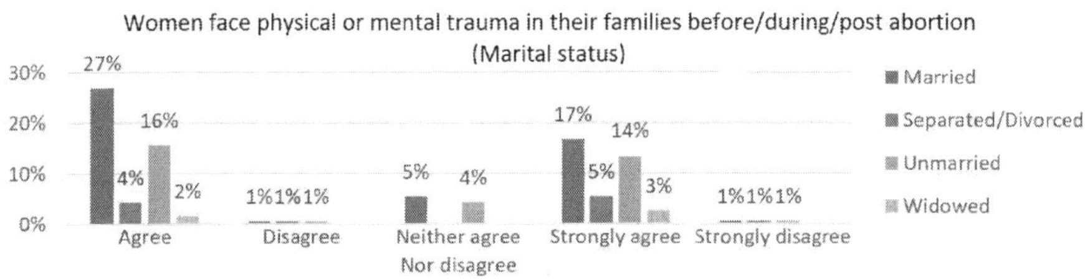

Figure 75: Marital Status and Trauma during Abortion

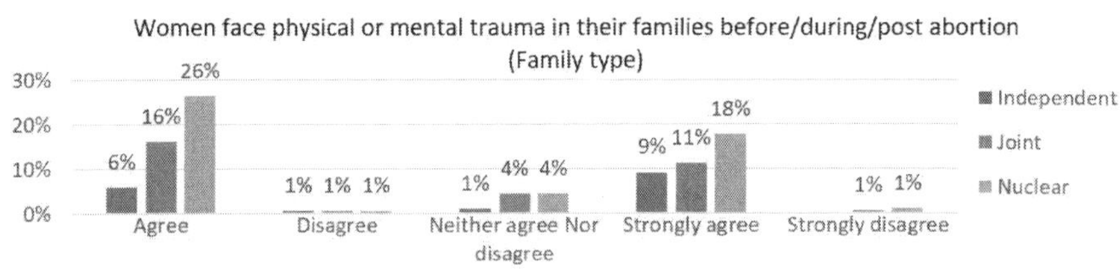

Figure 76: Family Type and Trauma during Abortion

Analysis: Regarding Women Facing Physical and Mental Trauma in their Families Before/During/Post Abortion

- **Age:** 86% of women agreed or strongly agreed that women undergo physical and mental trauma during abortion.
- **Education:** 87% of women with various educational qualifications agreed/strongly agreed with the premise.
- **Religion:** 88% of respondents irrespective of their religion agreed/strongly agreed that women faced mental trauma in their respective families pre/post-abortion.
- **Source of income:** 86% of women from various economic backgrounds agreed or strongly agreed on the matter.
- **Marital status:** 44% of married and 44% of unmarried/separated/divorced women agreed to the premise.
- **Family type:** 59% of respondents from nuclear families and independent setups and 27% of women from joint families agreed/strongly agreed with the same.

Women's mental health is dependent upon the reasons behind opting for the termination and the quality of service received. The attitude and socio-economic background of the family also matter. Also, the degree of autonomy the woman has in the decision-making impacts her physical or mental health status.

Mandatory Court Permission for Abortion after 24 Weeks of Pregnancy

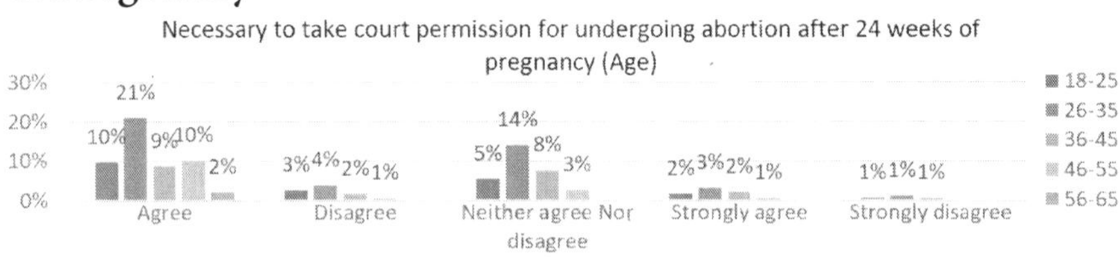

Figure 77: Age and Court Permission for Abortion under the MTP Act

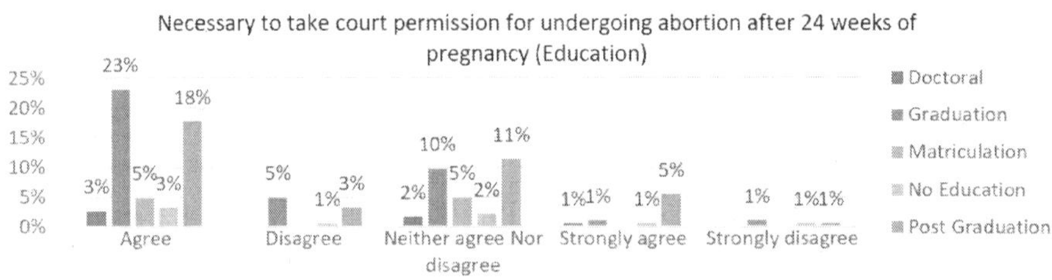

Figure 78: Education and Court Permission for Abortion under the MTP Act

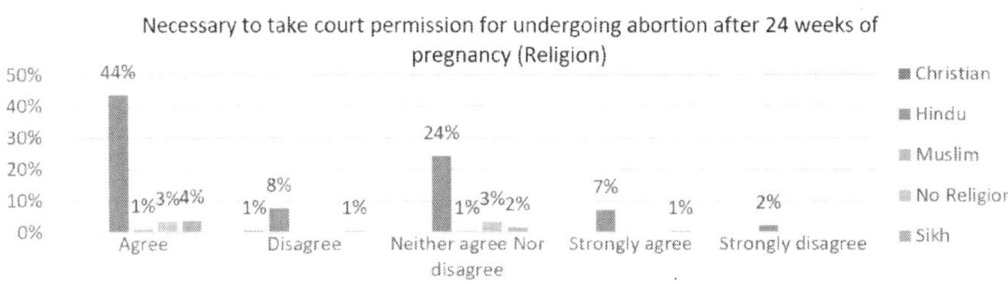

Figure 79: Religion and Court Permission for Abortion under the MTP Act

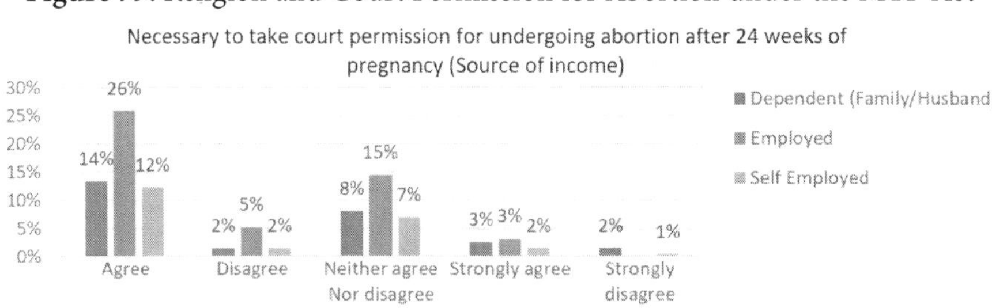

Figure 80: Source of Income and Court Permission for Abortion under the MTP Act

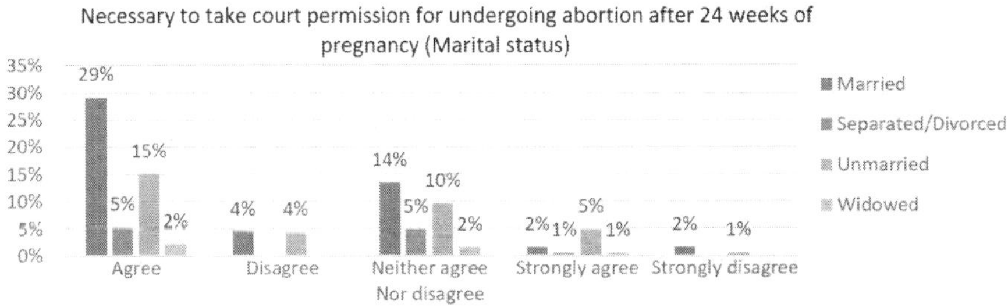

Figure 81: Marital Status and Court Permission for Abortion under the MTP Act

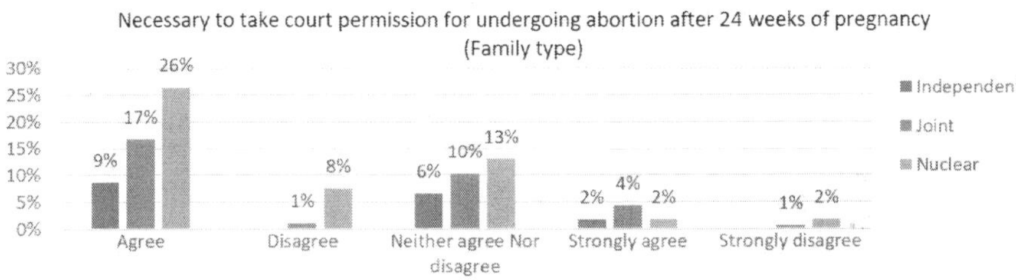

Figure 82: Family Type and Court Permission for Abortion under the MTP Act

Analysis: Regarding the Knowledge of the Necessity to have Court Permission to Undergo Abortion after 24 Weeks of Pregnancy under the MTP Act, 2021

- **Age:** 60% of women agreed/strongly agreed that court permission is necessary in certain cases (mentioned under the MTP Act) where women want to abort beyond 24 weeks of pregnancy.
- **Education:** 24% of graduates and 23% of postgraduates were aware that court permission is mandatory for abortion after 24 weeks of gestation under the MTP Act.
- **Religion:** 60% of respondents from various religions agreed to the premise, whereas 30% were neutral and 12% disagreed with it.
- **Source of income:** 29% of employed and 31% of dependent and self-employed women agreed/strongly agreed with the statement.
- **Marital status**: 31% of married and 29% of separated/divorced/widowed and unmarried women had knowledge about the same.
- **Family type:** 39% of women from independent and nuclear families and 21% from joint families agreed/strongly agreed that court permission is necessary in such cases.

The knowledge about the necessity to approach the court was found to be reasonably good.

Delays by Courts in Granting Permission for Abortion

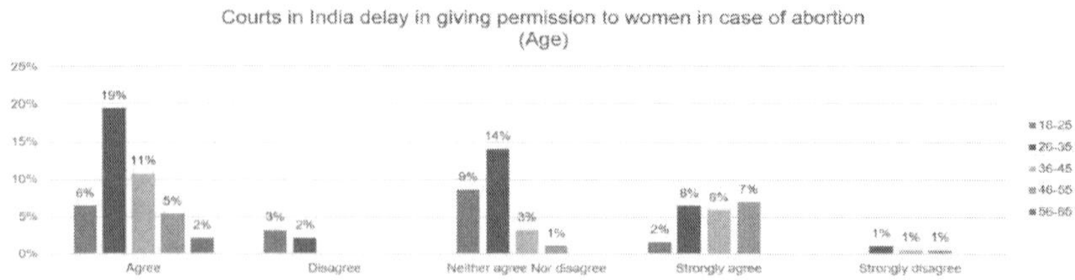

Figure 83: Age and Delays in Court Permission

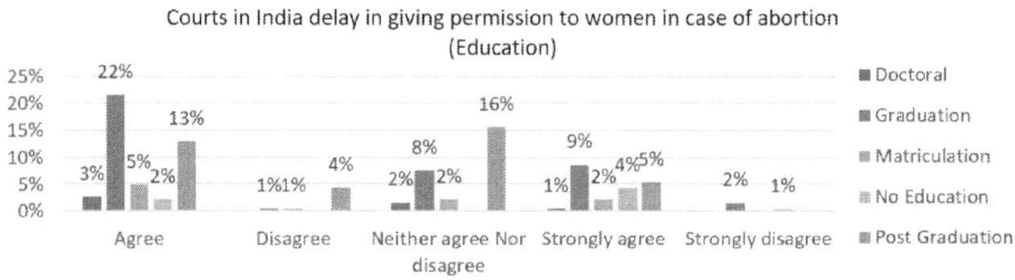

Figure 84: Education and Delays in Court Permission

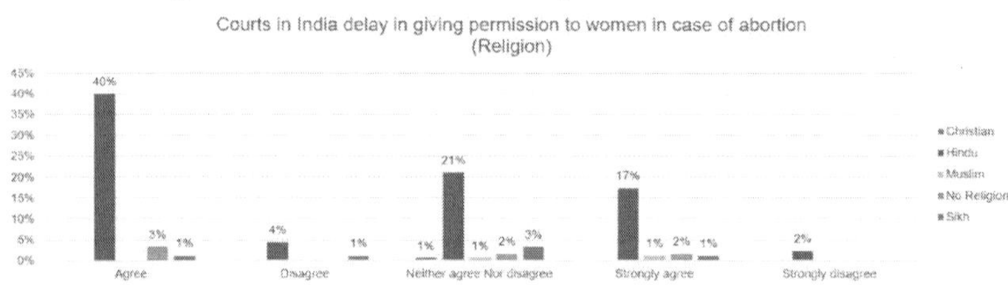

Figure 85: Religion and Delays in Court Permission

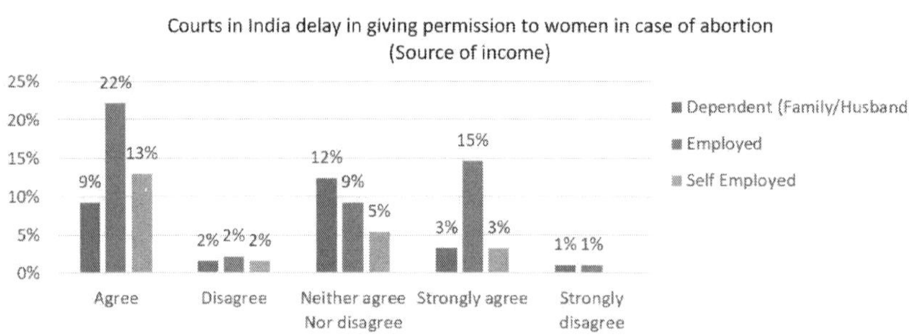

Figure 86: Source of Income and Delays in Court Permission

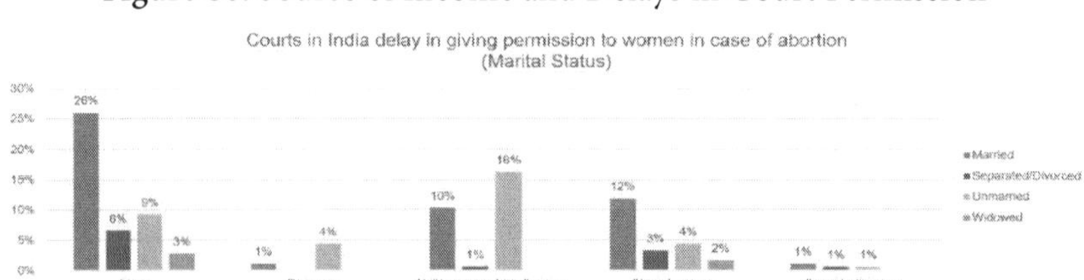

Figure 87: Marital Status and Delays in Court Permission

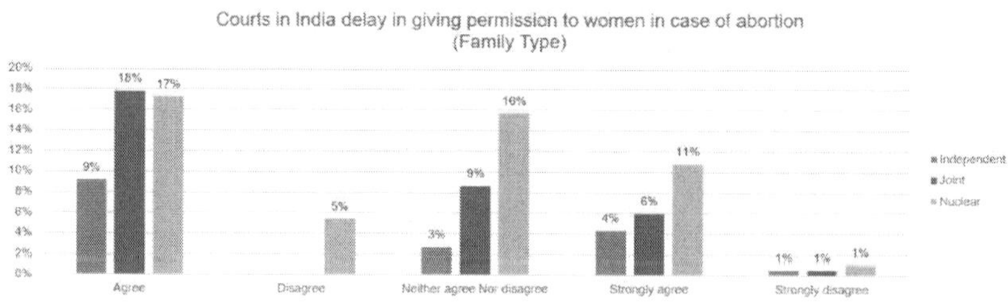

Figure 88: Family Type and Delays in Court Permission

Analysis: Regarding the Delays in Approval by Courts for Abortion in India

- **Age:** 64% of women agreed/strongly agreed that there are delays in getting permission for an abortion from courts.
- **Education:** 66% of respondents from uneducated and educated groups agreed/strongly agreed with the premise.
- **Religion:** 65% of women belonging to various religions strongly agreed with this issue, while 28% neither agreed nor disagreed.
- **Source of income:** 37% of employed, 12% of dependent, and 16% of independent respondents agreed that courts take too long to grant permission for abortion to women.
- **Marital status:** 38% of married and 27% of separated/divorced/ widowed women believed that in cases of abortion, women suffer due to the court's delay in making a decision.
- **Family type:** 13% of women from independent, 24% from joint, and 28% from nuclear families agreed/strongly agreed with the premise.

In addition to the mental stress that comes with the delay, there is also a risk to the physical health of the mother and fetus, which sometimes leads to serious complications and even unwarranted deaths.

Finality of the Decision of the Doctor(s) Regarding Abortion under the MTP Act, 2021

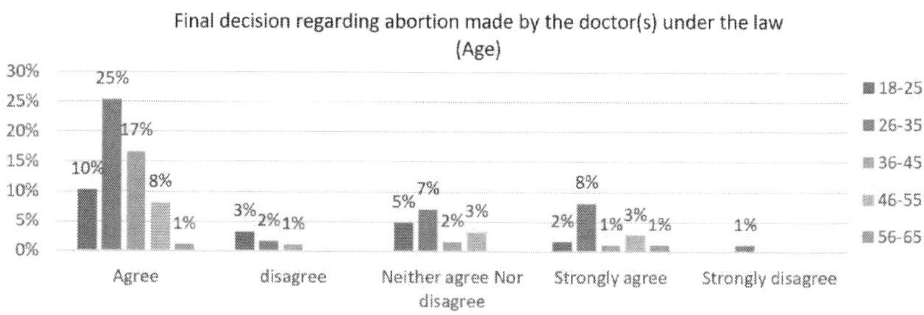

Figure 89: Age and Finality of Decision of Doctor(s)

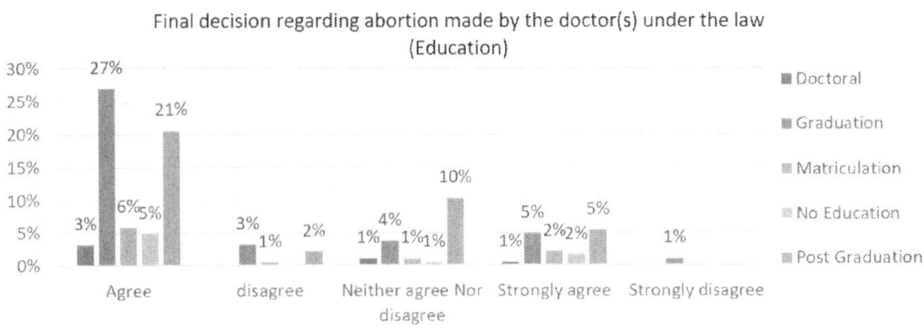

Figure 90: Education and Finality of Decision of Doctor(s)

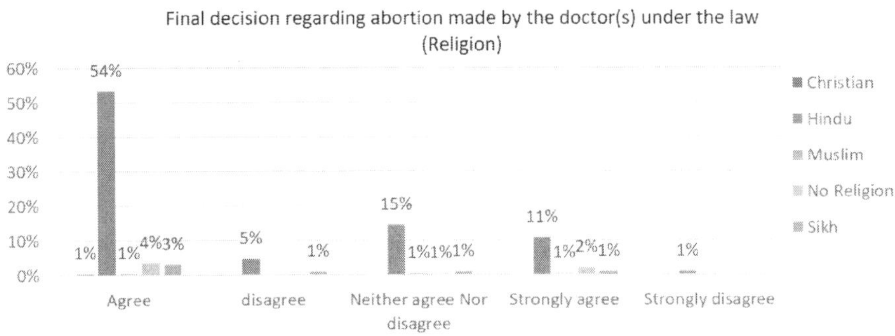

Figure 91: Religion and Finality of Decision of Doctor(s)

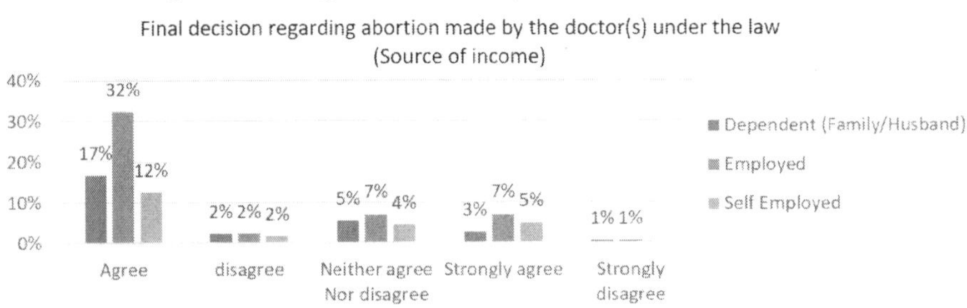

Figure 92: Source of Income and Finality of Decision of Doctor(s)

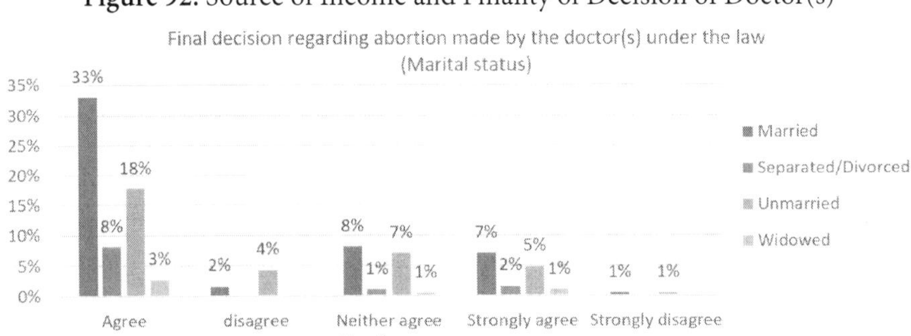

Figure 93: Marital Status and Finality of Decision of Doctor(s)

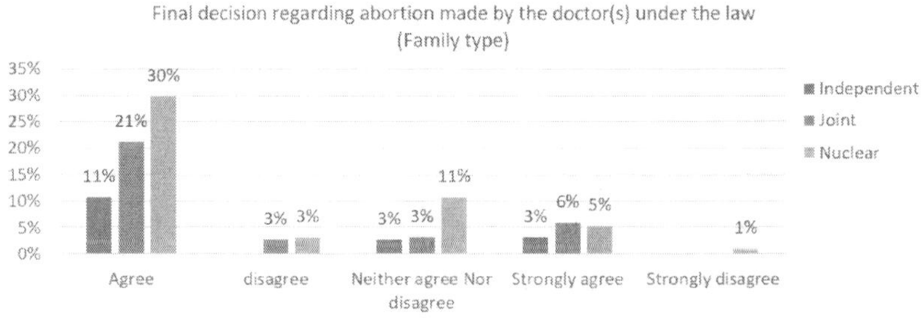

Figure 94: Marital Status and Finality of Decision of Doctor(s)

Analysis: Regarding the Finality of the Decision Made by the Doctor(s) for Abortion between the Gestation Period of 20–24 Weeks under the MTP Act, 2021

- **Age:** 76% of women of 18–65 years of age agreed/strongly agreed that the sole decision of the doctors is final under the law.
- **Education:** 32% of graduates, 26% of postgraduates, and 19% of women from other educational backgrounds agreed/strongly agreed with the same.
- **Religion:** 78% of the respondents from various religions agreed with the statement.
- **Source of income**: 76% of respondents irrespective of their source of income agreed/strongly agreed with the premise.
- **Marital status:** 40% of married and 37% of unmarried/divorced/separated women agreed that it was the sole discretion of the doctors to decide on the abortion.
- **Family type**: 49% of women from nuclear and independent families and 27% from joint families agreed/strongly agreed with the premise.

The MTP Act, 2021 lays that two doctors must agree to the termination of pregnancy between 20 and 24 weeks of gestation period, making the requirements for abortion more difficult.

Awareness about Abortion Laws in India

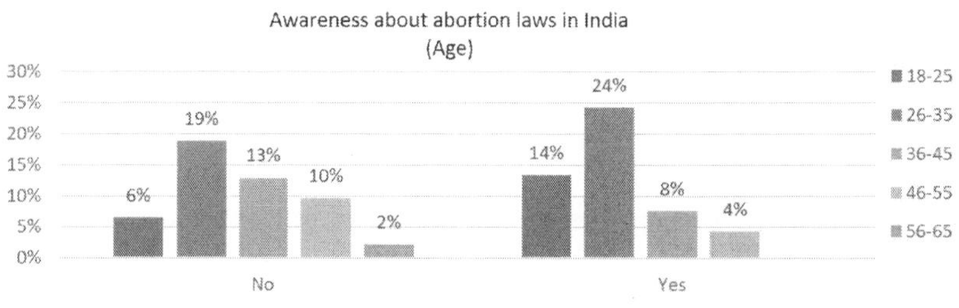

Figure 95: Age and Awareness of Abortion Laws

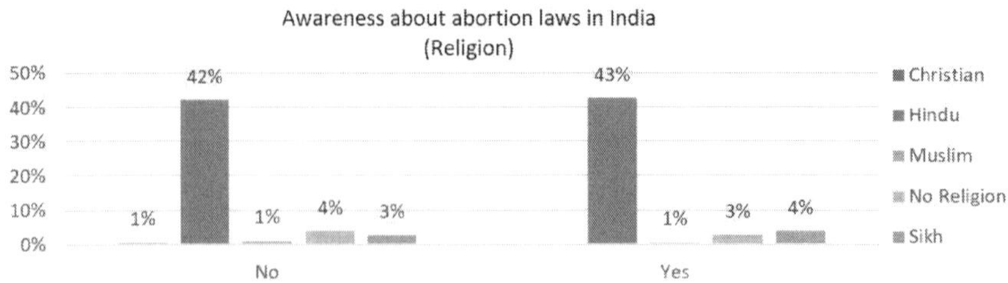

Figure 96: Religion and Awareness of Abortion Laws

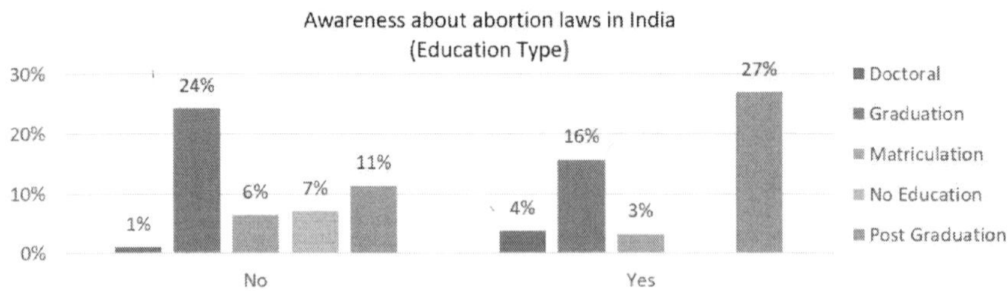

Figure 97: Education and Awareness of Abortion Laws

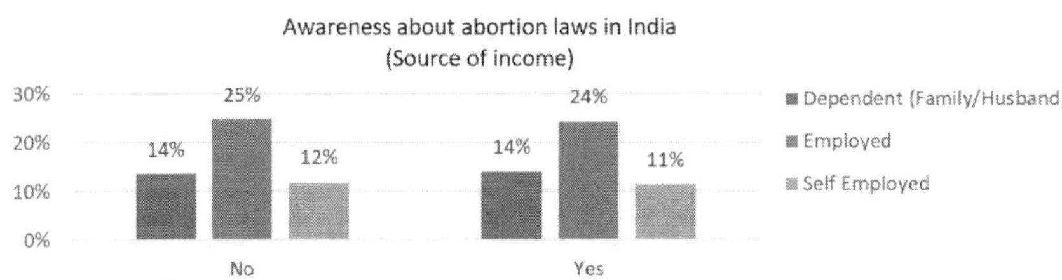

Figure 98: Source of Income and Awareness of Abortion Laws

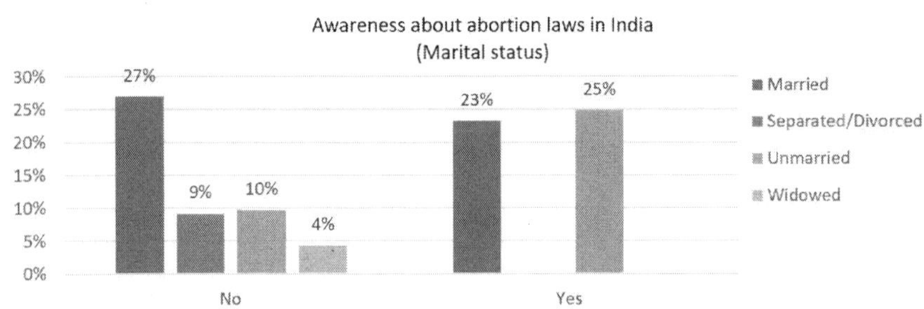

Figure 99: Marital Status and Awareness of Abortion Laws

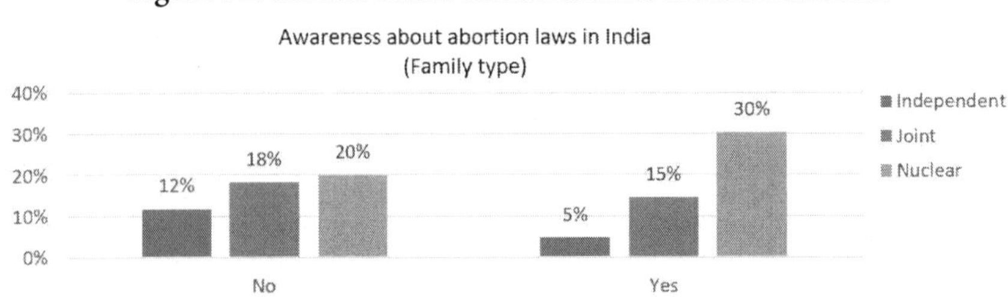

Figure 100: Family Type and Awareness of Abortion Laws

Analysis: Regarding Awareness about Abortion Laws in India

- **Age:** 50% of women were unaware of the existing laws.
- **Religion:** 42% of Hindu women and 9% women belonging to other religions were unaware of laws on abortion in India.
- **Education:** 49% of respondents from different educational backgrounds had the least awareness.
- **Source of income:** 25% of employed, 14% of dependent, and 12% of self-employed women were unaware about the laws.
- **Marital status:** 50% of respondents irrespective of their marital status were also unaware.
- **Family type:** 50% of women from different familial structures were unaware of the abortion laws. However, 5% of women from independent setups and 15% from joint families were aware about them.

Thus, there is low awareness amongst women of the present laws for abortion (the MTP Act and the PCPNDT Act) in India.

Awareness about Abortion Rights

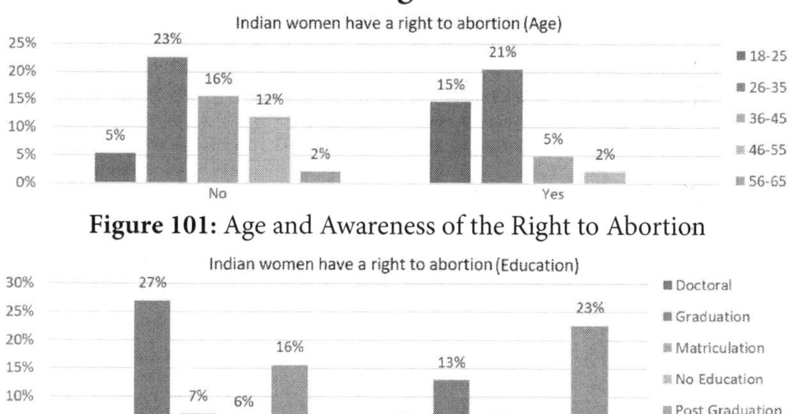

Figure 101: Age and Awareness of the Right to Abortion

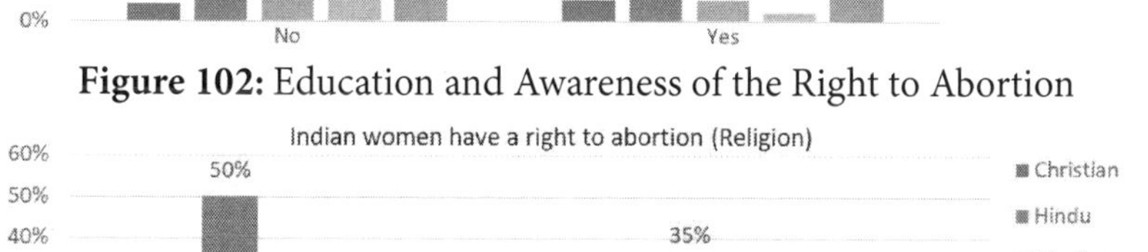

Figure 102: Education and Awareness of the Right to Abortion

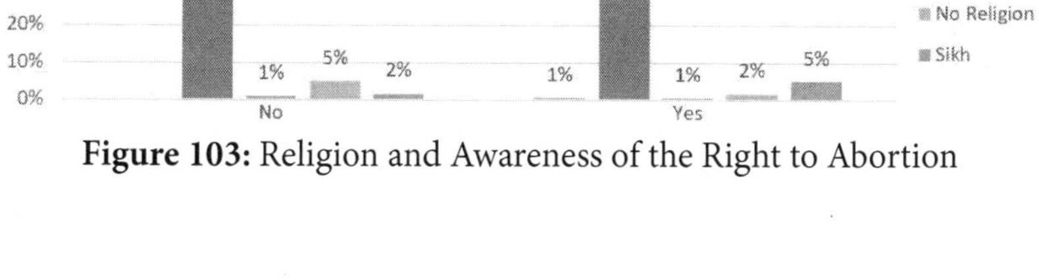

Figure 103: Religion and Awareness of the Right to Abortion

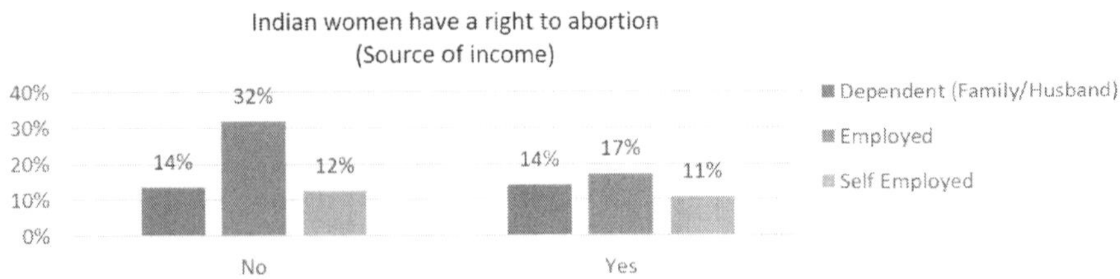

Figure 104: Source of Income and Awareness of the Right to Abortion

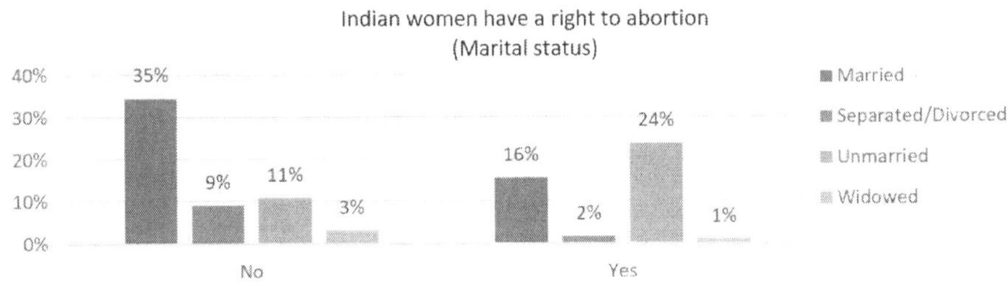

Figure 105: Marital Status and Awareness of the Right to Abortion

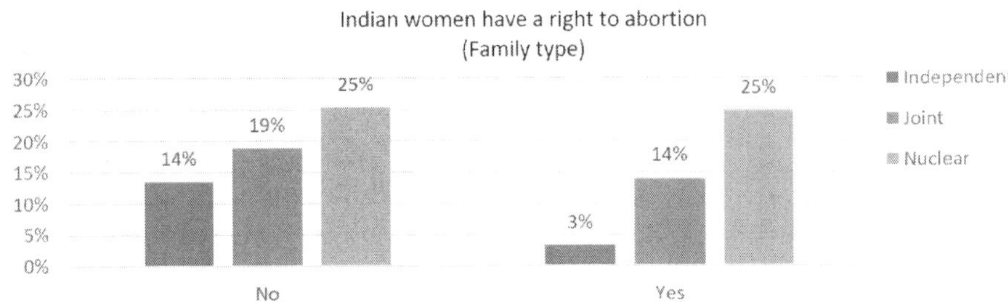

Figure 106: Family Type and Awareness of the Right to Abortion

Analysis: Regarding the Awareness about Abortion Rights of Women in India

- **Age:** 58% of women were unaware of their abortion rights.
- **Education:** 27% of graduates, 16% of postgraduates, and 6% of uneducated women were found unaware of abortion rights.
- **Religion:** 58% of respondents irrespective of religion were unaware.
- **Source of income:** Overall, 58% of respondents were also unaware.
- **Marital status:** 35% of married, 11% of unmarried, and 12% of divorced/separated women were unaware of their abortion rights.
- **Family type:** 25% of women from nuclear families, 19% of women from joint families, and 14% of women living independently were unaware of their rights.

The data shows that women are less aware of their right to abortion.

Awareness about the Favorability of Abortion Laws

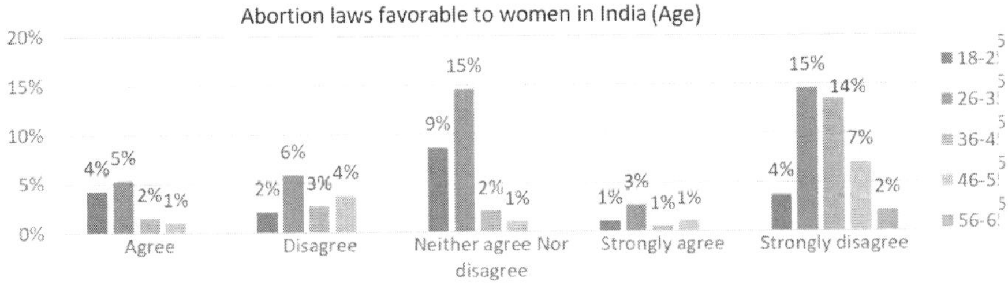

Figure 107: Age and Awareness of Favorability of Abortion Laws

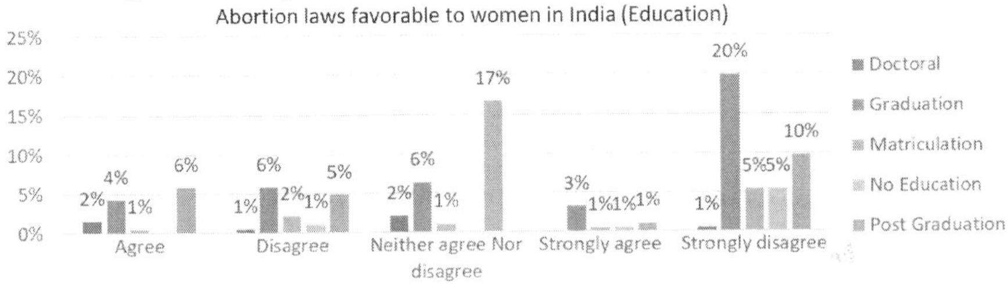

Figure 108: Education and Awareness of Favorability of Abortion Laws

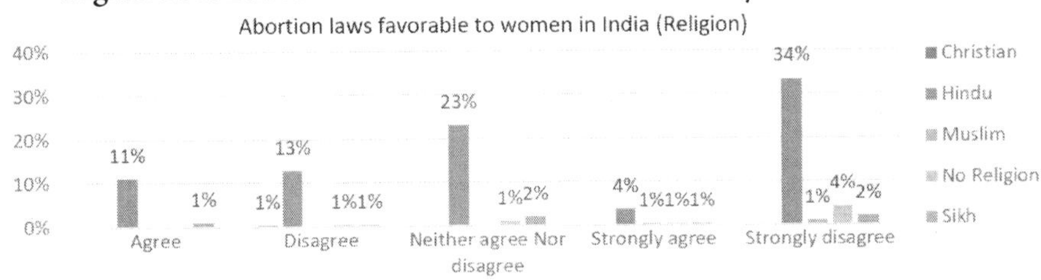

Figure 109: Religion and Awareness of Favorability of Abortion Laws

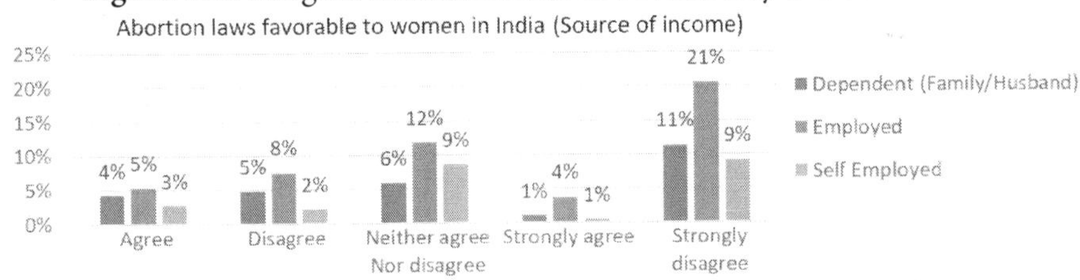

Figure 110: Source of Income and Awareness of Favorability of Abortion Laws

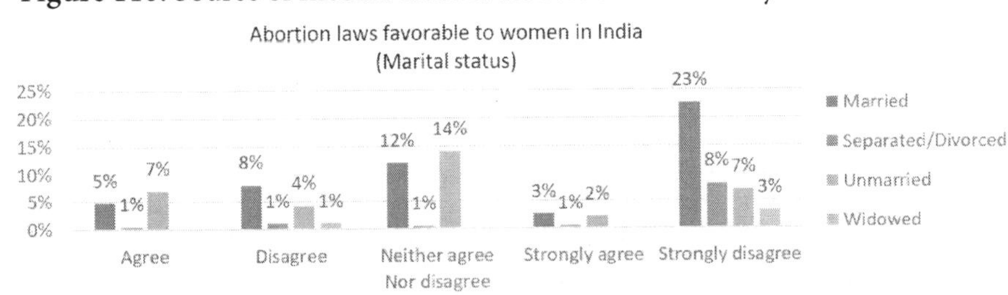

Figure 111: Marital Status and Awareness of Favorability of Abortion Laws

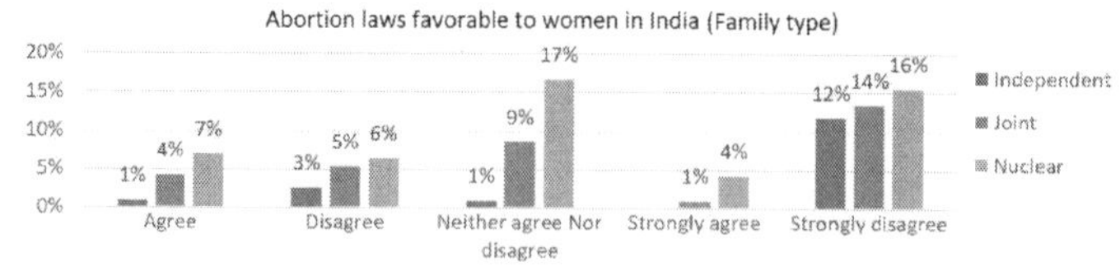

Figure 112: Source of Income and Awareness of Favorability of Abortion Laws

Analysis: Regarding the Favorability of Abortion Laws for Women

- **Age:** 57% of women strongly disagreed with the idea that Indian abortion laws are favorable to women.
- **Education:** 56% of women from diverse educational backgrounds disagreed/strongly disagreed with the premise that abortion laws are favorable to women.
- **Religion:** 57% of women belonging to different religions also disagreed/strongly disagreed.
- **Source of income:** Overall, 56% of respondents disagreed/strongly disagreed with the premise.
- **Marital status**: 31% of married and 24% of unmarried/separated/divorced women strongly disagreed with the statement.
- **Family type**: 22% of women from nuclear and 34% from joint and independent families disagreed that abortion laws are favourable to women.

As per the data, the respondents confirm extremely less favorability of abortion laws for women.

Suggestive Changes in the Legal Framework

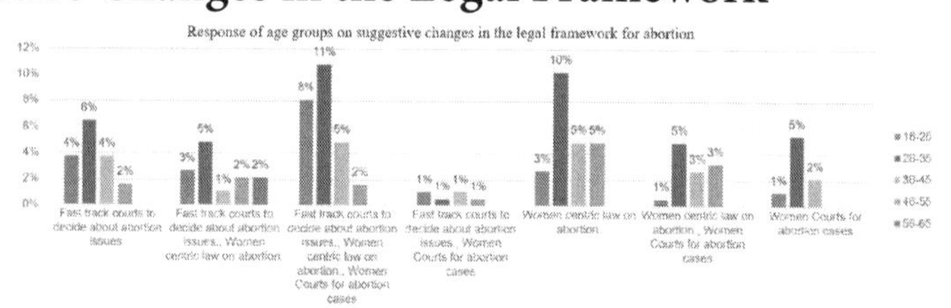

Figure 113: Age and Suggestive Changes

Figure 114: Religion and Suggestive Changes

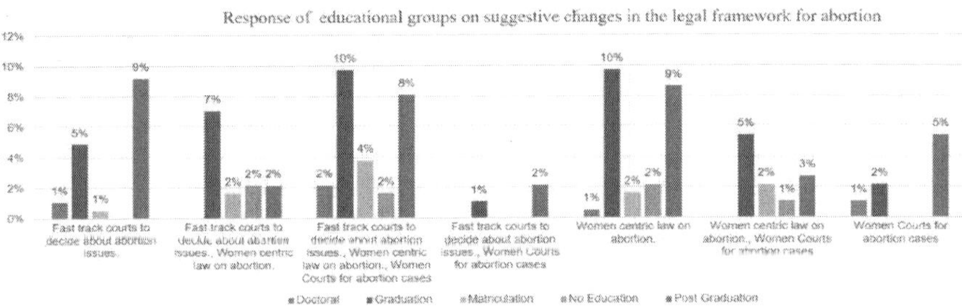

Figure 115: Education and Suggestive Changes

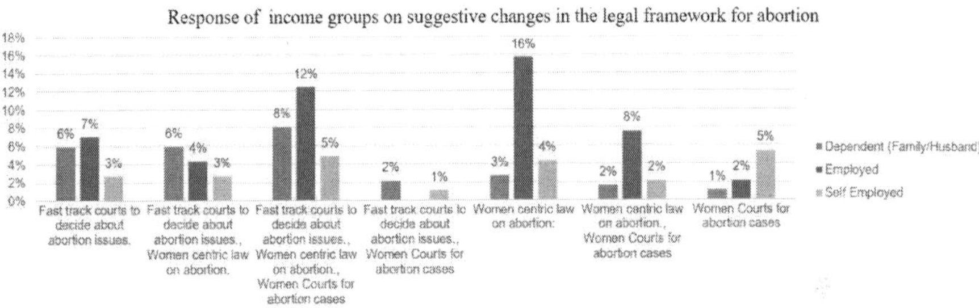

Figure 116: Source of Income and Suggestive Changes

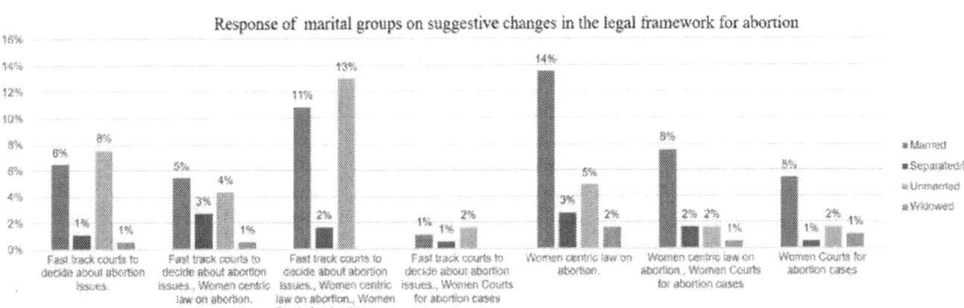

Figure 117: Marital Status and Suggestive Changes

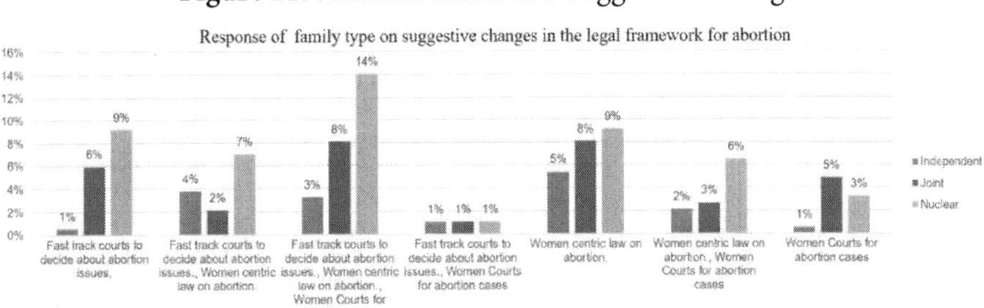

Figure 118: Family Type and Suggestive Changes

Analysis: Regarding the Suggestions for Changes in the Legal Framework

- **Age:** 16% of women suggested only the need for fast-track courts to decide about cases on abortion, and 12% confirmed the need for women-centric laws and women's courts for cases of abortion. 26% of women respondents suggested all three options.

- **Religion:** 16% of respondents chose the need for fast-track courts, 22% chose the need for women-centric laws, and 8% selected the need for women's courts for cases of abortion. 26% of women suggested all three options.
- **Education:** 16% of respondents from different educational backgrounds suggested a need for fast-track courts, while 32% suggested the framing of women-centric laws on abortion and setting up of women's courts for cases of abortion.
- **Source of income:** 23% of women suggested women-centric laws, 16% suggested fast-track courts, and 8% suggested women's courts for cases of abortion.
- **Marital status:** 16% of women suggested fast-track courts, 24% of women suggested women-centric laws on abortion, and 9% of women suggested women's court for abortion cases. 26% of women opted for the consolidated viewpoint.
- **Family type:** 25% of women opted for consolidated suggestions. 16% of women opted for fast-track courts, 22% of women for women-centric laws on abortion, and 9% of women suggested women's courts for cases of abortion.

Thus, fast-track and women's courts for abortion cases and women-centric laws are the need of the hour.

ELEVEN

Findings of the Empirical Study

A woman has the right to make a choice to carry the pregnancy; at the same time, it is her right not to carry a pregnancy, however, subject to conditions and restrictions enumerated under the provisions of the MTP Act, 1971.

– *XXX v. State of Telangana*[1]

The preceding chapter etched out the dynamics of reproductive rights *vis-a-vis* the constraints in achieving abortion rights. The analysis of the quantitative survey gave a glimpse of the lived experiences of women with regard to the barriers faced by them while exercising their reproductive rights. Women's reproductive autonomy is strategically ignored by the policies that govern reproductive procedures.

This concluding chapter primarily summarizes the findings based on the data gathered from the survey. Further, the chapter discusses in greater detail the social and familial barriers that prevent women from exercising their legal right to an abortion. It also examines the MTP Amendment Act, 2021 in relation to other relevant laws and the judiciary's role in advancing reproductive rights jurisprudence. It then concludes that the legislative mandate and even the judiciary have not been successful in fully addressing the barriers to women's reproductive rights. Lastly, it puts forth various suggestions for empowering women with absolute autonomy over their reproductive rights.

Key Findings of the Study

The survey data shows that Indian women do not have a real say on matters related to pregnancy. However, it also shows that educated women have some degree of choice as compared to rural women. Further, women find the decision-making process for pregnancy-related matters difficult. Surprisingly, women living in metropolitan cities also find the

[1] WP No. 24850 of 2021.

process hard. Another noteworthy finding of the study is that women do not easily opt for abortion due to concerns about morality.

The data reflects that women feel that they should have the power to make decisions regarding their pregnancy. They should be allowed to terminate the pregnancy at any stage as long as their health permits. Overall, the awareness level of the respondents about the law and rights was found to be mediocre. Some of the major findings from the study have been discussed below:

- **The social stigma of abortion:** As per the data, 79% of women in the age group of 26–65 years considered abortion to be a social stigma. A significant 80% of Hindu women surveyed believed that termination of pregnancy is still a social stigma. Surprisingly, similar responses were recorded from educated and financially independent women living in Delhi NCR (50%). In terms of marital status, 40% married women and 23% unmarried women agreed or strongly agreed that abortion is a stigma, while 26% of the respondents belonging to joint families and 38% of respondents from nuclear families also believed the same. This shows that abortion remains, by and large, a social stigma and does not find easy acceptance in society.
- **Morality as an obstruction to the exercise of the right to abortion**: 80% of the women respondents based in Delhi agreed or strongly agreed that morality is one of the barriers preventing the exercise of the right to abortion. 64% of Hindu women, 88% of respondents (both educated and uneducated), 40% of married women, 38% of divorced/separated women, and 77% of respondents from independent, nuclear as well as joint family setups strongly agreed that morality is an important reason that holds back women from terminating a pregnancy.
- **Religion as an impediment to the exercise of the right to abortion:** The data shows that irrespective of their marital status, women considered religion to be an important factor while deciding to opt for termination of pregnancy. 83% of the respondents agreed or strongly agreed that religion prohibits the killing of an unborn child and thus acts as a barrier to the free exercise of abortion rights. Further, 42% of employed women, 41% of women from nuclear families, and 27% of women living independently agreed that religion had an impact on the exercise of their abortion rights. In a country like India, where religious and cultural beliefs play a significant role in the minds of

the people, most religions hold that abortion is a sin, a prohibited practice, and also a crime.

- **Choice of women to decide on their pregnancy:** 65% of the respondents agreed that women do not have the choice to make decisions about their pregnancy. Almost 60% of Hindu respondents and 51% of graduate/post-graduate women respondents agreed that women did not have the authority to decide on their pregnancy solely. The decisions were found to be influenced by family and the overall social milieu. Only 36% of married respondents felt that women had a choice in deciding about their pregnancy.
- **Abortion-related decision-making:** 41% of the respondents from 26 to 35 years (the most (re)productive age group), 17% in the higher age group and 20% in the age group of 18–25 years believed that women did not have a superior say in the matters of termination of pregnancy. 63% of the respondents from Delhi NCR confirmed their lack of voice in this important decision. Responses based on the religious affiliation, educational background, and employment status of the respondents show that 80% of Hindu women, 74% of highly educated women (36% post-graduates and 38% graduates), and 73% of working women (48% employed and 25% self-employed) believed that women had less authority to decide about abortion. Not surprisingly, 34% of married, 46% of unmarried, and 10% of separated/divorced women did not find it easy to make their voices heard. Thus, having a negligible say in the decision for undergoing abortion presents a serious difficulty for women irrespective of their age, education, income, and the type of family structures they belong to.
- **Dependence on others regarding abortion:** A significant finding from the survey shows that merely 8% of respondents admitted that abortion was the sole decision of women, whereas 64% of the respondents irrespective of the age group confirmed that the decision regarding abortion was not taken by women independently and was mostly influenced by the extended family members. 48% of educated respondents agreed that there was greater involvement of the extended family in deciding about abortion. Thus, it was found that not only the closest family members such as spouses and parents from both sides but also the members of the extended family influenced the decision regarding abortion by a woman. Women have yet to claim

independence in such decisions based solely on the consideration of privacy, bodily integrity, and autonomy.

- **Forced pregnancy for having a male child:** The data highlighted a worrisome situation of forced pregnancies. Across all the age groups of 18–65 years, 82% agreed with the premise that women were forced to carry pregnancies until they delivered a male child. Almost 81% of the women respondents from Delhi NCR, 81% of Hindu respondents, and 80% of respondents (both educated and uneducated) agreed with the alarming practice of forced pregnancy for having a male child in the family. Sorted by family setup, 81% of respondents (26% of those living in joint families, 40% from nuclear families, and 15% of independent women) were of the same view.
- **Sterilization only after a male child:** The survey data revealed that sterilization was performed only after the birth of a male child. 46% of women respondents in all the age groups of 26 to 65 years agreed/strongly agreed with this social mindset. 45% of Hindu women and 10% of women respondents from other religious groups believed in the same premise. Further, 45% of educated and 11% of uneducated women respondents highlighted the same issue. A similar trend was apparent amongst those who had different sources of income (38%). 51% of women respondents from joint families/nuclear families/independent families believed the same. Thus, the data not only demonstrates the patriarchal mindset of the society but also reflects that the preference for a male child act as a barrier to a woman's bodily autonomy.
- **Intolerance for pregnancy of unmarried women in society:** 26% of respondents agreed and 66% strongly agreed that the pregnancy of unmarried women was unaccepted in society. Similarly, 99% of educated women supported the fact that there was a lack of acceptance of unmarried pregnancy in society. Even 46% of economically independent women agreed with this view. Almost 32% of unmarried women confirmed the same. 78% of women, especially those following the Hindu religion, believed that the pregnancy of an unmarried mother was stigmatic in society.
- **Expensive/unaffordable abortion services in Delhi NCR:** Among women of all age groups, 53% agreed that abortion services were expensive in Delhi NCR. A significant 67% of Hindu women and 58% of economically independent women also confirmed that they cannot afford abortion services independently. Similarly, 76% of women

living in joint and nuclear families confirmed the unaffordability of the services.

- **Preference for health providers for abortion:** The data reflects that the respondents strongly preferred health providers for abortion for different reasons. 31% of respondents demanded health providers primarily because of better facilities and 26% due to confidentiality. Based on marital status, 35% women preferred them because of better facilities, 10% of unmarried/divorced women chose them for reputation, 29% for confidentiality, and 14% due to vicinity. Irrespective of their economic status, 34% preferred health providers for better facilities, 29% for confidentiality, 11% for reputation, 8% for inexpensiveness, 7% for less time, and 13% for vicinity. Thus, maximum respondents preferred health providers for abortion due to better facilities.
- **Inadequate/unqualified staff in hospitals:** 67% of women of all age groups believed that there was inadequate/unqualified staff in hospitals who could perform safe abortions. Also, 65% of educated women respondents agreed and 45% uneducated respondents strongly agreed that there was a dearth of trained staff to conduct abortions. Similarly, 60% of employed women agreed and 20% of dependent women strongly agreed about the issue of unqualified staff. This indicates that there is a shortage of trained staff/service providers in hospitals in Delhi NCR.
- **Determination of preference for health providers for abortion services:** For abortion services, 25% of respondents from 25 to 36 years of age preferred to approach qualified private doctors, 20% preferred government facilities, and 15% inclined toward private hospitals in Delhi NCR. 10% of uneducated and 17% of graduate women had chosen quacks, though these constituted a small number. 40% of post-graduate and 30% of graduate women respondents preferred to consult qualified doctors. The data shows that women choose abortion services based on factors like location, affordability, methods, and sometimes legality. Women look for commitment, professionalism, skill, and accuracy when choosing a health provider.
- **Physical and mental trauma during abortion:** 86% of women of all ages strongly agreed that women experience physical and mental trauma before and after abortion. Similarly, 88% of women from all religions agreed that women face mental trauma in their families during the pre/post-abortion period. 72% of married/unmarried

women corroborated this fact. 50% of women from nuclear families and 38% of women living in joint families strongly agreed with the same. Women's mental health is largely impacted by the process and quality of abortion services as well as the behavior of those in close interaction with them such as family, friends, and health service providers. Further, women's socio-economic status and their say in the decision-making process impact their physical or mental health during the abortion.

- **Mandatory court permission for abortion after 24 weeks of pregnancy under the MTP (Amendment) Act, 2021:** 61% of women of all age groups strongly agreed with the premise that mandatory court permission was undesirable in cases where women were willing to abort pregnancy beyond 24 weeks. Also, 35% of women from various places in Delhi NCR agreed that the court's permission to undergo the procedure was unnecessary, and 20% of women remained neutral on this premise.
- **Delays by courts in granting permission for abortion:** 35% of women between 26 and 35 years agreed that there are delays by courts in approving abortion. 68% of educated respondents also strongly agreed with the situation. Further, 67% of married/separated/divorced/widowed women and 64% of women respondents from joint families, nuclear families, and independent families endorsed the same premise. Thus, the courts need to be more proactive in such cases of abortion which require urgent attention and where time is of the essence. Delays increase the risk to the health of the mother and fetus and sometimes even result in unwarranted deaths.
- **Finality of the doctor(s)' decision regarding abortion under the MTP Act, 2021:** 55% of women of all ages strongly agreed that in terms of the MTP Act, the finality of the decision lays with the doctors. From Delhi NCR, 50% of respondents acknowledged this perspective. Further, 50% of graduates and 45% of post-graduates also accepted that the final decision is made by the doctors. 95% of women from all religions also agreed with this premise. In addition, 60% of employed women and 62% of married/unmarried/divorced/separated respondents also agreed or strongly agreed to it. Similarly, 76% of women from various family backgrounds believed that abortion remained the sole discretion of the doctors. In all, abiding by the legislation, seeking the court's permission, and being completely

dependent on the discretion of doctors make it tougher for women to terminate a pregnancy between 20 and 24 weeks of gestation period.

- **Awareness about abortion laws in India:** The data highlights some noticeable gaps in awareness about the MTP Act and PCPNDT Act. 50% of women in the age group of 26 to 65 years were unaware of abortion laws. 14% of financially dependent women had the least amount of awareness. Overall, 40% of married women were unaware of abortion laws. 58% of women from various family backgrounds were also unaware.
- **Awareness about contraceptive pills:** 67% of women aged 18 to 35 years were most aware of contraception and contraceptive pills. 69% of women belonging to Delhi NCR had awareness about the same. 67% of unemployed/employed women, 64% of married/unmarried women, and 64% of women belonging to nuclear and joint families confirmed their awareness. However, women continue to have unintended pregnancies even though there is decent awareness about contraceptive pills.
- **Awareness about abortion rights in India:** 60% of women from all age groups were not aware that they have the right to abortion. 35% of younger women of 18 to 25 years of age were more aware. On the contrary, 40% of women from the age group of 26–35 years were unaware. A significant 61% of women belonging to Delhi NCR and 36% of graduates/post-graduates women respondents confirmed their awareness of the right to abortion. However, 59% of women from different religious backgrounds and 60% of women belonging to different economic statuses were unaware of their right to abortion. 47% of married and divorced/separated women and 58% of women irrespective of their family background were found unaware of the right to abortion. Thus, it is observed that most women were not aware of their reproductive rights, especially the right to abortion.
- **Awareness about the favorability of abortion laws:** 50% of women from the age group of 26–65 years strongly disagreed with the idea that abortion laws were favorable. A considerable 58% of women from all religions and 41% of graduates and postgraduate respondents also strongly disagreed with the statement that abortion laws favored women. Similarly, 55% of married/unmarried women respondents and 56% of respondents belonging to nuclear and joint families acknowledged that abortion laws did not favor women.

- **Suggestive changes by the respondents for the abortion practice in India:** Amongst women in the age group of 26–35 years, 19% suggested a need for fast-track courts to decide cases involving abortion along with the need for women-centric laws, whereas 11% of the respondents suggested setting up of women's courts for deciding cases of abortion. 21% of respondents belonging to different religions also voted for fast-track courts, 15% for women-centric laws, and 40% demanded special women's courts for such matters. 35% of women with different educational backgrounds also agreed with the need for fast-track courts. On the same lines, 30% of women from different income categories responded significantly to women-centric laws followed by a need for fast-track courts. Almost 25% of married women suggested women-centric laws on abortion and a notable 30% of unmarried women opted for the need for fast-track courts. Similarly, 25–30% of unmarried women and 35% of women respondents from diverse family backgrounds opted for the consolidated viewpoint. 40% of women from independent families favored women-centric laws on abortion.

TWELVE

Discussion and Observations

The ability of women to participate equally in the economic and social life of the nation has been facilitated by their ability to control their reproductive lives.

– Justice Sandra Day O' Connor[1]

The present study elaborates on why women have not been able to fully exercise their reproductive rights pertaining to abortion and what reform proposals need to be made to support women. It has also relied on previous literature and the empirical survey to document that women in the country are unable to comprehensively exercise their reproductive rights, particularly their decisional autonomy to seek abortions.

Based on the present study, it has been concluded that the social order in India has largely been sustained through religious sanctions and a strict moral code borne out of religion. Religions condemn abortion and Hindu religious texts are no exception. Even the legal perception of abortion remains largely influenced by moral and religious predicaments. It is therefore not surprising to find the common man equating abortion with sin and immorality.

On an assessment of the studies relied upon in the present research, it can be further concluded that in matters of termination of pregnancy, for a vast majority of women in India, the perception of herself takes a backseat, while factors such as cultural, religious, socio-economic and societal pressure – as detailed in this study – play a significant role in influencing her decision.

The remnants of colonialism, wherein women are regarded as serfs who either belong to the father or the husband, are reflected in different ways whereby the control over women's bodies is transferred into the

[1] Sandra Day O'Connor is an American retired attorney and politician who served as the first female associate justice of the Supreme Court of the United States from 1981 to 2006. She was both the first woman nominated and first confirmed to the court.

hands of parents or spouses. When every petty decision of a woman's life is subjected to the consent of the husband, family, and society, it is very difficult for her to exercise control over her womb. Further, procreation is seen as a societal expectation where individual rights are overlooked. This is why a normative pregnancy is regarded as desirable as against unmarried pregnancy. In the same vein, a women's right to abort is bound to the family, and a woman (married) is expected to not seek an abortion. But in the case of widows or unmarried females, abortion is more acceptable, in order to protect the family's honor.

Fertility behavior[2] in India indicates that women face several social and domestic constraints that limit their capacity to act upon reproductive decisions. These include early marriage and the social pressure for early childbearing, poor access to knowledge regarding contraception, lack of decision-making power in their household, limited physical mobility and access to services and providers, and physical violence and coercion in sexual and family relations. Gender equality is still a far cry for women in the current patriarchal society, which is characterized by exclusive male dominance by way of male control of female sexuality, fertility, mobility, and productivity.

Literature and findings referred to in this study show that strong son preference and other structural facets of patriarchy limit women's freedom to exercise choice even when it appears that they are doing so. Moreover, in India, State intervention has limited choices about reproduction, further minimizing the individual's right to self-determination.

Abortion laws in western countries were a result of the feminist struggle, based on the right to self-determination. Feminists recognized abortion as a woman's reproductive right as her right over her own body. In India, on the other hand, termination of pregnancy has never been recognized as a normal recourse for expecting mothers. Feminists in India have been divided into pro-life and pro-choice camps in matters of abortion as in developed countries. Thus, there has been no attempt to recognize 'abortion at will' at any stage of pregnancy in India. Abortion laws in India were introduced to curb the issue of overpopulation and did not prioritize the choice of women. The larger plan of the State in the implementation of the Medical Termination of Pregnancy Act was to

[2] Fertility behavior refers to the childbearing patterns of women or couples, including especially the number of births, the timing of births, and associated reproductive behaviors such as union formation (including marriage and cohabitation) and contraceptive behavior.

achieve population control and therefore abortion remained a qualified right only.

Exploring the legal framework in India and the long journey of legislating access to safe abortion which started in 1971, the present study shows that the MTP Act, 1971 is liberal mostly on paper. Analyzing the impact of the MTP Act, it can be said that the Act of 1971 created an exception to the offence of abortion under the Indian Penal Code, 1860. Since voluntarily causing a miscarriage was a crime under the IPC and women were also liable to be prosecuted, by formalizing the procedure, the MTP Act created a basis that allowed a woman to access medical assistance without fear of bodily harm at the hands of an inexperienced and unqualified person. It is said that approximately one-seventh of women who became pregnant resorted to unsafe termination methods at the hands of inexperienced persons and quacks and/or paramedical personnel like nurses and midwives who lacked the necessary experience, resulting in risks of high morbidity amongst pregnant women and children. The MTP Act took into consideration the mother's safety according to the medical technology available at the time. There was a reduced incidence of suicide and a betterment of the health and safety of women. The MTP Act set the gestational limit for abortions at 20 weeks, beyond which abortions were to be performed only when there was a risk to the life of the pregnant person.

In this sense, the MTP Act was progressive, yet the Act lacked a rights-based framework, and the legislative intent in passing it, as opined by the Supreme Court of India, was to provide a qualified 'right to abortion' where termination of pregnancy was never recognized as a normal recourse for expecting mothers. This law was doctor-centric and over-medicalized, stripping pregnant persons of their right to bodily and decisional autonomy. The medical boards set up were draconian and invasive. Additionally, the government failed to ensure that a sufficient number of public healthcare facilities were equipped to provide health abortion services. As a result, rather paradoxical to the goal of the act, the vast majority of Indian women got abortions outside the legal framework.

The issues concerning the implementation of the MTP Act (already complex with abortion being influenced by religion, moral or socio-political context, and sexual politics[3]) were and are further compounded

---

[3] Sexual politics, in general, are ideas and activities that are concerned with how power is shared between men and women, and how this affects their relationships.

by sex-selective abortion. Strong son preference in the society led to sex-selective abortion, which resulted in female feticide. As abortion before 20 weeks of pregnancy was legal in India, female feticide could not be banned per se; hence, the requirement of a new law was felt to prevent the misuse of the MTP Act for sex selection. Thus, the Pre-conception and Pre-natal Diagnostic Techniques (Prohibition of Sex Selection) Act was enacted in 1994. The PCPNDT Act, 1994 (as amended by the 2002 amendment) provided for the prohibition of sex selection, before or after conception, and for the regulation of pre-natal diagnostic techniques for the prevention of their misuse, thus preventing female feticide.

The MTP (Amendment) Act of 2021 was introduced after nearly five decades of the MTP Act of 1971. These amendments were brought in to remedy the ineffective abortion laws which led to illegal and unsafe abortions and followed the MTP Bills of 2014, 2017, and 2018, which were allowed to lapse in the Parliament. One of the key features of this Act has been the increase in the permissible upper limit of undergoing termination, without an order from the court concerned, from 20 weeks to 24 weeks of pregnancy. It includes another progressive feature that has ended the statutory discrimination against unmarried women by including all women and their partners notwithstanding the marital status between them. However, in light of the limitations of the Act as discussed in the previous chapters, the amendment at best remains a tight-fisted grant of fettered autonomy. Further, the government has still failed in ensuring that a sufficient number of public healthcare facilities are equipped to provide abortion services; as a result, a majority of abortions are being sought in the private sector.

Women's bodily autonomy when it comes to reproductive health has not only been wholly absent in the MTP Act, 2021, but the legislative approach has been inherently regressive. This framework requires an overhaul incorporating the spirit of the Constitution and the evolving rights that govern individual and bodily autonomy, where a pregnant woman has a final say on her choice of reproduction.

Moving from the legislative to the judicial sphere, it becomes evident that the recognition of reproductive rights as fundamental rights has created a mandate for the government to shift away from population control approaches, confront discrimination that limits women's authority, and instead center policies and health-related laws on women's right to dignity, autonomy, and bodily integrity. The Indian judiciary has no doubt carried forward reproductive rights jurisprudence based on the fundamental rights to autonomy, bodily integrity, and privacy, yet pregnant persons continue to face challenges in accessing reproductive health services.

This study examines the various judgments of the High Courts and the Supreme Court on various aspects of reproductive rights. Though there has been a significantly progressive and positive shift in the Indian reproductive rights discourse by the courts as highlighted in the judgments, a clear framework has not been established to determine when a medical termination of pregnancy is legal, how to eliminate the need for judicial and medical board authorization, and how to address the underlying issue of providers unwillingness to authorize legal abortions. Courts have been undertaking a case-by-case analysis in abortion cases and proclaiming varied judgments even for cases with similar facts, thereby following a subjective rather than an objective approach.

Typically, the judiciary has refused abortions in many cases except those which are strictly based on grounds mentioned in the MTP Act. Courts have primarily addressed the right to reproductive autonomy as a matter of life and personal liberty, but have yet to robustly address abortion or reproductive autonomy as an issue of equality and non-discrimination. Additionally, there remains a shortfall of surgeons, obstetricians, gynecologists, physicians, and pediatricians. The lack of doctors makes the setting up of medical boards infeasible. The authorization requirements often lead to delays, public scrutiny, and trauma.

Another prominent issue that constitutes a barrier to accessing abortion is obstetric violence. Mistreatment of pregnant women by health workers and doctors is common, which entails disrespect and physical abuse as well. This exacerbates the situation for women who are already vulnerable to discrimination and unable to access healthcare because of socio-economic disadvantages. The situation is even more challenging for women with disabilities. Services and care for people with psychosocial disabilities in healthcare facilities often involve the violation of their reproductive rights through coercive measures such as forced sterilization, hysterectomy, and medical examination following sexual assault.

The present study has addressed the fact that the bias against the allocation of resources necessary to provide health services to meet women's special needs is a form of gender discrimination. In the high numbers of deaths and complications related to pregnancy and childbirth, discrimination against women is a significant factor. Failure to provide maternal health services reflects the low priority attached to fulfilling women's specific needs.

The lack of awareness in women about their right to make autonomous and unhindered reproductive choices also acts as a serious barrier to abortion. This is especially true in the case of rural women and unmarried women, a majority of whom are unaware that they can legally abort an unwanted fetus. Most women in India have no control over the condition in which they have sexual intercourse and often abortion becomes the only form of birth control. Women also have abortions because of the stigma of illegitimacy or because they cannot afford another child or because they are at a stage in their careers where they cannot take the responsibility for another human life. The lack of safe, effective, accessible temporary methods of contraception is another barrier to the realization of reproductive rights.

Laws that criminalize health services that only women need whether aimed at the person who provides such services or the women who receive them are discriminatory. The criminalization of abortion is heinous because it not only impairs women's right to reproductive choice – to make free and responsible decisions concerning matters that are key to the control of their lives – but also exposes them to the serious health risks of unsafe abortion, violating their rights to bodily integrity and, in extreme cases, to life itself.

The study concludes by highlighting the fact that in a world where a woman's rights are so severely curtailed; where her sexuality is not hers to have a say over; where she does not have access to equal opportunity or healthcare; where the State is determined to interfere in when and how many children she has; where social sector cuts, shrinking work opportunities and wages, and dwindling food security systems are hitting women the hardest, it is clear that her reproductive rights in the community and the family need to be located within the broader system of needs as perceived by women and cannot be discussed in isolation.

At the policy level, the interdependence of reproductive health, general health, and socio-economic conditions needs to be recognized. The focus cannot only be on regulating women's fertility, a concept that is advanced by the State and other agencies while dealing with reproductive health. What has to be kept in mind is a development-led perspective. Upholding women's reproductive rights would encompass a society free from the ills of prejudice, malpractice, coercion, and compulsion.

Thus, after the detailed analysis of reproductive rights, the study enumerates certain suggestions for the fuller recognition of reproductive rights.

What is thus required is that the reproductive rights framework be more fully integrated into future policies and judgments if the State is to understand and respectfully address the issues surrounding women. A shift in the law from restrictive to permissive will pave the way to show women that the moral ban on abortion has been lifted and that those who want an abortion for whatever reason have the approval and support of society at large. This will lessen the social pressure and stigma surrounding abortion. Finally, the government must make genuine efforts to raise awareness about women's right to make autonomous and unrestricted reproductive decisions.